Taste of Home

5 INGREDIENT HEALTHY

TASTE OF HOME BOOKS • RDA ENTHUSIAST BRANDS, LLC • MILWAUKEE, WI

Taste of Home

© 2021 RDA Enthusiast Brands, LLC.
1610 N. 2nd St., Suite 102,
Milwaukee WI 53212-3906
All rights reserved. Taste of Home
is a registered trademark of RDA
Enthusiast Brands, LLC.
Visit us at tasteofhome.com for other
Taste of Home books and products.

ISBN: 978-1-61765-956-0
LOCC: 2020946116

EXECUTIVE EDITOR: Mark Hagen
SENIOR ART DIRECTOR:
Raeann Thompson
EDITOR: Amy Glander
ART DIRECTOR: Maggie Conners
DESIGNER: Jazmin Delgado
DEPUTY EDITOR, COPY DESK:
Dulcie Shoener
COPY EDITOR: Sara Strauss
SENIOR EDITOR/FOOD:
Peggy Woodward, RDN

COVER
PHOTOGRAPHER: Dan Roberts
SET STYLIST: Stacey Genaw
FOOD STYLIST: Josh Rink

PICTURED ON FRONT COVER:
Sheet Pan Sausage
& Potato Dinner, p. 86

PICTURED ON TITLE PAGE:
Carolina-Style Vinegar
BBQ Chicken, p. 82

Printed in USA
1 3 5 7 9 10 8 6 4 2

P. 89

CONTENTS

SHORT ON TIME?

Keep an eye out for these handy icons to help you quickly identify recipes that fit your schedule and dietary needs.

Fast Fix Dishes are table-ready in 30 minutes (or less!)—from the time you open the fridge to when you put the meal on the table!

Power Packed Each dish contains a whole grain or legume, a lean protein, and a healthy dose of fruits and vegetables.

MORE WAYS TO CONNECT WITH US:

Here's What "Healthy" Means at *Taste of Home*

We're here to help you navigate the options with *5 Ingredient Healthy*.

If you think trying to eat healthy is overwhelming, you are not alone. There are a lot of factors to consider, research is constantly uncovering new information, and there's still a lot that science doesn't know about how food and nutrition affect our health.

Since "healthy" covers such a wide spectrum, we take a middle-of-the-road approach at *Taste of Home*. Organizations that make recommendations rooted in proven science, such as the USDA, FDA, WHO, NIH, plus the American Heart Association, the American Diabetes Association and the Academy of Nutrition and Dietetics, help guide us.

HOW WE DEFINE HEALTHY

We believe "healthy" foods are those that nourish us with vitamins, minerals, protein, fiber and healthy fats. And it's important to remember that it is not just about what's in our food but what's *not* in our food, too. It's widely recommended to limit saturated fat, trans fat and sodium for optimal health and disease prevention. At the same time, healthy eating doesn't mean cutting out entire food groups, feeling deprived or eating food that doesn't taste good!

IT'S ABOUT BALANCE

Healthy eating is about balance. Nutritious recipes can include butter and sugar, just as healthy meals can include an indulgent dessert—it's all about moderation and keeping a healthy big picture in mind.

NO LONG SHOPPING LISTS!

For today's busy home cooks, saving time is another top priority. Luckily, it doesn't take a lot of time or a whole shopping cart full of expensive ingredients to create a healthy meal. Every recipe in this book requires a handful of kitchen staples and comes together with no fuss, hassle or wasted effort.

Whether you're serving up dinner on a busy weeknight or planning a party for friends, you'll find everything you're looking for in this new collection of healthy favorites. Submitted by savvy home cooks across North America, the 300-plus recipes in this book will help you create wholesome meals your family will love.

Happy Cooking,

Peggy

Peggy Woodward, RDN
Senior Editor/Food

ABOUT OUR NUTRITION FACTS

The *5 Ingredient Healthy* cookbook provides a variety of recipes to fit in a healthy lifestyle. Here's how we arrive at the serving-size nutritional information listed at the end of each recipe.

- Whenever a choice of ingredients is given (such as ½ cup sour cream or plain yogurt), we use the first ingredient in our calculations.

- When a range is given for an ingredient, we calculate using the first amount.

- Only the amount of a marinade absorbed is calculated.

- Optional ingredients are not included in our calculations.

- Sugars provided in the Nutrition Facts represent both added and naturally occurring sugars.

P. 209

HOW DO YOU COUNT TO 5?

You'll notice throughout this book that some recipe lists run longer than five lines. That's because there are a few items we don't include in our five-ingredient counts. These are essentials that are so basic we feel comfortable assuming every kitchen always has them on hand. What are they? There are four items on the list, some of which you can customize as you wish.

1. WATER

P. 232

2. SALT

When we say "salt," we're referring to traditional table salt, and we don't count it. Many cooks regularly use kosher salt instead, preferring it for its more predictable "pinch" measure—feel free to do so. But if a particular recipe requires kosher salt, we'll name it specifically and include it in our count.

3. PEPPER

Black pepper is a go-to kitchen staple, and we don't count it. However, if a recipe demands freshly cracked black pepper, we will name it and count it. Cracked pepper gives the freshest flavor, but not everyone owns a pepper mill.

4. OIL

P. 16

Three oils make our "don't count" list: vegetable oil, canola oil and regular olive oil. Vegetable and canola oils are highly versatile and can be used interchangeably. They don't have a strong flavor and do have a high smoke point, which makes them ideal for frying, sauteing and baking. Regular olive oil adds a hint of fruity flavor and can be used for light sauteing and roasting, and for dressings and sauces. Extra virgin olive oil, on the other hand, has more specialized uses due to its low smoke point and will be specified (and counted!) when it's needed for a recipe.

We also don't include optional items when counting ingredients. We view these items as suggestions—either as garnishes or as complements—but they aren't necessary to make the recipe, so you can easily leave them out. Also, you can always swap them for your own preferred finishing touches.

5 TIPS FOR MAKING THE MOST OF 5 INGREDIENTS

1. THINK FRESH. Many of the most famous classic dishes have short ingredient lists and rely on a few distinctive flavors to carry the day. Start with quality ingredients and don't overcook, and you won't need a lot of extras.

2. CONSIDER COMMERCIALLY AVAILABLE INGREDIENTS THAT PILE ON THE FLAVOR. Jarred sauces, packaged rice mixes, seasoning blends, tomatoes with herbs, and canned soups let you get a head start.

3. USE MIXES IN NEW WAYS. A cake mix can be a good basis for cookies or bars. Biscuit and cookie mixes can also provide inspiration for a new recipe.

4. CHECK OUT PREPARED FOODS. Just because food is already prepared doesn't mean you need to serve it as is! Pre-cut fruit and veggies from the salad bar, rotisserie chicken from the deli—use these as starting points for your own dishes.

5. MAKE CONVENIENCE PRODUCTS YOUR OWN. Rice, stuffing and pasta mixes are ideal for experimentation. Try adding chopped fresh apple, celery and onion to a stuffing mix, for example, or add shrimp to a rice mix. Take a second look at convenience breads, such as crescent rolls, biscuits and frozen bread dough. You don't have to make bread with them—they also work with some well-chosen ingredients to make appetizers, casseroles or calzones.

Stocking Your Pantry

The key to the magic of being able to pull together a terrific meal on short notice (and prevent an unexpected grocery run) is to have a well-stocked pantry. If you cover your bases, you'll always have things in the cupboard that will work well together. Here are some suggestions for a few basic ingredients to always have on hand.

Chicken stock or broth • vinegar (red wine, white wine and/or balsamic) • eggs • milk • condensed soup (cream of mushroom and/or chicken) • salsa • all-purpose flour • a selection of herbs and spices • lemons • garlic • pastas • tomato sauce or paste • canned tomatoes (diced) • canned beans (garbanzo beans, white beans, kidney beans and/or black beans) • bread or rolls • rice mixes • onions • shredded cheese (cheddar, Italian blend or Mexican blend) • butter • frozen vegetables (mixed veggies, frozen peas, spinach) • prepared salad dressings • rice • bacon • honey • hot sauce/Tabasco sauce • bread crumbs • prepared mustard • bacon

BREAKFAST

BREAKFAST SWEET POTATOES
P. 11

1

2

3

4

5

WAKE UP TO GOOD MORNINGS WITH THESE
BETTER-FOR-YOU BREAKFAST RECIPES.
INCLUDING JUST A FEW INGREDIENTS, EACH
DISH IS A SMART WAY TO START YOUR DAY!

RISE & SHINE PARFAIT

MINI HAM & CHEESE FRITTATAS

I found this recipe a few years ago and made some little changes to it. I'm diabetic, and it fits into my low-carb and low-fat diet. Every time I host brunch, the frittatas are the first item to disappear, and nobody knows they are low in fat!

—Susan Watt, Basking Ridge, NJ

Prep: 15 min. • **Bake:** 25 min.
Makes: 8 servings

- 6 large eggs
- 4 large egg whites
- 2 Tbsp. fat-free milk
- ¼ tsp. salt
- ¼ tsp. pepper
- 3 Tbsp. minced fresh chives
- ¾ cup cubed fully cooked ham (about 4 oz.)
- 1 cup shredded fat-free cheddar cheese

1. Preheat oven to 375°. In a bowl, whisk the first 5 ingredients until blended; stir in chives. Divide ham and cheese among 8 muffin cups coated with cooking spray. Top with egg mixture, filling muffin cups three-fourths full.

2. Bake 22-25 minutes or until a knife inserted in the center comes out clean. Carefully run a knife around the sides to loosen.

1 mini frittata: 106 cal., 4g fat (1g sat. fat), 167mg chol., 428mg sod., 2g carb. (1g sugars, 0 fiber), 14g pro.
Diabetic exchanges: 2 medium-fat meat.

RISE & SHINE PARFAIT

Start your day with a smile. This fruit, yogurt and granola parfait is easy to make and good for you, too. Use whatever favorite fresh fruit is in season.

—Diana Laskaris, Chicago, IL

Takes: 15 min.
Makes: 4 servings

- 4 cups fat-free vanilla yogurt
- 2 medium peaches, chopped
- 2 cups fresh blackberries
- ½ cup granola without raisins or Kashi Go Lean Crunch cereal

Layer half the yogurt, peaches, blackberries and granola into 4 parfait glasses. Repeat layers.

1 serving: 259 cal., 3g fat (0 sat. fat), 7mg chol., 6mg sod., 48g carb. (27g sugars, 7g fiber), 13g pro.

MINI HAM &
CHEESE FRITTATAS

ITALIAN CLOUD EGGS

ITALIAN CLOUD EGGS

Drop egg yolks on nests of whipped Italian-seasoned egg whites, then bake in a cast-iron skillet. Dreamy!
—Matthew Hass, Ellison Bay, WI

- -

Takes: 25 min. • **Makes:** 4 servings

- **4 large eggs, separated**
- **¼ tsp. Italian seasoning**
- **⅛ tsp. salt**
- **⅛ tsp. pepper**
- **¼ cup shredded Parmesan cheese**

- **1 Tbsp. minced fresh basil**
- **1 Tbsp. finely chopped oil-packed sun-dried tomatoes**

1. Preheat oven to 450°. Separate the eggs; place whites in a large bowl and yolks in 4 separate small bowls. Beat egg whites, Italian seasoning, salt and pepper until stiff peaks form.
2. In a 9-in. cast-iron skillet generously coated with cooking spray, drop egg white mixture into 4 mounds. With the back of a spoon, create a small well in the center of each mound. Sprinkle with cheese. Bake until light brown, about 5 minutes. Gently slip an egg yolk into each of the mounds. Bake until yolks are set, 3-5 minutes longer. Sprinkle with basil and tomatoes. Serve immediately.

1 serving: 96 cal., 6g fat (2g sat. fat), 190mg chol., 234mg sod., 1g carb. (0 sugars, 0 fiber), 8g pro.
Diabetic exchanges: 1 medium-fat meat.

BREAKFAST SWEET POTATOES

Baked sweet potatoes aren't just for dinner anymore. Top them with breakfast favorites to power up your morning.
—*Taste of Home* Test Kitchen

Prep: 10 min. • **Bake:** 45 min.
Makes: 4 servings

- 4 **medium sweet potatoes (about 8 oz. each)**
- ½ **cup fat-free coconut Greek yogurt**
- 1 **medium apple, chopped**
- 2 **Tbsp. maple syrup**
- ¼ **cup toasted unsweetened coconut flakes**

1. Preheat oven to 400°. Place the potatoes on a foil-lined baking sheet. Bake until tender, 45-60 minutes.
2. With a sharp knife, cut an "X" in each potato. Fluff pulp with a fork. Top with remaining ingredients.

1 stuffed sweet potato: 321 cal., 3g fat (2g sat. fat), 0 chol., 36mg sod., 70g carb. (35g sugars, 8g fiber), 7g pro.

TEST KITCHEN TIP
To microwave the potatoes, scrub them, pierce them with a fork and place them on a microwave-safe plate. Microwave, uncovered, on high for 12-14 minutes or until tender, turning once. If you have a sweet tooth, add some chocolate chips to the topping.

BREAKFAST SWEET POTATOES

GOAT CHEESE & HAM OMELET

I often combine the egg mixture for this omelet beforehand and refrigerate it overnight. Then all I have to do in the morning is heat up my skillet. My favorite part is the goat cheese filling, which gets nice and creamy from the heat of the omelet.
—Lynne Dieterle, Rochester, MI

Takes: 20 min. • **Makes:** 1 serving

- 4 **large egg whites**
- 2 **tsp. water**
- ⅛ **tsp. pepper**
- 1 **slice deli ham, finely chopped**
- 2 **Tbsp. finely chopped green pepper**
- 2 **Tbsp. finely chopped onion**
- 2 **Tbsp. crumbled goat cheese**
  Minced fresh parsley, optional

1. In a small bowl, whisk egg whites, water and pepper until blended; stir in the ham, green pepper and onion. Heat a large nonstick skillet coated with cooking spray over medium-high heat. Pour in egg white mixture. Mixture should set immediately at edges. As egg whites set, push the cooked portions toward the center of the skillet, letting the uncooked egg flow underneath.
2. When no liquid egg remains, sprinkle goat cheese on 1 side. Fold omelet in half; slide onto a plate. If desired, sprinkle with parsley.

1 omelet: 143 cal., 4g fat (2g sat. fat), 27mg chol., 489mg sod., 5g carb. (3g sugars, 1g fiber), 21g pro.
Diabetic exchanges: 3 lean meat, ½ fat.

POTATO OMELET

POTATO OMELET

Even folks who don't care for eggs will enjoy this dish. The fantastic taste of potatoes, onions and garlic come through.
—Edie DeSpain, Logan, UT

Takes: 30 min. • **Makes:** 4 servings

- 2   medium potatoes, peeled and diced
- 2   Tbsp. olive oil
- ½   cup sliced green onions
- ¼   cup minced fresh parsley
- 1   garlic clove, minced
- 6   large eggs
- ¼   cup water
- ½   tsp. salt
- ⅛   tsp. pepper
       Optional: Sour cream and crumbled cooked bacon

1. In a 10-in. skillet, cook potatoes in oil over medium-high heat for 10 minutes or until golden brown, stirring occasionally. Add the onions, parsley and garlic; cook until tender. Reduce heat to medium.
2. In a bowl, beat the eggs, water, salt and pepper. Pour over the potato mixture; cover and cook for 8-10 minutes or until completely set. Cut into wedges. Serve with sour cream and bacon as desired.

1 piece: 236 cal., 14g fat (3g sat. fat), 279mg chol., 408mg sod., 16g carb. (2g sugars, 1g fiber), 11g pro.
Diabetic exchanges: 1½ fat, 1 starch, 1 medium-fat meat.

WHOLE WHEAT PANCAKES

WHOLE WHEAT PANCAKES

To fix a large batch of tender pancakes for my big family, I rely on this fuss-free recipe. It calls for whole wheat flour and buttermilk, which make the pancakes filling but light. Serve them with hot chocolate for a breakfast that's sure to delight little ones.
—Line Walter, Wayne, PA

Takes: 25 min. • **Makes:** 20 pancakes

- 2   cups whole wheat flour
- ½   cup toasted wheat germ
- 1   tsp. baking soda
- ½   tsp. salt
- 2   large eggs, room temperature
- 3   cups buttermilk
- 1   Tbsp. canola oil

In a large bowl, combine the flour, wheat germ, baking soda and salt. In another bowl, whisk the eggs, buttermilk and oil. Stir into the dry ingredients just until blended. Pour the batter by ¼ cupfuls onto a hot griddle coated with cooking spray; turn when bubbles form on top. Cook until the second side of the pancake is golden brown.

Freeze option: Freeze cooled pancakes between layers of waxed paper in an airtight freezer container. To use, place the pancakes on an ungreased baking sheet, cover with foil and reheat in a preheated 375° oven 6-10 minutes. Or place a stack of 3 pancakes on a microwave-safe plate and microwave on high until heated through, 45-90 seconds.

2 pancakes: 157 cal., 4g fat (1g sat. fat), 45mg chol., 335mg sod., 24g carb. (4g sugars, 4g fiber), 9g pro.

MAPLE NUT BAGEL SPREAD

You won't believe how easy it is to whip up this creamy bagel spread. It's also wonderful on toast or muffins.
—*Taste of Home* Test Kitchen

- -

Takes: 10 min. • **Makes:** 1¼ cups

- 1 **carton (8 oz.) reduced-fat spreadable cream cheese**
- 3 **Tbsp. maple syrup**
- ⅛ **tsp. ground cinnamon**
- ¼ **cup finely chopped walnuts, toasted**
  Bagels, split

In a large bowl, beat the cream cheese, syrup and cinnamon until smooth; stir in walnuts. Chill until serving. Serve with bagels.

2 Tbsp.: 84 cal., 5g fat (3g sat. fat), 11mg chol., 107mg sod., 6g carb. (5g sugars, 0 fiber), 3g pro.
Diabetic exchanges: 1 fat, ½ starch.

SOUTHWEST TORTILLA SCRAMBLE

Here is my tasty version of a deconstructed breakfast burrito. Go for hefty corn tortillas in this recipe. Flour ones can get lost in the scramble.
—Christine Schenher, Exeter, CA

- -

Takes: 15 min. • **Makes:** 2 servings

- 4 **large egg whites**
- 2 **large eggs**
- ¼ **tsp. pepper**
- 2 **corn tortillas (6 in.), halved and cut into strips**
- ¼ **cup chopped fresh spinach**
- 2 **Tbsp. shredded reduced-fat cheddar cheese**
- ¼ **cup salsa**

1. In a large bowl, whisk egg whites, eggs and pepper. Stir in tortilla strips, spinach and cheese.

2. Heat a large skillet coated with cooking spray over medium heat. Pour in egg mixture; cook and stir until eggs are thickened and no liquid egg remains. Top with salsa.

1 cup: 195 cal., 7g fat (3g sat. fat), 217mg chol., 391mg sod., 16g carb. (2g sugars, 2g fiber), 17g pro.
Diabetic exchanges: 2 lean meat, 1 starch.

SOUTHWEST TORTILLA SCRAMBLE

OVERNIGHT CHERRY-
ALMOND OATMEAL

OVERNIGHT CHERRY-ALMOND OATMEAL

Would you like breakfast ready for you when the sun comes up? If so, try my hot cereal. It's so simple—just place the ingredients in the slow cooker and turn it on before you go to bed. In the morning, you can enjoy a warm and satisfying dish.
—Geraldine Saucier, Albuquerque, NM

- -

Prep: 10 min. • **Cook:** 7 hours
Makes: 6 servings

4   **cups vanilla almond milk**
1   **cup steel-cut oats**
1   **cup dried cherries**
⅓   **cup packed brown sugar**
½   **tsp. salt**
½   **tsp. ground cinnamon**
     Additional almond milk, optional

1. In a 3-qt. slow cooker coated with cooking spray, combine all the ingredients. Cook, covered, on low until oats are tender, 7-8 hours.
2. Stir before serving. If desired, serve with additional milk.

¾ **cup:** 276 cal., 4g fat (0 sat. fat), 0 chol., 306mg sod., 57g carb. (35g sugars, 4g fiber), 5g pro.

TEST KITCHEN TIP
Nutritionally, steel-cut oats are about the same as rolled oats, so take your pick. Skip instant oatmeal mixes, which have a lot of added sugar.

APPLE CINNAMON OVERNIGHT OATS

FRESH FRUIT BOWL

The glorious colors of the fruit make this a festive salad. Slightly sweet and chilled, it makes a nice accompaniment to almost any entree.
—Marion Kirst, Troy, MI

Prep: 15 min. + chilling
Makes: 16 servings

8 cups fresh melon cubes
1 to 2 Tbsp. corn syrup
1 pint fresh strawberries, halved
2 cups fresh pineapple chunks
2 oranges, sectioned
Fresh mint leaves, optional

In a large bowl, combine melon cubes and corn syrup. Cover and refrigerate overnight. Just before serving, stir in the remaining fruit. If desired, garnish with the fresh mint leaves.
¾ cup: 56 cal., 0 fat (0 sat. fat), 0 chol., 14mg sod., 14g carb. (11g sugars, 2g fiber), 1g pro.
Diabetic exchanges: 1 fruit.

APPLE CINNAMON OVERNIGHT OATS

Many folks love this oatmeal cold, but I heat it up a little since I'm not a big fan of it right out of the fridge. Add a handful of nuts for crunch, flavor and extra health benefits.
—Sarah Farmer, Waukesha, WI

Prep: 5 min. + chilling
Makes: 1 serving

½ cup old-fashioned oats
½ medium Gala or Honeycrisp apple, chopped
1 Tbsp. raisins
1 cup 2% milk
¼ tsp. ground cinnamon
Dash salt
Toasted chopped nuts, optional

In a small container or Mason jar, combine all the ingredients. Seal; refrigerate overnight.
1½ cups: 349 cal., 8g fat (4g sat. fat), 20mg chol., 263mg sod., 59g carb. (28g sugars, 7g fiber), 14g pro.

FRESH FRUIT
BOWL

LANCE'S OWN FRENCH TOAST

LANCE'S OWN FRENCH TOAST

When my young son, Lance, helps me make this French toast, he knows in what order to add the ingredients and even how much to measure out. This dish is perfect for the whole family!
—Janna Steele, Magee, MS

- -

Takes: 25 min. • **Makes:** 6 servings

 4 **large eggs**
 1 **cup 2% milk**
 1 **Tbsp. honey**
 ½ **tsp. ground cinnamon**
 ⅛ **tsp. pepper**
 12 **slices whole wheat bread**
  Optional: Cinnamon sugar or vanilla frosting

In a shallow bowl, whisk eggs, milk, honey, cinnamon and pepper. Dip both sides of bread in the egg mixture. Cook on a greased hot griddle 3-4 minutes on each side or until golden brown. If desired, sprinkle with cinnamon sugar or frost with vanilla icing.

Freeze option: Cool French toast on wire racks. Freeze between layers of waxed paper in a resealable freezer container. To use, reheat French toast in a toaster oven on medium setting. Or microwave each French toast on high for 30-60 seconds or until heated through.

2 slices: 218 cal., 6g fat (2g sat. fat), 144mg chol., 331mg sod., 28g carb. (8g sugars, 4g fiber), 13g pro.
Diabetic exchanges: 2 starch, 1 medium-fat meat.

RHUBARB COMPOTE WITH YOGURT & ALMONDS

My Grandma Dot used to make rhubarb compote and always had some in the freezer when I came to visit. This breakfast is a tribute to her. No two stalks of rhubarb are exactly alike, so make sure to taste the compote before you chill it. It should be tart, but sometimes it needs a little extra sugar.
—Michael Hoffman, Brooklyn, NY

- -

Prep: 10 min.
Cook: 15 min. + chilling
Makes: 6 servings

- **2 cups finely chopped fresh rhubarb**
- **¼ cup sugar**
- **2 Tbsp. water**
- **3 cups reduced-fat plain Greek yogurt**
- **2 Tbsp. honey**
- **¾ cup sliced almonds, toasted**

1. In a small saucepan, combine rhubarb, sugar and water. Bring to a boil. Reduce heat; simmer, uncovered, 10-15 minutes or until the rhubarb is tender, stirring occasionally. Transfer to a bowl; cool slightly. Refrigerate until cold.
2. In a small bowl, whisk the yogurt and honey until blended. Spoon into serving dishes. Top with compote; sprinkle with almonds.

½ cup yogurt with about 2 Tbsp. compote and 2 Tbsp. almonds: 218 cal., 8g fat (2g sat. fat), 7mg chol., 49mg sod., 23g carb. (20g sugars, 2g fiber), 14g pro.
Diabetic exchanges: 1 starch, 1 reduced-fat milk, 1 fat.

SCRUMPTIOUS SCRAMBLE

By substituting 4 egg whites for the 4 whole eggs in this recipe, you save 25 calories, 3g fat and a whopping 141mg cholesterol per serving! And since the eggs are seasoned with veggies and dill, you won't miss the flavor at all.
—Lynn Winkler, Chatsworth, GA

- -

Takes: 15 min. • **Makes:** 3 servings

- **½ cup finely chopped red onion**
- **1 tsp. olive oil**
- **1 medium tomato, seeded and finely chopped**
- **4 large eggs**
- **4 large egg whites**
- **2 Tbsp. water**
- **1½ tsp. snipped fresh dill or ½ tsp. dill weed**
- **¼ tsp. salt**
- **⅛ tsp. pepper**

1. In a large nonstick skillet coated with cooking spray, saute the onion in oil for 2 minutes. Add the tomato; saute 1-2 minutes longer or until the vegetables are tender. Transfer to a small bowl; set aside.
2. In a large bowl, whisk remaining ingredients. Coat the same skillet with additional cooking spray; add the egg mixture. Cook and stir over medium heat until eggs are nearly set. Add the reserved onion mixture; cook and stir until heated through and eggs are completely set.
¾ cup: 156 cal., 8g fat (2g sat. fat), 283mg chol., 359mg sod., 6g carb. (4g sugars, 1g fiber), 14g pro.

RHUBARB COMPOTE WITH YOGURT & ALMONDS

VEGETABLE
SCRAMBLED EGGS

VEGETABLE SCRAMBLED EGGS

I like to have friends and family over for a special Sunday brunch, especially when there's a big game on television. These colorful eggs go perfectly with sausage, fresh fruit and toasted English muffins.

—Marilyn Ipson, Rogers, AR

- -

Takes: 10 min. • **Makes:** 2 servings

- 4 large eggs, lightly beaten
- ¼ cup fat-free milk
- ½ cup chopped green pepper
- ¼ cup sliced green onions
- ¼ tsp. salt
- ⅛ tsp. pepper
- 1 small tomato, chopped and seeded

In a small bowl, combine the eggs and milk. Add green pepper, onions, salt and pepper. Pour into a lightly greased skillet. Cook and stir over medium heat until eggs are nearly set, 2-3 minutes. Add tomato; cook and stir until eggs are completely set.
¾ cup: 173 cal., 10g fat (3g sat. fat), 373mg chol., 455mg sod., 7g carb. (4g sugars, 2g fiber), 15g pro.
Diabetic exchanges: 2 medium-fat meat, 1 vegetable.

PEANUT BUTTER BANANA OATMEAL

PEANUT BUTTER BANANA OATMEAL

The classic flavors of bananas and peanut butter come together in this yummy oatmeal. It's a healthy recipe that fits in my diet and satisfies my husband's taste buds at the same time. We enjoy it often.

—Deborah Purdue, Westland, MI

- -

Takes: 15 min. • **Makes:** 4 servings

- 3 cups fat-free milk or water
- ¼ tsp. salt
- 1½ cups quick-cooking oats
- 2 large bananas, sliced
- 2 Tbsp. peanut butter
- ½ tsp. vanilla extract

Place the milk and salt in a large saucepan; bring just to a boil. Stir in the oats; cook until thickened, 1-2 minutes, stirring occasionally. Remove from heat; stir in the remaining ingredients.
1 cup: 284 cal., 7g fat (1g sat. fat), 4mg chol., 260mg sod., 47g carb. (19g sugars, 5g fiber), 13g pro.

WAFFLE-IRON FRENCH TOAST

Are waffles too much trouble on a busy morning? Try this quick and clever alternative. I drizzle crispy slices of whole wheat bread with a yummy strawberry sauce that combines pancake syrup and fresh sliced berries. It's sure to become a breakfast must at your house, too!
—Martha Osborne, Jackson, MI

- -

Takes: 25 min. • **Makes:** 2 servings

- 1 **large egg**
- 1 **large egg white**
- ¼ **cup fat-free milk**
- 4 **slices whole wheat or white bread**
- 1 **cup sliced fresh strawberries**
- ¼ **cup reduced-calorie pancake syrup**

1. In a shallow dish, beat the egg, egg white and milk. Dip bread into egg mixture, coating both sides. Bake in a preheated waffle iron according to the manufacturer's directions until golden brown.

2. For sauce, in a bowl, crush the strawberries; stir in the pancake syrup. Serve French toast with the strawberry sauce.

2 pieces: 261 cal., 5g fat (1g sat. fat), 107mg chol., 401mg sod., 45g carb. (0 sugars, 4g fiber), 11g pro.
Diabetic exchanges: 2½ starch, 1 lean meat, ½ fruit.

NUTTY FLAX OATMEAL

My son and I eat this every day for breakfast. It's a hearty, healthy meal to jump-start our day.
—Elisabeth Reitenbach, Terryville, CT

- -

Takes: 15 min. • **Makes:** 2 servings

- 1¾ **cups water**
- ⅛ **tsp. salt**
- 1 **cup old-fashioned oats**
- 2 **Tbsp. creamy peanut butter**
- 2 **Tbsp. honey**
- 2 **tsp. ground flaxseed**
- ½ **to 1 tsp. ground cinnamon**
  Chopped apple, optional

In a small saucepan, bring water and salt to a boil. Stir in the oats; cook 5 minutes over medium heat, stirring occasionally. Transfer oatmeal to 2 bowls; in each bowl, stir half each peanut butter, honey, flaxseed, cinnamon and, if desired, apple. Serve immediately.

¾ cup: 323 cal., 12g fat (2g sat. fat), 0 chol., 226mg sod., 49g carb. (19g sugars, 6g fiber), 11g pro.

NUTTY FLAX OATMEAL

BERRY SMOOTHIE BOWL

BERRY SMOOTHIE BOWL

We turned one of our most-loved smoothies into a smoothie bowl and topped it with even more fresh fruit and a few toasted almonds for a little crunch.
—*Taste of Home* Test Kitchen

Takes: 5 min. • **Makes:** 2 servings

- 1 cup fat-free milk
- 1 cup frozen unsweetened strawberries
- ½ cup frozen unsweetened raspberries
- 3 Tbsp. sugar
- 1 cup ice cubes
  Optional: Sliced fresh strawberries, fresh raspberries, chia seeds, fresh pumpkin seeds, unsweetened shredded coconut and sliced almonds

Place the milk, berries and sugar in a blender; cover and process until smooth. Add ice cubes; cover and process until smooth. Divide mixture between 2 serving bowls. Add optional toppings as desired.

1½ cups: 155 cal., 0 fat (0 sat. fat), 2mg chol., 54mg sod., 35g carb. (30g sugars, 2g fiber), 5g pro.

BLUEBERRY CORNMEAL PANCAKES

MAKEOVER
HASH & EGGS

A diner classic goes home-style in this better-than-ever version that delivers fresh flavors with a wonderful dose of fiber.
—*Taste of Home* Test Kitchen

- -

Takes: 30 min. • **Makes:** 4 servings

1   large onion, chopped
1   Tbsp. canola oil, divided
6   medium red potatoes
    (about 1½ lbs.),
    cut into ½-in. cubes
¼   cup water
3   pkg. (2 oz. each) thinly sliced
    deli corned beef,
    coarsely chopped
¼   tsp. pepper
4   large eggs
    Additional pepper, optional

1. In a large nonstick skillet, saute onion in 2 tsp. oil until tender. Stir in potatoes and water. Bring to a boil. Reduce heat; cover and simmer for 15-20 minutes or until potatoes are tender. Stir in corned beef and pepper; heat through.
2. Meanwhile, in a large nonstick skillet, fry the eggs in remaining oil as desired. Season with additional pepper if desired. Serve with corned beef hash.

1 egg with 1 cup hash: 301 cal., 12g fat (3g sat. fat), 239mg chol., 652mg sod., 31g carb. (4g sugars, 4g fiber), 18g pro. **Diabetic exchanges:** 2 starch, 2 medium-fat meat, ½ fat.

BLUEBERRY CORNMEAL PANCAKES

These pancakes are one of my family's favorite breakfasts. No time to make them from scratch? No problem! Store-bought corn muffin mix works, too.
—Carolyn Eskew, Dayton, OH

- -

Takes: 30 min.
Makes: 10 corncakes

1   pkg. (8½ oz.) cornbread/
    muffin mix
1   cup fresh or frozen
    blueberries
⅓   cup canned white or
    shoepeg corn
    Maple syrup

In a large bowl, prepare muffin mix according to package directions. Gently stir in blueberries and corn. Lightly grease a griddle; warm over medium heat. Pour the batter by ¼ cupfuls onto griddle; flatten slightly. Cook until bottoms are golden brown. Turn; cook until second sides are golden brown. Serve with syrup.

2 cakes: 251 cal., 7g fat (2g sat. fat), 39mg chol., 454mg sod., 41g carb. (14g sugars, 4g fiber), 6g pro.

MAKEOVER
HASH & EGGS

CURRY SCRAMBLE

CURRY SCRAMBLE

I have eggs every morning, and this is a delightful change of pace from the classic scrambled mixture. I add sliced peppers on top if I have them on hand.
—Valerie Belley, St. Louis, MO

- -

Takes: 15 min. • **Makes:** 4 servings

   8   **large eggs**
   ¼   **cup fat-free milk**

   ½   **tsp. curry powder**
   ¼   **tsp. salt**
   ⅛   **tsp. pepper**
   ⅛   **tsp. ground cardamom, optional**
   2   **medium tomatoes, sliced or chopped**

1. In a large bowl, whisk eggs, milk, curry powder, salt, pepper and, if desired, cardamom until blended.
2. Place a lightly greased large nonstick skillet over medium heat.

Pour in egg mixture; cook and stir until eggs are thickened and no liquid egg remains. Serve with tomatoes.

1 serving: 160 cal., 10g fat (3g sat. fat), 372mg chol., 299mg sod., 4g carb. (3g sugars, 1g fiber), 14g pro. **Diabetic exchanges:** 2 medium-fat meat.

WARM GRAPEFRUIT WITH GINGER-SUGAR

Sweetly broiled grapefruit is a morning specialty at my bed-and-breakfast. It also makes a fabulous light snack or dessert.
—Stephanie Levy, Lansing, NY

- -

Takes: 15 min. • **Makes:** 2 servings

- 1 large red grapefruit
- 2 to 3 tsp. chopped crystallized ginger
- 2 tsp. sugar

1. Preheat broiler. Cut grapefruit crosswise in half. With a small knife, cut around the membrane in the center of each half and discard. Cut around each section to loosen fruit. Place on a baking sheet, cut side up.
2. Mix ginger and sugar; sprinkle over fruit. Broil 4 in. from heat until sugar is melted, about 4 minutes.
½ grapefruit: 85 cal., 0 fat (0 sat. fat), 0 chol., 3mg sod., 22g carb. (17g sugars, 2g fiber), 1g pro. **Diabetic exchanges:** 1 fruit, ½ starch.

EGG-FREE SPICED PANCAKES

Golden brown and fluffy, these pancakes are ideal served with syrup or berries. You'll never guess the eggs are missing!
—*Taste of Home* Test Kitchen

- -

Prep: 10 min. • **Cook:** 10 min./batch
Makes: 8 pancakes

- 1 cup all-purpose flour
- 2 Tbsp. brown sugar
- 2½ tsp. baking powder
- ½ tsp. pumpkin pie spice
- ¼ tsp. salt
- 1 cup fat-free milk
- 2 Tbsp. canola oil
   Maple syrup, optional

1. In a large bowl, combine the flour, brown sugar, baking powder, pie spice and salt. In another bowl, combine milk and oil; stir into dry ingredients just until moistened.
2. Pour batter by ¼ cupfuls onto a hot griddle coated with cooking spray; turn when bubbles form on top. Cook until the second side is golden brown. Serve with syrup if desired.
2 pancakes: 223 cal., 7g fat (1g sat. fat), 1mg chol., 427mg sod., 34g carb. (10g sugars, 1g fiber), 5g pro. **Diabetic exchanges:** 2 starch, 1½ fat.

WARM GRAPEFRUIT WITH GINGER-SUGAR

**FETA SCRAMBLED
EGG WRAPS**

FETA SCRAMBLED EGG WRAPS

My daughter jokes that I am so predictable when it comes to dining out. I always order chicken souvlaki. So I figured, why not incorporate my favorite Greek dish into a breakfast wrap? It's healthy, tasty and easy to make.

—Mary Jo Kempf, West Seneca, NY

- -

Takes: 15 min. • **Makes:** 4 servings

- 1½ cups Southwestern-style egg substitute
- ¾ cup crumbled feta cheese
- 2 Tbsp. sliced pepperoncini, chopped
- 4 whole wheat tortillas (8 in.), warmed

Place a large nonstick skillet coated with cooking spray over medium heat. Pour in egg substitute; cook and stir until thickened and no liquid egg remains. Gently stir in cheese and pepperoncini; heat through. Serve in tortillas.

1 wrap: 239 cal., 6g fat (2g sat. fat), 11mg chol., 560mg sod., 24g carb. (3g sugars, 3g fiber), 17g pro.
Diabetic exchanges: 2 lean meat, 1½ starch.

YOGURT & HONEY FRUIT CUPS

YOGURT & HONEY FRUIT CUPS

This tasty combo of fresh fruit and creamy orange-kissed yogurt is guaranteed to disappear fast from your breakfast table.

—*Taste of Home* Test Kitchen

- -

Takes: 10 min. • **Makes:** 6 servings

- 4½ cups cut-up fresh fruit (pears, apples, bananas, grapes, etc.)
- ¾ cup mandarin orange, vanilla or lemon yogurt
- 1 Tbsp. honey
- ½ tsp. grated orange zest
- ¼ tsp. almond extract

Divide fruit among 6 individual serving bowls. Combine the yogurt, honey, orange zest and extract; spoon over the fruit.

¾ cup: 97 cal., 0 fat (0 sat. fat), 2mg chol., 22mg sod., 23g carb. (9g sugars, 2g fiber), 2g pro.
Diabetic exchanges: 1 fruit, ½ starch.

HOMEMADE YOGURT

It is almost too simple to make homemade yogurt. Top with granola and your favorite berries.
—*Taste of Home* Test Kitchen

Prep: 5 min. + chilling
Cook: 20 min. + standing
Makes: about 2 qt.

2 qt. pasteurized whole milk
2 Tbsp. plain yogurt with live active cultures

1. In a Dutch oven, heat milk over medium heat until a thermometer reads 200°, stirring occasionally to prevent scorching. Remove from the heat; let stand until a thermometer reads 112°-115°, stirring occasionally. (If desired, place pan in an ice-water bath for faster cooling.)
2. Whisk 1 cup warm milk into the yogurt until smooth; return all to pan, stirring gently. Transfer mixture to warm, clean jars, such as 1-qt. canning jars.
3. Cover jars; place in oven. Turn on oven light to keep mixture warm, about 110°. Let stand, undisturbed, 6-24 hours or until yogurt is set, tilting jars gently to check. (Yogurt will become thicker and more tangy as it stands.)
4. Refrigerate, covered, until cold. Store in refrigerator up to 2 weeks.
1 cup: 151 cal., 8g fat (5g sat. fat), 25mg chol., 107mg sod., 12g carb. (12g sugars, 0 fiber), 8g pro.
Diabetic exchanges: 1 whole milk.

SAVORY APPLE-CHICKEN SAUSAGE

These robust sausages taste incredible, and they make an elegant brunch dish. The recipe can be doubled or tripled for a crowd, and the sausages freeze well either cooked or raw.
—Angela Buchanan, Longmont, CO

Takes: 25 min. • **Makes:** 8 patties

1 large tart apple, peeled and diced
2 tsp. poultry seasoning
1 tsp. salt
¼ tsp. pepper
1 lb. ground chicken

1. In a large bowl, combine the first 4 ingredients. Crumble chicken over the mixture and mix well. Shape into eight 3-in. patties.
2. In a large, greased cast-iron or other heavy skillet, cook patties over medium heat until no longer pink, 5-6 minutes on each side. Drain if necessary.
1 sausage patty: 92 cal., 5g fat (1g sat. fat), 38mg chol., 328mg sod., 4g carb. (3g sugars, 1g fiber), 9g pro.
Diabetic exchanges: 1 medium-fat meat.

SAVORY APPLE-CHICKEN SAUSAGE

WAFFLE SANDWICH

WAFFLE SANDWICH

Keep 'em going right through to lunchtime with this quick and easy breakfast idea. I serve it with crisp, juicy apples on the side.
—Michele McHenry, Bellingham, WA

- -

Takes: 20 min. • **Makes:** 1 serving

- 1   slice Canadian bacon
- 1   large egg
- 1   green onion, chopped
- 2   frozen low-fat multigrain waffles
- 1   Tbsp. shredded reduced-fat cheddar cheese
     Sliced tomato, optional

1. In a nonstick skillet, cook the Canadian bacon over medium-high heat 1-2 minutes on each side or until lightly browned. Remove and keep warm.

2. In a small bowl, whisk the egg and the green onion; add to the same pan. Cook and stir until the egg is thickened and no liquid egg remains.

3. Meanwhile, prepare waffles according to package directions. Place 1 waffle on a plate. Top with Canadian bacon, scrambled egg, cheese and, if desired, tomato. Top with remaining waffle.

1 sandwich: 261 cal., 10g fat (3g sat. fat), 223mg chol., 733mg sod., 30g carb. (5g sugars, 3g fiber), 16g pro. **Diabetic exchanges:** 2 starch, 2 medium-fat meat.

**VANILLA
FRENCH TOAST**

QUINOA BREAKFAST BOWL

Quinoa has been around for a while, but I'm just now jumping on the quinoa breakfast bowl bandwagon. I've made it several times as a savory side or salad— never as a warm breakfast cereal. I finally gave it a try last weekend and loved it!
—Erica Schmidt, Kansas City, KS

- -

Takes: 20 min. • **Makes:** 4 servings

- 2 **cups 2% or coconut milk**
- 1 **cup quinoa, rinsed**
     Optional: Ground cinnamon, vanilla Greek yogurt, sugar substitute blend, honey, brown sugar, raisins, fresh blueberries, chopped apple, chia seeds and fresh mint leaves

In a large saucepan, bring milk to a boil over medium heat, stirring occasionally. Add quinoa. Reduce heat; simmer, covered, until liquid is absorbed, 12-15 minutes. Remove from the heat; fluff with a fork. If desired, stir in any combination of optional ingredients.
¾ cup: 217 cal., 5g fat (2g sat. fat), 10mg chol., 59mg sod., 33g carb. (6g sugars, 3g fiber), 10g pro.
Diabetic exchanges: 1½ starch, ½ reduced-fat milk.

VANILLA FRENCH TOAST

We discovered this recipe in Mexico. We couldn't figure out what made the French toast so delicious until we learned the secret was vanilla—it's one of Mexico's most popular flavorings. Now we add a touch of vanilla to our waffle and pancake recipes, and it makes all the difference.
—Joe and Bobbi Schott, Castroville, TX

- -

Takes: 15 min. • **Makes:** 6 servings

- 4 **large eggs, lightly beaten**
- 1 **cup 2% milk**
- 2 **Tbsp. sugar**
- 2 **tsp. vanilla extract**
- ⅛ **tsp. salt**
- 12 **slices day-old sandwich bread**
     Optional toppings: Butter, maple syrup, fresh berries and confectioners' sugar

1. In a shallow dish, whisk together the first 5 ingredients. Preheat a greased griddle over medium heat.
2. Dip bread in egg mixture, allowing to soak 30 seconds on each side. Cook on griddle until golden brown on both sides. Serve with toppings as desired.
2 slices: 218 cal., 6g fat (3g sat. fat), 127mg chol., 376mg sod., 30g carb. (9g sugars, 1g fiber), 10g pro.
Diabetic exchanges: 2 starch, 1 medium-fat meat.

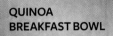

QUINOA
BREAKFAST BOWL

**BANANA
OATMEAL
PANCAKES**

BANANA OATMEAL PANCAKES

*These whole wheat pancakes
have less sodium per serving than
other pancakes made from mixes.
Decrease the sodium per serving
even more by stretching the mix
with banana, oats and walnuts.
The fruit is so sweet you don't
need syrup.*

— Patricia Swart, Galloway, NJ

- -

Prep: 10 min. • **Cook:** 5 min./batch
Makes: 16 pancakes

2 **cups complete whole wheat
    pancake mix**
1 **large firm banana,
    finely chopped**
½ **cup old-fashioned oats**
¼ **cup chopped walnuts**

Prepare pancake batter according
to the package directions. Stir in
the banana, oats and walnuts. Pour
the batter by ¼ cupfuls onto a hot
griddle coated with cooking spray;
turn when bubbles form on top.
Cook until the second side is
golden brown.

2 pancakes: 155 cal., 4g fat (0 sat.
fat), 0 chol., 293mg sod., 28g carb.
(4g sugars, 4g fiber), 7g pro.
Diabetic exchanges: 2 starch.

SWEET ONION PIE

Loaded with sweet onions, this creamy pie makes a scrumptious addition to a brunch buffet. I cut calories and fat by using less butter to cook the onions and substituting lighter ingredients.
—Barbara Reese, Catawissa, PA

- -

Prep: 35 min. • **Bake:** 30 min.
Makes: 8 servings

- 2 **sweet onions, halved and sliced**
- 1 **Tbsp. butter**
- 1 **frozen deep-dish pie crust**
- 1 **cup egg substitute**
- 1 **cup fat-free evaporated milk**
- 1 **tsp. salt**
- ¼ **tsp. pepper**

1. In a large nonstick skillet, cook onions in butter over medium-low heat until very tender, 30 minutes. Meanwhile, line unpricked crust with a double thickness of heavy-duty foil.
2. Bake at 450° for 6 minutes. Remove foil; cool on a wire rack. Reduce heat to 425°.
3. Spoon onions into crust. In a small bowl, whisk the egg substitute, milk, salt and pepper; pour over onions. Bake until a knife inserted in center comes out clean, 30-35 minutes. Let the pie stand for 5-10 minutes before cutting.

1 piece: 169 cal., 7g fat (2g sat. fat), 5mg chol., 487mg sod., 21g carb. (8g sugars, 1g fiber), 7g pro. **Diabetic exchanges:** 1 starch, 1 lean meat, 1 fat.

SWEET ONION PIE

SAUSAGE & SALSA BREAKFAST BURRITOS

The best of breakfast gets wrapped up snugly in a whole wheat tortilla for a hand-held feast for a meal on the go.
—Michelle Burnett, Eden, UT

- -

Takes: 20 min. • **Makes:** 6 servings

- 5 **breakfast turkey sausage links**
- 2 **cartons (8 oz. each) egg substitute**
- ½ **cup salsa**
- ¼ **tsp. pepper**
- 6 **whole wheat tortilla (8 in.), warmed**
- ½ **cup shredded reduced-fat cheddar cheese**

1. Cook sausage links according to package directions. Meanwhile, in a large bowl, whisk the egg substitute, salsa and pepper. Pour into a large nonstick skillet coated with cooking spray. Cook and stir over medium heat until eggs are nearly set. Chop the sausage links. Add to egg mixture; cook and stir until completely set.
2. Spoon ⅓ cup egg mixture off center on each tortilla and sprinkle with 4 tsp. cheese. Fold sides and ends over filling and roll up.

1 burrito: 265 cal., 10g fat (3g sat. fat), 25mg chol., 602mg sod., 25g carb. (3g sugars, 2g fiber), 18g pro. **Diabetic Exchanges:** 2 lean meat, 1½ starch, 1 fat.

WHOLESOME SNACKS

TURKEY & APRICOT WRAPS
P. 53

1

2

3

4

5

KISS THAT GREASY BAG OF CHIPS GOODBYE!
THESE TASTY AND SATISFYING BITES PROVE
THAT SNACK TIME CAN BE FUN *AND* GOOD
FOR YOU, TOO!

ROSEMARY
WALNUTS

ROSEMARY WALNUTS

My Aunt Mary started making this recipe years ago. Each time we visited, she would have a batch ready for us. Cayenne adds an unexpected zing to the savory combo of rosemary and walnuts. When you need a housewarming or hostess gift, double the batch and save one for yourself.
—Renee Ciancio, New Bern, NC

- -

Takes: 20 min. • **Makes:** 2 cups

- 2 **cups walnut halves**
  Cooking spray
- 2 **tsp. dried rosemary, crushed**
- ½ **tsp. kosher salt**
- ¼ **to ½ tsp. cayenne pepper**

1. Place the walnuts in a small bowl. Spritz with cooking spray. Add the seasonings; toss to coat. Place in a single layer on a baking sheet.
2. Bake at 350° for 10 minutes. Serve warm, or cool completely and store in an airtight container.
¼ cup: 166 cal., 17g fat (2g sat. fat), 0 chol., 118mg sod., 4g carb. (1g sugars, 2g fiber), 4g pro. **Diabetic exchanges:** 3 fat.

DID YOU KNOW?
Walnuts have hard outer shells that contain light brown kernels. These can be used raw or in sweet and savory recipes.

SPICY EDAMAME

SPICY EDAMAME

Edamame (pronounced ay-duh-MAH-may) are young soybeans in their pods. We boiled and seasoned them with salt, ginger, garlic powder and red pepper flakes.
—*Taste of Home* Test Kitchen

- -

Takes: 20 min. • **Makes:** 6 servings

- 1 **pkg. (16 oz.) frozen edamame pods**
- 2 **tsp. kosher salt**
- ¾ **tsp. ground ginger**
- ½ **tsp. garlic powder**
- ¼ **tsp. crushed red pepper flakes**

Place edamame in a large saucepan and cover with water. Bring to a boil. Cover and cook until tender, 4-5 minutes; drain. Transfer to a large bowl. Add the seasonings; toss to coat.
1 serving: 52 cal., 2g fat (0 sat. fat), 0 chol., 642mg sod., 5g carb. (1g sugars, 2g fiber), 4g pro.

CHOCOLATE-HAZELNUT FRUIT PIZZA

This snackable pizza takes only 10 minutes to prepare! It is a fun way to get in those daily fruit servings.

—Dalynn Dowling,
Grand Forks AFB, ND

Takes: 10 min. • **Makes:** 4 servings

- 1   whole wheat tortilla (8 in.)
- 2   Tbsp. Nutella
- 3   to 4 fresh strawberries, sliced
- ½   medium firm banana,
       peeled and sliced
- ½   medium kiwifruit,
       peeled and sliced

Spread the tortilla with Nutella. Arrange the fruits over the top. Cut into 4 wedges. Serve immediately.
1 wedge: 103 cal., 4g fat (0 sat. fat), 0 chol., 47mg sod., 17g carb. (8g sugars, 2g fiber), 2g pro.

SLOW-COOKED APPLESAUCE

My sweet, chunky applesauce makes a perfect snack or side dish with your favorite entree. It's prepared in the slow cooker, so you can let it cook while you and your family head out for some fun.

—Susanne Wasson,
Montgomery, NY

Prep: 20 min. • **Cook:** 6 hours
Makes: 12 cups

- 6   lbs. apples
       (about 18 medium),
       peeled and sliced
- 1   cup sugar
- 1   cup water
- 1   tsp. salt
- 1   tsp. ground cinnamon
- ¼   cup butter, cubed
- 2   tsp. vanilla extract

1. In a 5-qt. slow cooker, combine the apples, sugar, water, salt and cinnamon. Cover and cook on low for 6-8 hours or until tender.
2. Turn off heat; stir in the butter and vanilla. Mash if desired. Serve warm or cold.
½ cup: 105 cal., 2g fat (1g sat. fat), 5mg chol., 112mg sod., 23g carb. (20g sugars, 2g fiber), 0 pro.
Diabetic exchanges: 1 fruit, ½ starch, ½ fat.

SLOW-COOKED APPLESAUCE

PEANUT BUTTER, HONEY & PEAR OPEN-FACED SANDWICHES

PEANUT BUTTER, HONEY & PEAR OPEN-FACED SANDWICHES

I work a 12-hour night shift at a hospital, and when I come home in the morning, I don't want to cook a big breakfast. I love these sandwiches because they are easy and versatile. Sometimes I use apples instead of pears and different cheeses, such as Brie or grated Parmesan. The creative possibilities are endless!
—L. J. Washington, Carpinteria, CA

Takes: 10 min. • **Makes:** 4 servings

- ¼ cup chunky peanut butter
- 4 slices honey whole wheat bread, toasted
- 1 medium pear, thinly sliced
- ¼ tsp. salt
- 4 tsp. honey
- ½ cup shredded cheddar cheese

Spread peanut butter over the toast slices. Top with the pear, salt, honey and cheese. Place on a microwave-safe plate; microwave on high until cheese is melted, 20-25 seconds.

1 open-faced sandwich: 268 cal., 14g fat (4g sat. fat), 14mg chol., 446mg sod., 28g carb. (13g sugars, 4g fiber), 11g pro.

DID YOU KNOW?
Pears are available year-round, but their peak season is July through January. Pears do their best ripening after they are picked—a rare phenomenon among fruits.

HERBED COTTAGE CHEESE

I don't miss the fat in this tasty version of light cottage cheese. Serve it with canned tuna and crackers for a light lunch.
—Traci Hirstein, Western Springs, IL

Takes: 5 min. • **Makes:** 4 servings

- 2 cups 1% cottage cheese
- 1 Tbsp. minced chives
- ¼ tsp. garlic powder
- ¼ tsp. onion powder
- ¼ tsp. salt
- ⅛ tsp. celery seed
- ⅛ tsp. pepper

In a bowl, combine all of the ingredients. Serve immediately.
½ cup: 83 cal., 1g fat (1g sat. fat), 5mg chol., 607mg sod., 3g carb. (0 sugars, 0 fiber), 14g pro.

BERRY SMOOTHIES

HARD-BOILED EGGS

Here's a foolproof technique for making hard-boiled eggs to eat plain or to use in other recipes.
—*Taste of Home* Test Kitchen

Prep: 20 min. + cooling
Makes: 12 servings

  12 **large eggs**
      Cold water

1. Place eggs in a single layer in a large saucepan; add enough cold water to cover by 1 in. Cover and quickly bring to a boil. Remove from heat. Let stand for 15 minutes for large eggs (18 minutes for extra-large eggs and 12 minutes for medium eggs).
2. Rinse eggs in cold water and place in ice water until completely cooled. Drain and refrigerate.
1 hard-boiled egg: 75 cal., 5g fat (2g sat. fat), 213mg chol., 63mg sod., 1g carb. (1g sugars, 0 fiber), 6g pro.
Diabetic exchanges: 1 medium-fat meat.

BERRY SMOOTHIES

Enjoy these bright smoothies for breakfast or any time you crave a healthy snack. They're delicious and nourishing, and no one can tell there's tofu in the silky blend.
—Sonya Labbe,
West Hollywood, CA

Takes: 10 min. • **Makes:** 2 servings

 ½ **cup pomegranate juice**
 1 **Tbsp. agave syrup or honey**
 3 **oz. silken firm tofu**
     (about ½ cup)
 1 **cup frozen unsweetened mixed berries**
 1 **cup frozen unsweetened strawberries**

Place all ingredients in a blender; cover and process until blended. Serve immediately.
1 cup: 157 cal., 1g fat (0 sat. fat), 0 chol., 24mg sod., 35g carb. (29g sugars, 3g fiber), 4g pro.

HARD-BOILED EGGS

HOMEMADE PEANUT BUTTER

HOMEMADE PEANUT BUTTER

We eat a lot of peanut butter, so I decided to make my own. My homemade version is easier on my wallet, and I know what ingredients are in it. It's also a lot tastier!
—Marge Austin, North Pole, AK

- -

Takes: 15 min. • **Makes:** about 1 cup

- 2 **cups unsalted dry roasted peanuts**
- ½ **tsp. salt**
- 1 **Tbsp. honey**

Process peanuts and salt in a food processor until desired consistency, about 5 minutes, scraping down the sides as needed. Add honey; process just until blended. Store in an airtight container in refrigerator.

1 Tbsp.: 111 cal., 9g fat (1g sat. fat), 0 chol., 75mg sod., 5g carb. (2g sugars, 2g fiber), 4g pro. **Diabetic exchanges:** 2 fat.

BLACK TEA WITH LEMON BALM

Try this recipe for a delicious tea that boasts a wonderful lemony flavor. It's perfect to slowly sip while enjoying a warm muffin or scone on a cool day.
—*Taste of Home* Test Kitchen

- -

Takes: 10 min. • **Makes:** 1 serving

- 1 **cup water**
- 1 **individual bag of black tea**
- 1 **tsp. dried lemon balm**
  Lemon peel

In a saucepan, bring water to a boil. Remove from heat. Add the tea, lemon balm and lemon peel. Let stand 5 minutes. Remove tea bag and strain tea into a teacup or mug.

1 cup: 3 cal., 0 fat (0 sat. fat), 0 chol., 8mg sod., 1g carb. (0 sugars, 0 fiber), 0 pro. **Diabetic exchanges:** 1 free food.

LEMON THYME GREEN TEA

Fresh sprigs of lemon thyme make this citrusy beverage so refreshing—it's like sipping summer from a cup. My family and I enjoy it so much that it's a staple on our southern porch.
—Melissa Pelkey Hass, Waleska, GA

- -

Takes: 20 min. • **Makes:** 8 servings

2 qt. water
8 individual green tea bags
12 fresh lemon thyme sprigs or
    8 fresh thyme sprigs plus
    ½ tsp. grated lemon peel
¼ cup honey
3 Tbsp. lemon juice
    Sugar, optional

In a large saucepan, bring water to a boil; remove from heat. Add the tea bags and lemon thyme sprigs; steep, covered, 3 minutes. Discard tea bags; steep, covered, 3 minutes longer. Strain tea. Add the honey and lemon juice; stir until honey is dissolved. Stir in sugar if desired. Serve immediately.

1 cup: 33 cal., 0 fat (0 sat. fat), 0 chol., 0 sod., 9g carb. (9g sugars, 0 fiber), 0 pro

LEMON THYME GREEN TEA

CASHEW BUTTER

Once you taste homemade cashew butter, you'll never go back to store-bought versions. The coconut oil makes the butter just a little creamier, but you can omit it if you don't normally keep the oil on hand.
—*Taste of Home* Test Kitchen

- -

Takes: 15 min. • **Makes:** about 1 cup

2 cups raw cashews
½ tsp. salt
3 tsp. coconut oil

Process cashews and salt in a food processor until desired consistency, about 5-7 minutes, scraping down sides as needed. Add coconut oil and process another 30 seconds. Store in an airtight container in refrigerator.

1 Tbsp.: 83 cal., 6g fat (1g sat. fat), 0 chol., 76mg sod., 4g carb. (1g sugars, 1g fiber), 3g pro.

DID YOU KNOW?
Cashews are a popular snack nut rich in flavor. They are often eaten raw, roasted and lightly salted. Cashews are common to Thai, Indian and Chinese cuisines and in vegetarian dishes.

**FRUITY PEANUT
BUTTER PITAS**

FRUITY PEANUT BUTTER PITAS

My kids ask for these pita sandwiches all the time. They haven't noticed that as good as they taste, they're also good for them.

—Kim Holmes, Emerald Park, SK

- -

Takes: 5 min. • **Makes:** 2 servings

- ¼ cup peanut butter
- ⅛ tsp. each ground allspice, cinnamon and nutmeg, optional
- 2 whole wheat pita pocket halves
- ½ medium apple, thinly sliced
- ½ medium firm banana, sliced

In a small bowl, blend the peanut butter with allspice, cinnamon and nutmeg if desired. Spread inside the pita bread halves; fill with the apple and banana slices.

1 pita half: 324 cal., 17g fat (4g sat. fat), 0 chol., 320mg sod., 36g carb. (13g sugars, 6g fiber), 12g pro. **Diabetic exchanges:** 3 fat, 1 starch, 1 lean meat, 1 fruit.

SPICED APPLESAUCE

SPICED APPLESAUCE

Every year we have an apple-picking party. I always look forward to making this with our bountiful harvest.

—Marian Platt, Sequim, WA

- -

Prep: 25 min. • **Cook:** 30 min.
Makes: 8 cups

- 5 lbs. tart apples (about 16 medium), peeled and sliced
- 1 cup apple juice
- 1 tsp. ground cinnamon
- ½ tsp. ground allspice
- ½ tsp. ground cloves

In a Dutch oven, combine all 5 ingredients; bring to a boil. Reduce heat; simmer, covered, 25-35 minutes or until apples are tender, stirring occasionally. Remove from heat; mash apples to desired consistency. Serve warm or cold.

Freeze option: Freeze cooled applesauce in freezer containers. To use, thaw in the refrigerator overnight. Serve cold or heat through in a saucepan, stirring occasionally. **⅔ cup:** 94 cal., 1g fat (0 sat. fat), 0 chol., 1mg sod., 24g carb. (20g sugars, 3g fiber), 0g pro. **Diabetic exchanges:** 1½ fruit.

GINGER CARDAMOM TEA

I add a little spice to my tea with ginger and cardamom. Kick up your feet and relax with a hot mug full of this comforting drink.
—Trisha Kruse, Eagle, ID

- -

Takes: 25 min. • **Makes:** 4 servings

- 2 **cups water**
- 4 **tsp. honey**
- 1 **Tbsp. minced fresh gingerroot**
- ½ **tsp. ground cardamom**
- 6 **tea bags**
- 1½ **cups fat-free milk**

1. In a small saucepan, combine the water, honey, ginger and cardamom; bring to a boil. Reduce heat; simmer 10 minutes.

2. Pour over tea bags in a 2-cup glass measuring cup. Steep 3-5 minutes according to taste. Strain tea back into saucepan, discarding ginger and tea bags. Stir in milk; heat through.

¾ cup: 55 cal., 0 fat (0 sat. fat), 2mg chol., 39mg sod., 11g carb. (10g sugars, 0 fiber), 3g pro.
Diabetic exchanges: ½ starch.

OLD BAY CRISPY KALE CHIPS

Here in East Hampton, New York, harvesttime means big bunches of kale from local growers. These crunchy veggie chips are healthy, easy and delicious. I make them with seafood seasoning to take the flavor up a notch. For extra zip, add a dash of cayenne pepper.
—Luanne Asta, Hampton Bays, NY

- -

Prep: 10 min. • **Cook:** 30 min.
Makes: 4 servings

- 1 **bunch kale, washed**
- 2 **Tbsp. olive oil**
- 1 **to 3 tsp. Old Bay Seasoning**
  Sea salt, to taste

1. Preheat oven to 300°. Remove tough stems from kale and tear leaves into large pieces. Place in a large bowl and toss with olive oil and seasonings. Arrange leaves in a single layer on greased baking sheets.

2. Bake, uncovered, 10 minutes and then rotate pans. Continue baking until crisp and just starting to brown, about 15 minutes longer. Let stand at least 5 minutes before serving.

1 serving: 101 cal., 7g fat (1g sat. fat), 0 chol., 202mg sod., 8g carb. (0 sugars, 2g fiber), 3g pro. **Diabetic exchanges:** 1½ fat, 1 vegetable.

OLD BAY CRISPY KALE CHIPS

**APPLE
CARTWHEELS**

APPLE CARTWHEELS

Stuff cored apples with a yummy filling, and then slice them into rings for an eye-appealing snack. The filling is an irresistible combo of creamy peanut butter, sweet honey, miniature chocolate chips and raisins.

—Miriam Miller, Thorp, WI

- -

Prep: 20 min. + chilling
Makes: about 2 dozen

- ¼ cup peanut butter
- 1½ tsp. honey
- ½ cup miniature semisweet chocolate chips
- 2 Tbsp. raisins
- 4 medium unpeeled Red Delicious apples, cored

1. In a small bowl, combine peanut butter and honey; fold in chocolate chips and raisins.
2. Fill centers of apples with peanut butter mixture; refrigerate for at least 1 hour. Cut into ¼-in. rings.

1 piece: 50 cal., 3g fat (1g sat. fat), 0 chol., 13mg sod., 7g carb. (6g sugars, 1g fiber), 1g pro.

HONEY CINNAMON MILK

Having trouble falling asleep? Use this milk to help you find your way to dreamland.

—Leony Santoso, Winchester, VA

- -

Takes: 10 min. • **Makes:** 1 serving

- 1 cup fat-free milk
- 1 cinnamon stick (3 in.)
  Dash ground nutmeg
  Dash ground allspice
- 1½ tsp. honey

1. In a small saucepan, combine the milk, cinnamon stick, nutmeg and allspice.
2. Cook and stir over medium heat until heated through; whisk in honey.
3. Serve warm in a mug; garnish with cinnamon stick.

1 cup: 117 cal., 0 fat (0 sat. fat), 5mg chol., 103mg sod., 21g carb. (21g sugars, 0 fiber), 8g pro.
Diabetic exchanges: 1 fat-free milk, ½ starch.

ROASTED PUMPKIN SEEDS

AVOCADO EGG SALAD TOAST

I had a surplus of avocados after purchasing too many for an event. A few days later, I was making egg salad sandwiches for lunch and had the fantastic idea to use avocado to bind it together instead of traditional mayo. Not only was this version unbelievably delicious but the healthy fats in the avocado make this a much better option than the traditional mayo-laden version.
—Shannon Dobos, Calgary, AB

Takes: 20 min. • **Makes:** 4 servings

- 1   medium ripe avocado, peeled and cubed
- 6   hard-boiled large eggs, chopped
- 1   green onion, finely chopped
- 1   tsp. lemon juice
- ¼   tsp. salt
- ⅛   tsp. pepper
- 4   large slices sourdough bread, halved and toasted

In a large bowl, mash avocado to desired consistency. Gently stir in eggs, green onion, lemon juice, salt and pepper. Spread over toast. Serve immediately.

2 pieces: 367 cal., 15g fat (4g sat. fat), 280mg chol., 671mg sod., 41g carb. (4g sugars, 4g fiber), 18g pro.

ROASTED PUMPKIN SEEDS

Roasted pumpkin seeds are a festive fall snack. Just scoop them out of the pumpkin, add butter and seasoning, and bake!
—Dawn Fagerstrom, Warren, MN

Prep: 20 min. • **Bake:** 50 min.
Makes: 2 cups

- 2   cups fresh pumpkin seeds
- 3   Tbsp. butter, melted
- 1   tsp. salt
- 1   tsp. Worcestershire sauce

1. Preheat oven to 250°. Toss seeds with remaining ingredients; spread evenly into a greased foil-lined 15x10x1-in. pan.

2. Bake for 45 minutes, stirring occasionally. Increase oven setting to 325°. Bake until dry and lightly browned, about 5 minutes.

3. Serve warm or at room temperature. Cool completely before storing in an airtight container.

¼ cup: 110 cal., 7g fat (3g sat. fat), 11mg chol., 339mg sod., 9g carb. (0 sugars, 3g fiber), 3g pro.
Diabetic exchanges: 1½ fat, ½ starch.

**AVOCADO
EGG SALAD
TOAST**

**CHILI-LIME
ROASTED CHICKPEAS**

CHILI-LIME
ROASTED CHICKPEAS

*Looking for a light snack that will
please a crowd? You've found it!
These zesty chickpeas will have
everyone happily munching.*
—Julie Ruble, Charlotte, NC

- -

Prep: 10 min.
Bake: 40 min. + cooling
Makes: 2 cups

- 2 **cans (15 oz. each) chickpeas
  or garbanzo beans, rinsed,
  drained and patted dry**
- 2 **Tbsp. olive oil**
- 1 **Tbsp. chili powder**
- 2 **tsp. ground cumin**
- 1 **tsp. grated lime zest**
- 1 **Tbsp. lime juice**
- ¾ **tsp. sea salt**

1. Preheat oven to 400°. Line
a 15x10x1-in. baking sheet with
foil. Spread the chickpeas in a
single layer over foil, removing
any loose skins. Bake until very
crunchy, 40-45 minutes, stirring
every 15 minutes.
2. Meanwhile, whisk together
remaining ingredients. Remove
the chickpeas from oven; let
cool 5 minutes. Drizzle with the
oil mixture; shake pan to coat.
Cool completely. Store in an
airtight container.
⅓ cup: 178 cal., 8g fat (1g sat. fat),
0 chol., 463mg sod., 23g carb. (3g
sugars, 6g fiber), 6g pro. **Diabetic
exchanges:** 1½ starch, 1½ fat.
Rosemary-Sea Salt variation:
Prepare the chickpeas according to
step 1 in the recipe. Toss beans with

2 Tbsp. extra virgin olive oil, 1 Tbsp.
minced fresh rosemary and ½ tsp.
sea salt. Toss beans with the oil
mixture. Cool completely.
Orange-Curry variation: Prepare
the chickpeas according to step 1 in
the recipe. Whisk 2 Tbsp. extra virgin
olive oil, 1 tsp. grated orange peel and
1 Tbsp. curry powder. Toss the beans
with the oil mixture. Cool completely.
Lemon-Pepper variation: Prepare
the chickpeas according to step 1 in
the recipe. Whisk 2 Tbsp. extra virgin
olive oil, 1 tsp. grated lemon peel
and 2 tsp. freshly cracked pepper.
Toss the beans with the oil mixture.
Cool completely.

PB&J TO GO!

These PB&J bites are fun to make and fun to eat! For a change of pace, replace the jam with Nutella and the rolled oats with sugar or crushed puffed rice cereal.
—Kelly Ward, Stratford, ON

- -

Takes: 20 min. • **Makes:** 1 dozen

1½ cups quick-cooking oats,
      divided
1   cup creamy peanut butter
½   cup confectioners' sugar
6   tsp. favorite jam

1. Combine 1 cup oats, peanut butter and confectioners' sugar until well blended. Shape the dough into 1¼-in. balls; flatten into ¼-in.-thick circles. Place ½ tsp. of jam in center of circle; wrap peanut butter dough around jam. Pinch edges to seal; shape into ball. Repeat with the remaining jam and dough. Roll balls in remaining oats.

2. Refrigerate for 30 minutes on parchment-lined baking sheet.

1 cookie: 186 cal., 12g fat (2g sat. fat), 0 chol., 91mg sod., 18g carb. (9g sugars, 2g fiber), 6g pro.

TURKEY & APRICOT WRAPS

(PICTURED ON P. 36)

I combined two favorites to come up with these easy snack wraps: the classic southern appetizer of fruit jam and cream cheese on crackers with the turkey, apple and Brie sandwiches served at my bridal luncheon. I sneak fresh spinach into all sorts of recipes because it has such a mild flavor.
—Kim Beavers,
North August, SC

- -

Takes: 15 min. • **Makes:** 4 servings

½   cup reduced-fat
      cream cheese
3   Tbsp. apricot preserves
4   whole wheat tortillas
      (8 in.), room temperature
½   lb. sliced reduced-sodium
      deli turkey
2   cups fresh arugula or
      baby spinach

In a small bowl, mix cream cheese and preserves. Spread about 2 Tbsp. over each tortilla to within ½ in. of edges. Layer with turkey and arugula. Roll up tightly. Serve immediately, or cover and refrigerate until serving.

1 wrap: 312 cal., 10g fat (4g sat. fat), 41mg chol., 655mg sod., 33g carb. (8g sugars, 2g fiber), 20g pro.
Diabetic exchanges: 2 starch, 2 lean meat, 1 fat.

PB&J TO GO!

PEANUT BUTTER
GRANOLA
PINWHEELS

PEANUT BUTTER GRANOLA PINWHEELS

I came across this easy and tasty snack while searching online for healthy munchies for kids. The rolls are quick to make and keep little ones satisfied until dinner.
—Mary Haluch, Ludlow, MA

- -

Takes: 5 min. • **Makes:** 16 pinwheels

- 4 Tbsp. creamy peanut butter
- 2 flour tortillas (8 in.)
- 2 tsp. honey
- ½ cup granola without raisins

Spread peanut butter over each tortilla; drizzle with honey and sprinkle with granola. Roll up; cut into slices.

1 pinwheel: 60 cal., 3g fat (1g sat. fat), 0 chol., 48mg sod., 7g carb. (2g sugars, 1g fiber), 2g pro.

SUNBURST SPICED TEA

SUNBURST SPICED TEA

Oranges and lemon lend a lovely citrus flavor to ordinary black tea.
—*Taste of Home* Test Kitchen

- -

Takes: 25 min. • **Makes:** 4 servings

- 2 medium oranges
- 1 medium lemon
- 4 cardamom pods
- 4 whole cloves
- 4 tsp. English breakfast tea leaves or other black tea leaves
- 4 cups boiling water
   Lemon slices, optional

1. Using a citrus zester, remove the peels from oranges and lemon in long narrow strips. (Save fruit for another use.) Place peel strips, cardamom and cloves in a large bowl. With the end of a wooden spoon handle, crush mixture until aromas are released.

2. Add tea leaves and boiling water. Cover and steep for 6 minutes. Strain tea, discarding peel mixture. Serve immediately. Serve with lemon slices if desired.

1 serving: 0 cal., 0 fat (0 sat. fat), 0 chol., 0 sod., 0 carb. (0 sugars, 0 fiber), 0 pro.

SOUPS & SANDWICHES

TOMATO & AVOCADO SANDWICHES P. 72

1

2

3

4

5

LOOKING FOR SOME HEALTHY SOUP AND SANDWICH IDEAS YOU CAN WHIP UP IN A FLASH? THESE SIMPLE RECIPES ARE AS DELICIOUS AS THEY ARE EASY.

CHICKEN PARMESAN PATTY MELTS

GREEK TOMATO SOUP WITH ORZO

My recipe for manestra, which means orzo in Greek, is so easy. Just follow these simple steps for a creamy, tomato-y soup that everyone is sure to love.
—Kiki Vagianos, Melrose, MA

- -

Prep: 10 min. • **Cook:** 25 min.
Makes: 4 servings

- 2 Tbsp. olive oil
- 1 medium onion, chopped
- 1¼ cups uncooked whole wheat orzo pasta
- 2 cans (14½ oz. each) whole tomatoes, undrained, coarsely chopped
- 3 cups reduced-sodium chicken broth
- 2 tsp. dried oregano
- ¼ tsp. salt
- ¼ tsp. pepper
  Optional: Crumbled feta cheese and minced fresh basil

1. In a large saucepan, heat oil over medium heat; saute the onion until tender, 3-5 minutes. Add orzo; cook and stir until lightly toasted.
2. Stir in the tomatoes, broth and seasonings; bring to a boil. Reduce the heat; simmer, covered, until the orzo is tender, 15-20 minutes, stirring occasionally. If desired, top with feta and basil.
Freeze option: Freeze cooled soup in freezer containers. To use, partially thaw in the refrigerator overnight. Heat through in a saucepan, stirring occasionally; add a little broth or water if necessary.
1 cup: 299 cal., 8g fat (1g sat. fat), 0 chol., 882mg sod., 47g carb. (7g sugars, 12g fiber), 11g pro.

CHICKEN PARMESAN PATTY MELTS

I came up with these open-faced melts to re-create the flavors of a restaurant-style sandwich. Now it's my husband's favorite dinner.
—Deborah Biggs, Omaha, NE

- -

Takes: 30 min. • **Makes:** 4 servings

- 5 Tbsp. grated Parmesan cheese, divided
- 1 cup marinara sauce, divided
- ¼ tsp. pepper
- ⅛ tsp. salt
- 1 lb. lean ground chicken
- 2 oz. fresh mozzarella cheese, thinly sliced
- 2 ciabatta rolls, split and toasted

1. In a large bowl, combine 3 Tbsp. Parmesan cheese, 2 Tbsp. marinara sauce, pepper and salt. Crumble the chicken over the mixture and mix well. Shape into 4 patties.
2. Place on a baking sheet coated with cooking spray. Broil 4 in. from the heat for 4-6 minutes on each side or until a thermometer reads 165° and juices run clear.
3. Top with remaining marinara, the mozzarella and remaining Parmesan. Broil 1-2 minutes longer or until the cheeses are melted. Top each roll half with a patty.
1 sandwich: 420 cal., 13g fat (5g sat. fat), 98mg chol., 658mg sod., 43g carb. (8g sugars, 3g fiber), 34g pro.
Diabetic exchanges: 4 lean meat, 2½ starch, 1 fat.

**GREEK
TOMATO SOUP
WITH ORZO**

SPICY PUMPKIN & CORN SOUP

SPICY PUMPKIN & CORN SOUP

Here's a seriously quick dish—it can satisfy a hungry crew in about 20 minutes. It freezes well, too. My family enjoys this delicious soup with cornbread.
—Heather Rorex, Winnemucca, NV

- -

Takes: 20 min. • **Makes:** 8 servings

- 1 **can (15 oz.) pumpkin**
- 1 **can (15 oz.) black beans,**
  rinsed and drained
- 1 **can (10 oz.) diced tomatoes**
  and green chiles

- 1½ **cups frozen corn**
- 2 **cans (14½ oz. each)**
  reduced-sodium
  chicken broth
- ¼ **tsp. pepper**

In a large saucepan, mix all the ingredients. Bring to a boil. Reduce the heat; simmer, uncovered, 10-15 minutes or until slightly thickened, stirring occasionally.

Freeze option: Freeze cooled soup in freezer containers. To use, partially thaw in the refrigerator overnight. Heat through in a saucepan, stirring occasionally; add a little broth if necessary.

¾ cup: 100 cal., 0 fat (0 sat. fat), 0 chol., 542mg sod., 20g carb. (3g sugars, 5g fiber), 6g pro.
Diabetic exchanges: 1 starch.

PEPPERED PORK PITAS

Cracked black pepper is all it takes to give my pork pitas some pop. I often fill them with caramelized onions and garlic mayo.

—Katherine White, Henderson, NV

- -

Takes: 20 min. • **Makes:** 4 servings

- 1 **lb. boneless pork loin chops, cut into thin strips**
- 1 **Tbsp. olive oil**
- 2 **tsp. coarsely ground pepper**
- 2 **garlic cloves, minced**
- 1 **jar (12 oz.) roasted sweet red peppers, drained and julienned**
- 4 **whole pita breads, warmed Optional: Garlic mayonnaise and torn leaf lettuce**

In a small bowl, combine the pork, oil, pepper and garlic; toss to coat. Place a large skillet over medium-high heat. Add pork mixture; cook and stir until no longer pink. Stir in red peppers; heat through. Serve on pita breads. Top with mayonnaise and lettuce if desired.

1 sandwich: 380 cal., 11g fat (3g sat. fat), 55mg chol., 665mg sod., 37g carb. (4g sugars, 2g fiber), 27g pro. **Diabetic exchanges:** 3 lean meat, 2 starch, 1 fat.

LACTOSE-FREE POTATO SOUP

This is a terrific way for my husband and me to enjoy a rich and creamy soup without worrying about my lactose intolerance.

—Lisanne Heyward, Richmond, VA

- -

Takes: 30 min. • **Makes:** 6 servings

- 3 **medium onions, chopped**
- 2 **celery ribs, chopped**
- 2 **Tbsp. canola oil**
- 4 **cups reduced-sodium chicken broth**
- 4 **medium potatoes, peeled and cubed**

1. In a large saucepan, saute the onions and celery in oil until tender. Add broth and potatoes; bring to a boil. Reduce heat; cover and simmer 15-20 minutes or until the potatoes are tender.

2. Cool slightly. In a blender, process half the soup until smooth. Return to pan; heat through.

1 cup: 166 cal., 5g fat (0 sat. fat), 0 chol., 396mg sod., 27g carb. (7g sugars, 3g fiber), 5g pro. **Diabetic exchanges:** 1 starch, 1 vegetable, 1 fat.

PEPPERED PORK PITAS

CHICKEN CORDON BLEU STROMBOLI

CHICKEN CORDON BLEU STROMBOLI

If chicken cordon bleu and Stromboli had a baby, this would be it. Serve with jarred Alfredo sauce, homemade Alfredo sauce or classic Mornay sauce on the side if desired.
—Cyndy Gerken, Naples, FL

- -

Takes: 30 min. • **Makes:** 6 servings

- 1 **tube (13.8 oz.) refrigerated pizza crust**
- 4 **pieces thinly sliced deli ham**
- 1½ **cups shredded cooked chicken**
- 6 **slices Swiss cheese**
- 1 **Tbsp. butter, melted**
  Roasted garlic Alfredo sauce, optional

1. Preheat oven to 400°. Unroll pizza dough onto a baking sheet. Layer with the ham, chicken and cheese to within ½ in. of edges. Roll up jelly-roll style, starting with a long side; pinch seam to seal and tuck ends under. Brush with melted butter.
2. Bake until the crust is dark golden brown, 18-22 minutes. Let stand for 5 minutes before slicing. If desired, serve with Alfredo sauce for dipping.
1 slice: 298 cal., 10g fat (4g sat. fat), 53mg chol., 580mg sod., 32g carb. (4g sugars, 1g fiber), 21g pro.

TEST KITCHEN TIP
Don't let this stand too long before slicing and eating. The underside of the crust will get soft. Leftover rotisserie chicken is an excellent alternative in this Stromboli.

VEGAN CARROT SOUP

VEGAN CARROT SOUP

Yukon Gold potatoes—instead of cream—make a smooth carrot soup vegan and add a mild sweetness. If you don't have Yukon Golds on hand, russet potatoes will work, too.
—*Taste of Home* Test Kitchen

- -

Takes: 30 min. • **Makes:** 6 servings

- 1 **medium onion, chopped**
- 2 **celery ribs, chopped**
- 1 **Tbsp. canola oil**
- 4 **cups vegetable broth**
- 1 **lb. carrots, sliced**
- 2 **large Yukon Gold potatoes, peeled and cubed**
- 1 **tsp. salt**
- ¼ **tsp. pepper**
  Fresh cilantro leaves, optional

1. In a large saucepan, saute onion and celery in oil until tender. Add broth, carrots and potatoes; bring to a boil. Reduce heat; cover and simmer for 15-20 minutes or until vegetables are tender. Remove from the heat; cool slightly.
2. Transfer to a blender; cover and process until blended. Return to pan; stir in salt and pepper. Heat through. If desired, sprinkle with cilantro.
1 cup: 176 cal., 3g fat (0 sat. fat), 0 chol., 710mg sod., 35g carb. (7g sugars, 4g fiber), 4g pro.
Diabetic exchanges: 2 starch, ½ fat.

PORTOBELLO PIZZA BURGERS

Portobello mushrooms are a tasty meatless option, especially tucked inside a bun with melty mozzarella cheese.
—Sally Lauf, West Deptford, NJ

- -

Takes: 25 min. • **Makes:** 4 servings

- 4   **large portobello mushrooms (4 to 4½ in.)**
- 4   **tsp. plus 1 Tbsp. olive oil, divided**
- 1½ **cups finely chopped plum tomatoes**
- ¾   **cup shredded part-skim mozzarella cheese**
- 1½ **tsp. Italian seasoning**
- 4   **hamburger buns, split**

1. Preheat broiler. Remove and discard stems from mushrooms; with a spoon, scrape and remove gills. Brush caps with 4 tsp. oil. Place in an ungreased 15x10x1-in. baking pan, stem side down. Broil 4 in. from heat for 5 minutes.
2. In a small bowl, mix the tomatoes, cheese, Italian seasoning and the remaining oil. Remove mushrooms from broiler; turn over and fill caps with tomato mixture.
3. Broil 4-6 minutes longer or until mushrooms are tender and cheese is melted. Serve on buns.
1 burger: 284 cal., 13g fat (4g sat. fat), 12mg chol., 314mg sod., 29g carb. (7g sugars, 3g fiber), 12g pro.
Diabetic exchanges: 2 starch, 1½ fat, 1 medium-fat meat, 1 vegetable.
Note: Mushrooms may also be grilled. Place mushroom caps on grill rack over medium heat, stem side down. Grill, covered, 5 minutes. Remove

from grill; fill caps with the tomato mixture. Grill, covered, 4-6 minutes longer or until mushrooms are tender and cheese is melted. Serve on buns.

SIMPLE CHICKEN SOUP

I revised one of my family's favorite recipes so it would be lighter and easier to make. It's a hearty meal served with a green salad and crusty French bread.
—Sue West, Alvord, TX

- -

Takes: 20 min. • **Makes:** 6 servings

- 2   **cans (14½ oz. each) reduced-sodium chicken broth**
- 1   **Tbsp. dried minced onion**
- 1   **pkg. (16 oz.) frozen mixed vegetables**
- 2   **cups cubed cooked chicken breast**
- 2   **cans (10¾ oz. each) reduced-fat reduced-sodium condensed cream of chicken soup, undiluted**

In a large saucepan, bring broth and onion to a boil. Reduce heat. Add the vegetables; cover and cook for 6-8 minutes or until crisp-tender. Stir in chicken and soup; heat through.
1⅓ cups: 195 cal., 3g fat (1g sat. fat), 44mg chol., 820mg sod., 21g carb. (3g sugars, 3g fiber), 19g pro.

SIMPLE CHICKEN SOUP

SPICY FRENCH DIP

SPICY FRENCH DIP

If I'm cooking for a party or family get-together, I put this beef in the slow cooker in the morning and then turn my attention to other preparations. I love that it is a timesaver and a classic dish that never fails to draw rave reviews.

—Ginny Koeppen, Winnfield, LA

- -

Prep: 10 min. • **Cook:** 8 hours
Makes: 12 servings

- 1 **beef sirloin tip roast (3 lbs.), cut in half**
- ½ **cup water**
- 1 **can (4 oz.) diced jalapeno peppers, drained**
- 1 **envelope Italian salad dressing mix**
- 12 **crusty rolls (5 in.)**

1. Place beef in a 5-qt. slow cooker. In a small bowl, combine the water, jalapenos and dressing mix; pour over beef. Cover and cook on low 8-10 hours or until meat is tender.
2. Remove the beef and shred with 2 forks. Skim fat from cooking juices. Serve beef on rolls with juice.

1 sandwich: 315 cal., 8g fat (2g sat. fat), 72mg chol., 582mg sod., 31g carb. (2g sugars, 1g fiber), 28g pro.
Diabetic exchanges: 3 lean meat, 2 starch.

MINT-CUCUMBER TOMATO SANDWICHES

PEANUT BUTTER, STRAWBERRY AND HONEY SANDWICH

Who needs jam when you have fresh strawberries? A drizzle of honey and a bit of mint make this sandwich stand out.

— James Schend,
Pleasant Prairie, WI

Takes: 5 min. • **Makes:** 1 serving

- 1 Tbsp. creamy peanut butter
- 1 slice crusty white bread
- ¼ cup sliced fresh strawberries
- 1 tsp. thinly sliced fresh mint
- 1 tsp. honey

Spread peanut butter over bread. Top with strawberries and mint; drizzle with honey.

1 sandwich: 208 cal., 9g fat (2g sat. fat), 0 chol., 211mg sod., 27g carb. (11g sugars, 2g fiber), 6g pro.

TEST KITCHEN TIP
Don't wash fresh strawberries until you are ready to use them. Strawberries stay fresh longer if unwashed and kept with stems on in a sealed glass jar in the refrigerator. Strawberries soak up moisture from washing, which can make them spoil in a hurry. It's not a long way from wet berries to moldy berries.

MINT-CUCUMBER TOMATO SANDWICHES

I jazzed up the quintessential teatime cucumber sandwich to suit my family's tastes. This was my absolute go-to sandwich last summer when I was pregnant. It hit all the right spots!

—Namrata Telugu, Terre Haute, IN

Takes: 15 min. • **Makes:** 4 sandwiches

- 3 Tbsp. butter, softened
- 8 slices sourdough bread
- 1 large cucumber, thinly sliced
- 2 medium tomatoes, thinly sliced
- ¼ tsp. salt
- ⅛ tsp. pepper
- ¼ cup fresh mint leaves

Spread butter over 4 slices of bread. Layer with cucumber and tomatoes; sprinkle with salt, pepper and mint. Top with remaining bread. If desired, cut each sandwich into quarters.

1 sandwich: 286 cal., 10g fat (6g sat. fat), 23mg chol., 631mg sod., 42g carb. (5g sugars, 3g fiber), 9g pro.

PEANUT BUTTER, STRAWBERRY AND HONEY SANDWICH

**SLOW-COOKER
SHREDDED TURKEY
SANDWICHES**

SLOW-COOKER SHREDDED TURKEY SANDWICHES

This slow-cooked sandwich gets its zesty flavor from onion soup mix and beer. The recipe makes a big batch, so it's an ideal main dish for parties or potlucks.
—Werner Knuth, Owatonna, MN

- -

Prep: 15 minutes • **Cook:** 7 hours
Makes: 24 servings

- **2 boneless skinless turkey breast halves (2 to 3 lbs. each)**
- **1 bottle (12 oz.) beer or nonalcoholic beer**
- **½ cup butter, cubed**
- **1 envelope onion soup mix**
- **24 French rolls, split**

1. Place turkey in a 5-qt. slow cooker. Combine the beer, butter and soup mix; pour over the meat. Cover and cook on low for 7-9 hours or until meat is tender.

2. Shred meat and return to slow cooker; heat through. Serve on rolls.

1 sandwich: 294 cal., 7g fat (3g sat. fat), 57mg chol., 476mg sod., 31g carb. (2g sugars, 1g fiber), 24g pro.
Diabetic exchanges: 3 lean meat, 2 starch, ½ fat.

WEEKNIGHT GUMBO

My husband loves the kick that the smoked turkey sausage gives this quick, tasty gumbo.
—Amy Flack, Homer City, PA

- -

Takes: 20 min.
Makes: 6 servings (1½ qt.)

- **1 pkg. (13 oz.) smoked turkey sausage**
- **1 can (14½ oz.) diced tomatoes with green peppers and onions, undrained**
- **1 can (14½ oz.) reduced-sodium chicken broth**
- **½ cup water**
- **1 cup uncooked instant rice**
- **1 cup frozen corn**
  Sliced green onions, optional

In a large saucepan, cook sliced sausage until browned on both sides. Stir in tomatoes, broth and water; bring to a boil. Stir in rice and corn; cover and remove from the heat. Let stand for 5 minutes. If desired, top with sliced green onions.

1 cup: 183 cal., 4g fat (1g sat. fat), 38mg chol., 941mg sod., 23g carb. (4g sugars, 2g fiber), 13g pro.

SPINACH & WHITE BEAN SOUP

For me, a bowl of warm soup is love, comfort, happiness and memories. Chock-full of veggies and beans, this recipe appeals to my kitchen-sink style of cooking.
—Annette Palermo,
Beach Haven, NJ

Takes: 30 min. • **Makes:** 6 servings

- 2 **tsp. olive oil**
- 3 **garlic cloves, minced**
- 3 **cans (15 oz. each) cannellini beans, rinsed and drained, divided**
- ¼ **tsp. pepper**
- 1 **carton (32 oz.) vegetable or reduced-sodium chicken broth**
- 4 **cups chopped fresh spinach (about 3 oz.)**
- ¼ **cup thinly sliced fresh basil Shredded Parmesan cheese, optional**

1. In a large saucepan, heat oil over medium heat. Add garlic; cook and stir until tender, 30-45 seconds. Stir in 2 cans of beans, pepper and broth.

2. Puree mixture using an immersion blender. Or puree in a traditional blender and return to pan. Stir in the remaining can of beans; bring to a boil. Reduce the heat; simmer, covered, 15 minutes, stirring occasionally.

3. Stir in spinach and basil; cook, uncovered, until the spinach is wilted, 2-4 minutes. If desired, serve with cheese.

1¼ cups: 192 cal., 2g fat (0 sat. fat), 0 chol., 886mg sod., 33g carb. (1g sugars, 9g fiber), 9g pro.

TEST KITCHEN TIP
Reduced-sodium vegetable broth isn't always available. Organic vegetable broth, which is easier to find, is typically lower in sodium. Opt for organic if looking to cut salt.

SPINACH & WHITE BEAN SOUP

ARTICHOKE STEAK WRAPS

ARTICHOKE STEAK WRAPS

The whole family loves this simple, fast and flavorful dish. It's surprisingly easy to make, and you can broil the steak if you don't want to venture outside.
—Greg Fontenot, The Woodlands, TX

Takes: 30 min. • **Makes:** 6 servings

- 8 oz. frozen artichoke hearts (about 2 cups), thawed and chopped
- 2 medium tomatoes, chopped
- ¼ cup chopped fresh cilantro
- ¾ tsp. salt, divided
- 1 lb. beef flat iron or top sirloin steak (1¼ lbs.)
- ¼ tsp. pepper
- 6 whole wheat tortillas (8 in.), warmed

1. Toss the artichoke hearts and tomatoes with the cilantro and ¼ tsp. salt.

2. Sprinkle steak with pepper and remaining salt. Grill, covered, over medium heat or broil 4 in. from heat until meat reaches desired doneness (for medium-rare, a thermometer should read 135°; medium, 150°), 5-6 minutes per side. Remove from heat; let stand 5 minutes. Cut into thin slices. Serve steak and salsa in tortillas, folding bottoms and sides of tortillas to close.

1 wrap: 301 cal., 11g fat (4g sat. fat), 61mg chol., 506mg sod., 27g carb. (1g sugars, 5g fiber), 24g pro.
Diabetic exchanges: 3 lean meat, 1½ starch.

VEGAN CREAM OF BROCCOLI SOUP

VEGAN CREAM OF BROCCOLI SOUP

Pureed potatoes help give the vegan cream of broccoli soup a silky texture without the cream! This is a fantastic trick to make dairy-free soups super creamy.
—*Taste of Home* Test Kitchen

Prep: 45 min. • **Makes:** 8 servings

- 3 medium onions, chopped
- 2 celery ribs, chopped
- 2 Tbsp. canola oil
- 4 cups plus ½ cup vegetable broth
- 4 medium russet potatoes, peeled and cubed (about 4 cups)
- 6 cups chopped fresh broccoli (about 3 small heads)
- 1 tsp. salt
- ¼ tsp. pepper

1. In a large saucepan, saute the onions and celery in oil until tender. Add 4 cups broth and potatoes; bring to a boil. Reduce heat; cover and simmer for 15-20 minutes or until potatoes are tender.

2. Cool slightly. In a blender, process the soup in batches until smooth. Return to pan; add the remaining broth and bring to a boil. Add broccoli. Reduce heat; simmer, uncovered, 8-10 minutes or until broccoli is tender.

1 cup: 142 cal., 4g fat (0 sat. fat), 0 chol., 409mg sod., 24g carb. (5g sugars, 4g fiber), 4g pro.
Diabetic exchanges: 1½ starch, 1 vegetable, ½ fat.

TOMATO & AVOCADO SANDWICHES

(PICTURED ON P. 56)

I'm a vegetarian, and I could eat this tasty, healthy sandwich for almost every meal. At my house, we call it HATS: hummus, avocado, tomato and shallots. I almost always have these ingredients on hand.

—Sarah Jaraha, Moorestown, NJ

Takes: 10 min. • **Makes:** 2 servings

- ½   medium ripe avocado, peeled and mashed
- 4   slices whole wheat bread, toasted
- 1   medium tomato, sliced
- 2   Tbsp. finely chopped shallot
- ¼   cup hummus

Spread avocado over 2 slices of toast. Top with tomato and shallot. Spread hummus over remaining toast slices; place on top of the avocado toast, facedown on top of tomato layer.

1 sandwich: 278 cal., 11g fat (2g sat. fat), 0 chol., 379mg sod., 35g carb. (6g sugars, 9g fiber), 11g pro.
Diabetic exchanges: 2 starch, 2 fat.

COOL AS A CUCUMBER SOUP

Chilled soup makes a refreshing appetizer or side dish on a hot summer day. Bright bursts of dill provide pleasant contrasts to the mild cucumber.

—Deirdre Cox, Kansas City, MO

Prep: 15 min. + standing
Makes: 5 servings

- 1   lb. cucumbers, peeled, seeded and sliced
- ½   tsp. salt
- 1½ cups fat-free plain yogurt
- 1   green onion, coarsely chopped
- 1   garlic clove, minced
- 4½ tsp. snipped fresh dill
      Additional chopped green onion and snipped fresh dill

1. In a colander set over a bowl, toss the cucumbers with salt. Let stand for 30 minutes. Squeeze and pat dry.
2. Place cucumbers, yogurt, onion and garlic in a food processor; cover and process until smooth. Stir in the dill. Serve immediately in chilled bowls. Garnish with additional onion and dill.

⅔ cup: 40 cal., 0 fat (0 sat. fat), 2mg chol., 279mg sod., 8g carb. (5g sugars, 1g fiber), 3g pro.
Diabetic exchanges: ½ fat-free milk.

COOL AS A CUCUMBER SOUP

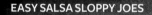
EASY SALSA SLOPPY JOES

EASY SALSA SLOPPY JOES

I created these sandwiches when I realized I did not have a can of sloppy joe sauce. The sweet brown sugar in this recipe complements the tangy salsa.
—Krista Collins, Concord, NC

- -

Takes: 20 min. • **Makes:** 8 servings

1   lb. ground beef
1⅓ cups salsa
1   can (10¾ ounces) condensed tomato soup, undiluted
1   Tbsp. brown sugar
8   hamburger buns, split

In a large skillet, cook beef over medium heat until no longer pink, breaking into crumbles; drain. Stir in salsa, soup and brown sugar. Cover and simmer 10 minutes or until heated through. Serve on buns.

Freeze option: Cool and place in a freezer container; freeze up to 3 months. To use, thaw beef mixture in refrigerator; place in a saucepan and heat through. Serve on buns.

1 sandwich: 271 cal., 8g fat (3g sat. fat), 35mg chol., 620mg sod., 32g carb. (9g sugars, 1g fiber), 15g pro.

**HEARTY
NAVY BEAN SOUP**

PEA SOUP WITH QUINOA

This smooth, fresh-tasting soup is low in fat and high in fiber. Best of all, it's simple to make.
—Jane Hacker, Milwaukee, WI

- -

Prep: 10 min. • **Cook:** 25 min.
Makes: 6 servings

- 1 **cup water**
- ½ **cup quinoa, rinsed**
- 2 **tsp. canola oil**
- 1 **medium onion, chopped**
- 2½ **cups frozen peas (about 10 oz.)**
- 2 **cans (14½ oz. each) reduced-sodium chicken broth or vegetable broth**
- ½ **tsp. salt**
- ¼ **tsp. pepper**
  Optional toppings: Plain yogurt, croutons, shaved Parmesan cheese and cracked pepper

1. In a small saucepan, bring water to a boil. Add quinoa. Reduce heat; simmer, covered, until water is absorbed, 12-15 minutes.
2. Meanwhile, in a large saucepan, heat the oil over medium-high heat; saute onion until tender. Stir in peas and broth; bring to a boil. Reduce heat; simmer, uncovered, until peas are tender, about 5 minutes.
3. Puree soup using an immersion blender. Or cool slightly and puree soup in a blender; return to pan. Stir in the quinoa, salt and pepper; heat through. Serve with toppings as desired.
1 cup: 126 cal., 3g fat (0 sat. fat), 0 chol., 504mg sod., 19g carb. (4g sugars, 4g fiber), 7g pro.

HEARTY NAVY BEAN SOUP

Take advantage of thrifty dried beans and a ham hock to create this comfort-food classic. This is a family favorite I make often.
—Mildred Lewis, Temple, TX

- -

Prep: 30 min. + soaking
Cook: 1¾ hours
Makes: 10 servings (2½ qt.)

- 3 **cups (1½ lbs.) dried navy beans**
- 1 **can (14½ oz.) diced tomatoes, undrained**
- 1 **large onion, chopped**
- 1 **meaty ham hock or 1 cup diced cooked ham**
- 2 **cups chicken broth**
- 2½ **cups water**
  Salt and pepper to taste
  Minced fresh parsley, optional

1. Rinse and sort the beans; soak according to package directions.
2. Drain and rinse beans, discarding liquid. Place in a Dutch oven. Add tomatoes with juice, onion, ham hock, broth, water, salt and pepper. Bring to a boil. Reduce heat; cover and simmer until beans are tender, about 1½ hours.
3. Add more water if necessary. Remove the ham hock and let it stand until cool enough to handle. Remove meat from bone; discard bone. Cut the meat into bite-sized pieces; set aside. (For a thicker soup, cool slightly, then puree the beans in a food processor or blender and return to the pan.) Return the ham to soup and heat through. Garnish with parsley if desired.
1 cup: 245 cal., 2g fat (0 sat. fat), 8mg chol., 352mg sod., 42g carb. (5g sugars, 16g fiber), 18g pro.
Diabetic exchanges: 3 starch, 2 lean meat.

**PEA SOUP
WITH QUINOA**

CRISP FINGER
SANDWICH

CRISP FINGER SANDWICH

*I love snacking on this delicious
sandwich with its crisp English
cucumber. I have also made
batches of these for parties
using a small loaf of whole
wheat or sourdough bread.*
—Missi Selin, Bothell, WA

Takes: 10 min. • **Makes:** 1 serving

- 1 slice whole wheat bread,
    toasted
- 2 Tbsp. reduced-fat spreadable
    garden vegetable
    cream cheese
- ⅓ cup thinly sliced
    English cucumber
- 3 Tbsp. alfalfa sprouts
    Dash coarsely ground pepper

Spread toast with cream cheese. Top
with cucumber, sprouts and pepper.
1 sandwich: 136 cal., 6g fat (3g sat.
fat), 15mg chol., 323mg sod., 13g
carb. (4g sugars, 2g fiber), 7g pro.

ZESTY HAMBURGERS

*These burgers get their zip from
horseradish. It's a quick and easy
way to add a little zing to dinner.*
—Sue Travnik Schiller,
Western Springs, IL

Takes: 25 min. • **Makes:** 4 servings

- 1 lb. ground beef or turkey
- 4 tsp. prepared horseradish
- 2 tsp. Dijon mustard
- 1 tsp. paprika
- ¼ tsp. pepper
- ⅛ tsp. salt, optional
- 4 hamburger buns, split

In a bowl, combine the first
6 ingredients; mix well. Shape
into 4 patties. Pan-fry, grill or broil
until no longer pink. Serve on buns.
1 hamburger: 240 cal., 4g fat (0 sat.
fat), 35mg chol., 355mg sod., 24g
carb. (0 sugars, 0 fiber), 31g pro.

CHORIZO & CHICKPEA SOUP

Chorizo sausage adds flavor and spice to the broth in this soup, creating a savory taste with no need for additional seasonings. The whole house smells amazing while it cooks.

—Jaclyn McKewan, Lancaster, NY

- -

Prep: 15 min. • **Cook:** 8¼ hours
Makes: 1½ qt.

- 3 **cups water**
- 2 **celery ribs, chopped**
- 2 **fully cooked Spanish chorizo links (3 oz. each), cut into ½-in. pieces**
- ½ **cup dried chickpeas or garbanzo beans**
- 1 **can (14½ oz.) petite diced tomatoes, undrained**
- ½ **cup ditalini or other small pasta**
- ½ **tsp. salt**

Place the water, celery, chorizo and chickpeas in a 4- or 5-qt. slow cooker. Cook, covered, on low until beans are tender, 8-10 hours. Stir in the tomatoes, pasta and salt; cook, covered, on high until the pasta is tender, 15-20 minutes.

Freeze option: Freeze cooled soup in freezer containers. To use, partially thaw in the refrigerator overnight. Heat in a saucepan, stirring occasionally; add a little water if necessary.

1 cup: 180 cal., 8g fat (3g sat. fat), 18mg chol., 569mg sod., 23g carb. (3g sugars, 6g fiber), 9g pro. **Diabetic exchanges:** 1½ starch, 1 high-fat meat.

TEST KITCHEN TIP
Chorizo is very flavorful but also high in fat. Using just a small amount, as this dish does, is a smart way to boost flavor without creating a high-fat soup.

CHORIZO & CHICKPEA SOUP

ENTREES

**SHEET PAN SAUSAGE
& POTATO DINNER
P. 86**

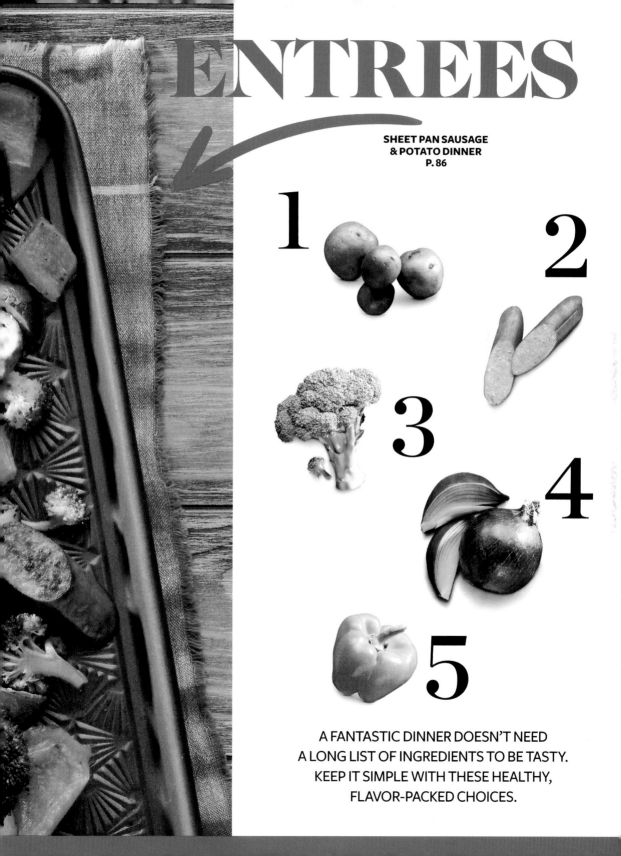

1

2

3

4

5

A FANTASTIC DINNER DOESN'T NEED
A LONG LIST OF INGREDIENTS TO BE TASTY.
KEEP IT SIMPLE WITH THESE HEALTHY,
FLAVOR-PACKED CHOICES.

GRILLED
TILAPIA
WITH MANGO

GRILLED TILAPIA WITH MANGO

Here's a new twist on tilapia that I created for my wife. She enjoys the combination of mango with Parmesan. Somehow it tastes even better outside on the deck with a cold glass of iced tea.
—Gregg May, Columbus, OH

Takes: 20 min. • **Makes:** 4 servings

- 4 tilapia fillets (6 oz. each)
- 1 Tbsp. olive oil
- ½ tsp. salt
- ½ tsp. dill weed
- ¼ tsp. pepper
- 1 Tbsp. grated
   Parmesan cheese
- 1 medium lemon, sliced
- 1 medium mango,
   peeled and thinly sliced

1. Brush fillets with oil; sprinkle with salt, dill and pepper.

2. Grill tilapia, covered, on a lightly oiled rack over medium heat for 5 minutes. Turn tilapia; top with cheese, lemon and mango. Grill 4-6 minutes longer or until fish flakes easily with a fork.

1 fillet: 213 cal., 5g fat (1g sat. fat), 84mg chol., 377mg sod., 10g carb. (8g sugars, 1g fiber), 32g pro.
Diabetic exchanges: 5 lean meat, ½ fruit, ½ fat.

> **TEST KITCHEN TIP**
> Add mango to your regular fruit rotation to boost your intake of important nutrients like vitamins C and A, and potassium.

GNOCCHI WITH PESTO SAUCE

GNOCCHI WITH PESTO SAUCE

Perk up gnocchi and vegetables with a flavorful pesto sauce.
—*Taste of Home* Test Kitchen

Takes: 25 min. • **Makes:** 4 servings

- 1 pkg. (16 oz.) potato gnocchi
- 2 tsp. olive oil
- 1 cup diced zucchini
- ½ cup chopped
   sweet yellow pepper
- ¼ cup prepared pesto
- 1 cup chopped tomatoes
   Toasted pine nuts, optional

1. Cook gnocchi according to the package directions; drain.

2. Meanwhile, in a large skillet, heat oil over medium-high heat; saute the zucchini and pepper until the zucchini is tender.

3. Add pesto and gnocchi, stirring gently to coat. Stir in tomatoes. If desired, top with pine nuts.

1 cup: 327 cal., 9g fat (2g sat. fat), 8mg chol., 682mg sod., 52g carb. (10g sugars, 4g fiber), 9g pro.

HAM & SPINACH COUSCOUS

Here's a simple way to dress up couscous. This foolproof dish makes a tasty one-pot meal when time is tight.

—Lisa Shannon, Cullman, AL

- -

Takes: 20 min. • **Makes:** 4 servings

- 2 **cups water**
- 1 **cup chopped fully cooked ham**
- 1 **cup chopped fresh spinach**
- ½ **tsp. garlic salt**
- 1 **cup uncooked couscous**
- ¼ **cup shredded cheddar cheese**

In a large saucepan, combine the water, ham, spinach and garlic salt. Bring to a boil. Stir in the couscous. Remove from heat; cover and let stand for 5-10 minutes or until water is absorbed. Fluff with fork. Sprinkle with cheese.

1 cup: 248 cal., 6g fat (3g sat. fat), 26mg chol., 727mg sod., 36g carb. (1g sugars, 2g fiber), 14g pro.
Diabetic exchanges: 2 starch, 1 lean meat, 1 fat.

CAROLINA-STYLE VINEGAR BBQ CHICKEN

I live in Georgia but I appreciate the tangy, sweet and slightly spicy taste of Carolina vinegar chicken. I make my version in the slow cooker. With the tempting aroma filling the house, your family will be at the dinner table in no time!

—Ramona Parris, Canton, GA

- -

Prep: 10 min. • **Cook:** 4 hours
Makes: 6 servings

- 2 **cups water**
- 1 **cup white vinegar**
- ¼ **cup sugar**
- 1 **Tbsp. reduced-sodium chicken base**
- 1 **tsp. crushed red pepper flakes**
- ¾ **tsp. salt**
- 1½ **lbs. boneless skinless chicken breasts**
- 6 **whole wheat hamburger buns, split, optional**

1. In a small bowl, mix the first 6 ingredients. Place chicken in a 3-qt. slow cooker; add the vinegar mixture. Cook, covered, on low 4-5 hours or until chicken is tender.
2. Remove the chicken; cool slightly. Reserve 1 cup cooking juices; discard remaining juices. Shred chicken with 2 forks. Return meat and reserved cooking juices to slow cooker; heat through. If desired, serve chicken mixture on buns.

½ cup: 134 cal., 3g fat (1g sat. fat), 63mg chol., 228mg sod., 3g carb. (3g sugars, 0 fiber), 23g pro.
Diabetic exchanges: 3 lean meat.

CAROLINA-STYLE VINEGAR BBQ CHICKEN

PORK CHOPS WITH DIJON SAUCE

Here's a main course that tastes rich but isn't high in saturated fat.
—Bonnie Brown-Watson, Houston, TX

- -

Takes: 25 min. • **Makes:** 4 servings

- 4 **boneless pork loin chops (6 oz. each)**
- ¼ **tsp. salt**
- ¼ **tsp. pepper**
- 2 **tsp. canola oil**
- ⅓ **cup reduced-sodium chicken broth**
- 2 **Tbsp. Dijon mustard**
- ⅓ **cup half-and-half cream**

1. Sprinkle pork chops with salt and pepper. In a large skillet coated with cooking spray, brown chops in oil for 4-5 minutes on each side or until a thermometer reads 145°. Remove and keep warm.

2. Stir the broth into skillet, scraping up any browned bits. Stir in mustard and half-and-half. Bring to a boil. Reduce heat; simmer, uncovered, until thickened, 5-6 minutes, stirring occasionally. Serve with pork chops.

1 pork chop: 283 cal., 14g fat (5g sat. fat), 92mg chol., 432mg sod., 1g carb. (1g sugars, 0 fiber), 34g pro.

Diabetic exchanges: 5 lean meat, 2 fat.

DID YOU KNOW?

Just like a good steak, a pork chop should rest before you cut into it. When cooking, the juices of the meat migrate away from the heat to the center of the pork chop. If you cut in too soon, all that flavorful juice will spill out. It's worth the wait!

PORK CHOPS WITH DIJON SAUCE

PESTO HALIBUT

ROAST PORK WITH APPLES & ONIONS

The sweetness of the apples and onions nicely complements the roast pork. With its crisp skin and melt-in-your-mouth flavor, this is one of our favorite dinners.

—Lily Julow, Lawrenceville, GA

Prep: 30 min.
Bake: 45 min. + standing
Makes: 8 servings

- 1 boneless pork loin roast (2 lbs.)
- ¼ tsp. salt
- ¼ tsp. pepper
- 1 Tbsp. olive oil
- 3 large Golden Delicious apples, cut into 1-in. wedges
- 2 large onions, cut into ¾-in. wedges
- 5 garlic cloves, peeled
- 1 Tbsp. minced fresh rosemary or 1 tsp. dried rosemary, crushed

1. Preheat oven to 350°. Sprinkle roast with salt and pepper. In a large nonstick skillet, heat oil over medium heat; brown the roast on all sides. Transfer to a roasting pan coated with cooking spray. Place the apples, onions and garlic around the roast; sprinkle with rosemary.

2. Roast 45-55 minutes or until a thermometer inserted in pork reads 145°, turning apples, onion and garlic once. Remove from oven; tent with foil. Let stand 10 minutes before slicing. Serve with apple mixture.

1 serving: 210 cal., 7g fat (2g sat. fat), 57mg chol., 109mg sod., 14g carb. (9g sugars, 2g fiber), 23g pro.
Diabetic exchanges: 3 lean meat, 1 starch, ½ fat.

PESTO HALIBUT

The mildness of halibut contrasts perfectly with the robust flavor of pesto in this recipe. It takes only minutes to get the fish ready for the oven, leaving you plenty of time to get started on your side dishes. Nearly anything goes well with this entree.

—April Showalter, Indianapolis, IN

Takes: 20 min. • **Makes:** 6 servings

- 2 Tbsp. olive oil
- 1 envelope pesto sauce mix
- 1 Tbsp. lemon juice
- 6 halibut fillets (4 oz. each)

1. Preheat oven to 450°. In a small bowl, combine oil, sauce mix and lemon juice; brush over both sides of fillets. Place in a greased 13x9-in. baking dish.

2. Bake, uncovered, until fish just begins to flake easily with a fork, 12-15 minutes.

1 fillet: 188 cal., 7g fat (1g sat. fat), 36mg chol., 481mg sod., 5g carb. (2g sugars, 0 fiber), 24g pro.
Diabetic exchanges: 3 lean meat, 1 fat.

ROAST PORK WITH APPLES & ONIONS

HADDOCK WITH LIME-CILANTRO BUTTER

HADDOCK WITH LIME-CILANTRO BUTTER

In Louisiana, the good times roll when we broil fish and serve it with lots of lime juice, cilantro and melted butter.

—Darlene Morris, Franklinton, LA

- -

Takes: 15 min. • **Makes:** 4 servings

- 4 haddock fillets (6 oz. each)
- ½ tsp. salt
- ¼ tsp. pepper
- 3 Tbsp. butter, melted
- 2 Tbsp. minced fresh cilantro
- 1 Tbsp. lime juice
- 1 tsp. grated lime zest

1. Preheat broiler. Sprinkle fillets with salt and pepper. Place on a greased broiler pan. Broil 4-5 in. from heat until fish flakes easily with a fork, 5-6 minutes.
2. In a small bowl, mix the remaining ingredients. Serve over fish.

1 fillet with 1 Tbsp. butter mixture: 227 cal., 10g fat (6g sat. fat), 121mg chol., 479mg sod., 1g carb. (0 sugars, 0 fiber), 32g pro.

SHEET PAN SAUSAGE & POTATO DINNER

(PICTURED ON P. 78)
Loaded with potatoes, sausage and fresh veggies, this fabulous toss-up makes a quick and easy weeknight dinner.

—Laurie Sledge, Brandon, MS

- -

Prep: 20 min. • **Bake:** 30 min.
Makes: 4 servings

- 1 lb. potatoes, cut into ½-in. pieces
- 1 pkg. (12 oz.) fully cooked andouille chicken sausage links or flavor of your choice, cut into 1-in. pieces
- 2 cups fresh broccoli florets
- 1 medium red onion, cut into wedges
- 1 medium sweet orange pepper, cut into 1-in. pieces
- 1 Tbsp. olive oil
- ¼ tsp. pepper
- ½ tsp. salt

1. Preheat oven to 400°. In a large bowl, combine potatoes, sausage, broccoli, onion and orange pepper. Add oil, pepper and salt; toss to coat.
2. Transfer to a 15x10x1-in. baking pan coated with cooking spray. Roast until vegetables are tender, stirring occasionally, 30-35 minutes.

1½ cups: 256 cal., 11g fat (3g sat. fat), 65mg chol., 789mg sod., 24g carb. (5g sugars, 3g fiber), 18g pro.

TOMATO & GARLIC BUTTER BEAN DINNER

On days I get home late and just want a warm meal, I stir together tomatoes, garlic and butter beans. Ladle it over noodles if you're in the mood for pasta.
—Jessica Meyers, Austin, TX

- -

Takes: 15 min. • **Makes:** 4 servings

- 1 Tbsp. olive oil
- 2 garlic cloves, minced
- 2 cans (14½ oz.) no-salt-added petite diced tomatoes, undrained
- 1 can (16 oz.) butter beans, rinsed and drained
- 6 cups fresh baby spinach (about 6 oz.)
- ½ tsp. Italian seasoning
- ¼ tsp. pepper
  Optional: Hot cooked pasta and grated Parmesan cheese

In a large skillet, heat the oil over medium-high heat. Add garlic; cook and stir until tender, 30-45 seconds. Add the tomatoes, beans, spinach, Italian seasoning and pepper; cook until the spinach is wilted, stirring occasionally. If desired, serve with pasta and cheese.

Freeze option: Freeze cooled bean mixture in freezer containers. To use, partially thaw mixture in refrigerator overnight. Heat in a saucepan, stirring occasionally; add water if necessary.

1¼ cups: 147 cal., 4g fat (1g sat. fat), 0 chol., 353mg sod., 28g carb. (8g sugars, 9g fiber), 8g pro. **Diabetic exchanges:** 2 starch, 1 lean meat, ½ fat.

MOIST LEMON HERB CHICKEN

I wanted a healthy, flavorful chicken recipe that was fast, simple and a crowd-pleaser. I got lucky and hit the jackpot with this one!
—Kali Wraspir, Lacey, WA

- -

Takes: 25 min. • **Makes:** 4 servings

- 4 boneless skinless chicken breast halves (6 oz. each)
- ½ tsp. salt
- ¼ tsp. pepper
- 1 Tbsp. olive oil
- 1 Tbsp. herbes de Provence
- 2 tsp. grated lemon zest
- 3 Tbsp. lemon juice

1. Sprinkle chicken with salt and pepper. In a large ovenproof skillet coated with cooking spray, brown chicken in oil. Sprinkle herbes de Provence and lemon zest over chicken; add lemon juice to pan.
2. Bake chicken, uncovered, at 375° until a thermometer reads 170°, 12-15 minutes.

1 chicken breast half: 220 cal., 7g fat (2g sat. fat), 94mg chol., 378mg sod., 2g carb. (0 sugars, 1g fiber), 35g pro. **Diabetic exchanges:** 5 lean meat, ½ fat.

TOMATO & GARLIC BUTTER BEAN DINNER

**GRILLED STEAK &
MUSHROOM SALAD**

GRILLED STEAK & MUSHROOM SALAD

My husband loves this salad, especially during summer. He says he feels as if he's eating a healthy salad and getting his steak, too! I always serve it with some fresh homemade bread.
—Julie Cashion, Sanford, FL

- -

Takes: 30 min. • **Makes:** 6 servings

- 6 Tbsp. olive oil, divided
- 2 Tbsp. Dijon mustard, divided
- ½ tsp. salt
- ¼ tsp. pepper
- 1 beef top sirloin steak (1½ lbs.)
- 1 lb. sliced fresh mushrooms
- ¼ cup red wine vinegar
- 1 medium bunch romaine, torn

1. In a small bowl, whisk 1 Tbsp. oil, 1 Tbsp. mustard, salt and pepper; set aside.

2. Grill the steak, covered, over medium-hot heat for 4 minutes. Turn; spread with mustard mixture. Grill 4 minutes longer or until the meat reaches desired doneness (for medium-rare, a thermometer should read 135°; medium, 140°; medium-well, 145°).

3. Meanwhile, in a large skillet, cook the mushrooms in 1 Tbsp. oil until tender. Stir in the vinegar and the remaining oil and mustard.

4. Thinly slice steak across the grain; add to mushroom mixture.

5. Serve over romaine.

1 serving: 299 cal., 20g fat (4g sat. fat), 63mg chol., 378mg sod., 6g carb. (1g sugars, 2g fiber), 25g pro.

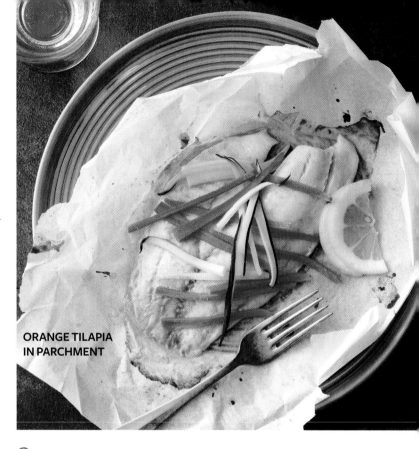

ORANGE TILAPIA
IN PARCHMENT

ORANGE TILAPIA IN PARCHMENT

Sweet orange juice and spicy cayenne pepper give this no-fuss dish fabulous flavor. A bonus? Cleanup is a breeze!
—Tiffany Diebold, Nashville, TN

- -

Takes: 30 min. • **Makes:** 4 servings

- ¼ cup orange juice
- 4 tsp. grated orange zest
- ¼ tsp. salt
- ¼ tsp. cayenne pepper
- ¼ tsp. pepper
- 4 tilapia fillets (6 oz. each)
- ½ cup julienned carrot
- ½ cup julienned zucchini

1. Preheat oven to 450°. In a small bowl, combine first 5 ingredients; set aside. Cut parchment or heavy-duty foil into four 18x12-in. lengths; place a fish fillet on each. Top with carrot and zucchini; drizzle with orange juice mixture.

2. Fold the parchment over the fish. Working from bottom inside corner, fold up about ¾ in. of the paper and crimp both layers to seal. Repeat, folding the edges up and crimping, until a half-moon-shaped packet is formed. Repeat for remaining packets. Place on baking sheets.

3. Bake until fish flakes easily with a fork, 12-15 minutes. Open packets carefully to allow steam to escape.

1 packet: 158 cal., 2g fat (1g sat. fat), 83mg chol., 220mg sod., 4g carb. (2g sugars, 1g fiber), 32g pro.

ROSEMARY PORK LOIN

I started growing rosemary in my garden after I discovered this pork recipe. My husband and I think it's restaurant quality, and we look forward to making it after work on weeknights.
—Judy Learned, Boyertown, PA

- -

Prep: 15 min. + standing
Grill: 20 min. • **Makes:** 4 servings

  1   garlic clove, minced
  ¾ tsp. salt
  1   Tbsp. olive oil
  2   tsp. minced fresh rosemary
  ¼ tsp. pepper
  1   pork tenderloin (1 lb.)

1. Place the garlic on a cutting board; sprinkle with salt. Using the flat side of a knife, mash the garlic. Continue to mash until it reaches a paste consistency. Transfer to a small bowl.
2. Stir in oil, rosemary and pepper; brush over the pork. Let stand for 20 minutes.
3. Grill the pork, covered, on a lightly oiled rack over medium heat or broil 4 in. from the heat 9-11 minutes on each side or until a thermometer reads 145°. Let stand for 5 minutes before slicing.

3 oz. cooked pork: 163 cal., 7g fat (2g sat. fat), 63mg chol., 488mg sod., 0 carb. (0 sugars, 0 fiber), 23g pro.
Diabetic exchanges: 3 lean meat, ½ fat.

GRILLED BUTTERMILK CHICKEN

I created this recipe years ago after one of our farmers market customers, a chef, shared the terrific idea of marinating chicken in buttermilk. The chicken is easy to prepare and always turns out moist and delicious. I bruise the thyme sprigs by twisting them before adding them to the buttermilk mixture; this tends to release the oils in the leaves and flavor the chicken nicely.
—Sue Gronholz, Beaver Dam, WI

- -

Prep: 10 min. + marinating
Grill: 10 min. • **Makes:** 12 servings

 1½ cups buttermilk
  4   fresh thyme sprigs
  4   garlic cloves, halved
  ½ tsp. salt
 12 boneless skinless chicken breast halves (about 4½ lbs.)

1. Place buttermilk, thyme, garlic and salt in a large bowl or shallow dish. Add chicken and turn to coat. Refrigerate 8 hours or overnight, turning occasionally.
2. Drain the chicken, discarding marinade. Grill, covered, over medium heat until a thermometer reads 165°, 5-7 minutes per side.

1 chicken breast half: 189 cal., 4g fat (1g sat. fat), 95mg chol., 168mg sod., 1g carb. (1g sugars, 0 fiber), 35g pro.
Diabetic exchanges: 5 lean meat.

GRILLED BUTTERMILK CHICKEN

EASY ASIAN BEEF & NOODLES

EASY ASIAN BEEF & NOODLES

I created this dish on a whim to feed my hungry teenagers. It's since become a dinnertime staple, and now two of my grandchildren make it, too.

—Judy Batson, Tampa, FL

Takes: 25 min. • **Makes:** 4 servings

- 1 **beef top sirloin steak (1 lb.), cut into ¼-in.-thick strips**
- 6 **Tbsp. reduced-sodium teriyaki sauce, divided**
- 8 **oz. uncooked whole grain thin spaghetti**
- 2 **Tbsp. canola oil, divided**
- 3 **cups broccoli coleslaw mix**
- 1 **medium onion, halved and thinly sliced**
  Chopped fresh cilantro, optional

1. Toss beef with 2 Tbsp. teriyaki sauce. Cook spaghetti according to package directions; drain.

2. In a large skillet, heat 1 Tbsp. oil over medium-high heat; stir-fry beef until browned, 1-3 minutes. Remove from pan.

3. In same skillet, heat the remaining oil over medium-high heat; stir-fry the coleslaw mix and onion until crisp-tender, 3-5 minutes. Add the spaghetti and remaining teriyaki sauce; toss and heat through. Stir in the beef. If desired, sprinkle with fresh cilantro.

2 cups: 462 cal., 13g fat (2g sat. fat), 46mg chol., 546mg sod., 52g carb. (9g sugars, 8g fiber), 35g pro.

SESAME NOODLES WITH SHRIMP & SNAP PEAS

SESAME NOODLES WITH SHRIMP & SNAP PEAS

Stir-fries and busy nights are a match made in heaven. For a boost of vibrant color and freshness, I sometimes stir in chopped cilantro just before I serve it from the pan.
—Nedra Schell, Fort Worth, TX

- -

Takes: 25 min. • **Makes:** 4 servings

- 8 **oz. uncooked whole wheat linguine**
- 1 **Tbsp. canola oil**
- 1 **lb. uncooked medium shrimp, peeled and deveined**
- 2 **cups fresh sugar snap peas, trimmed**
- ⅛ **tsp. salt**
- ⅛ **tsp. crushed red pepper flakes**
- ¾ **cup reduced-fat Asian toasted sesame salad dressing**

1. Cook linguine according to the package directions for al dente.
2. Meanwhile, in a large skillet, heat oil over medium-high heat. Add the shrimp, peas, salt and pepper flakes; stir-fry 2-3 minutes or until shrimp turn pink and peas are crisp-tender.
3. Drain linguine, reserving ¼ cup pasta water. Add pasta, pasta water and salad dressing to shrimp mixture; toss to combine.
1½ cups: 418 cal., 10g fat (1g sat. fat), 138mg chol., 646mg sod., 60g carb. (13g sugars, 8g fiber), 29g pro.

ASPARAGUS NICOISE SALAD

I've used my Nicoise as an appetizer or a main-dish salad, and it's a winner every time I put it on the table. Here's to a colorful, make-ahead salad!
—Jan Meyer, St. Paul, MN

- -

Takes: 20 min. • **Makes:** 4 servings

- 1 **lb. small red potatoes (about 10), halved**
- 1 **lb. fresh asparagus, trimmed and halved crosswise**
- 3 **pouches (2½ oz. each) albacore white tuna in water**
- ½ **cup pitted Greek olives, halved, optional**
- ½ **cup zesty Italian salad dressing**

1. Place the potatoes in a large saucepan; add water to cover by 2 in. Bring to a boil. Reduce heat; cook, uncovered, until tender, 10-12 minutes, adding asparagus during the last 2-4 minutes of cooking. Drain the potatoes and asparagus; immediately drop into ice water.
2. To serve, drain the potatoes and asparagus; pat dry and divide among 4 plates. Add the tuna and, if desired, olives. Drizzle with dressing.
1 serving: 233 cal., 8g fat (0 sat. fat), 22mg chol., 583mg sod., 23g carb. (4g sugars, 3g fiber), 16g pro.
Diabetic exchanges: 2 lean meat, 1½ starch, 1½ fat, 1 vegetable.

ASPARAGUS
NICOISE SALAD

SEARED SALMON
WITH
BALSAMIC SAUCE

SEARED SALMON WITH BALSAMIC SAUCE

A friend gave me this quick and easy salmon recipe. It has a mildly sweet sauce and is such a hit that I've passed it to other fish fans.
—Trish Horton,
Colorado Springs, CO

- - - - - - - - - - - - - - - - - - -

Takes: 30 min. • **Makes:** 4 servings

4	salmon fillets (4 oz. each)
½	tsp. salt
2	tsp. canola oil
¼	cup water
¼	cup balsamic vinegar
4	tsp. lemon juice
4	tsp. brown sugar
	Coarsely ground pepper

1. Sprinkle salmon with salt. In a large nonstick skillet, heat oil over medium heat. Place salmon in skillet, skin side up; cook until the fish just begins to flake easily with a fork, 4-5 minutes on each side. Remove from pan; keep warm.

2. In same skillet, combine the water, vinegar, lemon juice and brown sugar. Bring to a boil; cook until the liquid is reduced to about ⅓ cup, stirring occasionally. Serve the salmon with balsamic sauce; sprinkle with pepper.

1 fillet with about 1 Tbsp. sauce: 231 cal., 13g fat (2g sat. fat), 57mg chol., 353mg sod., 9g carb. (9g sugars, 0 fiber), 19g pro.
Diabetic exchanges: 3 lean meat, ½ starch, ½ fat.

CHICKEN & VEGETABLE CURRY COUSCOUS

For my busy family, a partly homemade one-pot meal is the best way to get dinner done in a hurry. Use your favorite blend of frozen veggies and serve with toasted pita bread for smiles all around.

—Elizabeth Hokanson, Arborg, MB

Takes: 25 min. • **Makes:** 6 servings

- 1 Tbsp. butter
- 1 lb. boneless skinless chicken breasts, cut into strips
- 1 pkg. (16 oz.) frozen vegetable blend of your choice
- 1¼ cups water
- 1 pkg. (5.7 oz.) curry-flavored couscous mix
- ½ cup raisins

1. In a cast-iron or other heavy skillet, heat butter over medium-high heat. Add chicken; cook and stir until no longer pink.

2. Add vegetable blend, water and contents of couscous seasoning packet. Bring to a boil; stir in the couscous and raisins. Remove from heat; let stand, covered, until water is absorbed, about 5 minutes. Fluff with a fork.

1 cup: 273 cal., 4g fat (2g sat. fat), 47mg chol., 311mg sod., 39g carb. (9g sugars, 4g fiber), 21g pro.

CHICKEN & VEGETABLE CURRY COUSCOUS

WALSH FAMILY GRILLED PORK TENDERLOINS

This is one of my friend's favorite family dinners, and one of my family's most loved, too. It's absolutely delicious, and even more so when cooked on a charcoal grill.

—Lisa Finnegan, Forked River, NJ

Prep: 10 min. + marinating
Grill: 20 min. • **Makes:** 8 servings

- ⅓ cup water
- ⅓ cup molasses
- ⅓ cup reduced-sodium soy sauce
- 2 Tbsp. minced fresh gingerroot
- 2 garlic cloves, minced
- ¼ tsp. salt
- ¼ tsp. pepper
- 2 pork tenderloins (1 lb. each)

1. In a bowl or shallow dish, combine the first 7 ingredients. Add pork and turn to coat. Cover and refrigerate for at least 8 hours or overnight.

2. Drain pork, discarding marinade. Place pork on an oiled grill rack. Grill, covered, over indirect medium-hot heat for 20-25 minutes or until a thermometer reads 145°. Let stand for 5 minutes before slicing.

3 oz. cooked pork: 143 cal., 4g fat (1g sat. fat), 63mg chol., 165mg sod., 3g carb. (2g sugars, 0 fiber), 23g pro.
Diabetic exchanges: 3 lean meat.

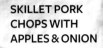

SKILLET PORK CHOPS WITH APPLES & ONION

SKILLET PORK CHOPS WITH APPLES & ONION

Simple recipes that land on the table fast are lifesavers. I serve skillet pork chops with veggies and, when there's time, cornbread stuffing.
—Tracey Karst, Ponderay, ID

- -

Takes: 20 min. • **Makes:** 4 servings

- **4** boneless pork loin chops (6 oz. each)
- **3** medium apples, cut into wedges
- **1** large onion, cut into thin wedges
- **¼** cup water
- **⅓** cup balsamic vinaigrette
- **½** tsp. salt
- **¼** tsp. pepper

1. Place a large nonstick skillet over medium heat; brown pork chops on both sides, about 4 minutes. Remove from pan.
2. In the same skillet, combine apples, onion and water. Place pork chops over apple mixture; drizzle chops with vinaigrette. Sprinkle with salt and pepper. Reduce heat; simmer, covered, until a thermometer inserted in chops reads 145°, 3-5 minutes.

1 pork chop with ¾ cup apple mixture: 360 cal., 15g fat (4g sat. fat), 82mg chol., 545mg sod., 22g carb. (15g sugars, 3g fiber), 33g pro. **Diabetic exchanges:** 5 lean meat, 1 fruit, 1 fat.

MANGO & GRILLED CHICKEN SALAD

MANGO & GRILLED CHICKEN SALAD

This fruity chicken salad is a weeknight standout, especially on hot days. I add salad greens and veggies for color and crunch.
—Sherry Little, Sherwood, AR

- -

Takes: 25 min. • **Makes:** 4 servings

- **1** lb. chicken tenderloins
- **½** tsp. salt
- **¼** tsp. pepper
- **SALAD**
- **6** cups torn mixed salad greens
- **¼** cup raspberry or balsamic vinaigrette
- **1** medium mango, peeled and cubed
- **1** cup fresh sugar snap peas, halved lengthwise

1. Toss the chicken with salt and pepper. Place on an oiled grill rack. Grill, covered, over medium heat or broil 4 in. from heat on each side until no longer pink, 3-4 minutes. Cut chicken into 1-in. pieces.
2. Divide greens among 4 plates; drizzle with vinaigrette. Top with chicken, mango and peas; serve immediately.

1 serving: 210 cal., 2g fat (0 sat. fat), 56mg chol., 447mg sod., 22g carb. (16g sugars, 4g fiber), 30g pro. **Diabetic exchanges:** 3 lean meat, 2 vegetable, ½ starch, ½ fat.

THAI SHRIMP PASTA

I came up with this recipe while my son was home from the Navy. He loves Thai food, and I wanted to make something special but simple. There wasn't a noodle left in the bowl.

—Jana Rippee, Casa Grande, AZ

Takes: 30 min. • **Makes:** 4 servings

- 8 oz. thin flat rice noodles
- 1 Tbsp. curry powder
- 1 lb. uncooked shrimp (31-40 per lb.), peeled and deveined
- 1 can (13.66 oz.) light coconut milk
- ¼ tsp. salt
- ¼ tsp. pepper
- ½ cup minced fresh cilantro
  Lime wedges, optional

1. Soak the noodles according to package directions. Meanwhile, in a large dry skillet over medium heat, toast curry powder until aromatic, about 1-2 minutes. Stir in shrimp, coconut milk, salt and pepper. Bring to a boil. Reduce the heat; simmer, uncovered, 5-6 minutes or until shrimp turn pink.

2. Drain noodles. Add noodles and cilantro to pan; heat through. If desired, serve with lime wedges.

1 cup: 361 cal., 9g fat (5g sat. fat), 138mg chol., 284mg sod., 44g carb. (2g sugars, 2g fiber), 22g pro.

Diabetic exchanges: 3 lean meat, 2½ starch, 1 fat.

THAI RED CURRY CHICKEN & VEGETABLES

The key to this curry chicken is achieving complex flavors without heaviness. For the vegetables, I add colorful pea pods, sweet red peppers and water chestnuts. Feel free to use your favorite store-bought blend of veggies.

—David Dahlman, Chatsworth, CA

Takes: 30 min. • **Makes:** 4 servings

- 1½ lbs. boneless skinless chicken breasts, cut into 1½-in. pieces
- 1⅓ cups light coconut milk
- 2 Tbsp. red curry paste
- ½ tsp. salt
- 1 pkg. (16 oz.) frozen stir-fry vegetable blend
- 3 cups hot cooked brown rice

1. Preheat oven to 425°. Place chicken in a greased 8-in. square baking dish. In a small bowl, mix coconut milk, curry paste and salt; pour over chicken.

2. Bake, covered, 18-22 minutes or until chicken is no longer pink. Meanwhile, cook the vegetables according to package directions; drain. Serve chicken with rice and vegetables.

1 cup chicken with ¾ cup rice and ¾ cup vegetables: 511 cal., 14g fat (6g sat. fat), 94mg chol., 606mg sod., 51g carb. (6g sugars, 5g fiber), 41g pro.

THAI RED CURRY CHICKEN & VEGETABLES

BALSAMIC CHICKEN WITH ROASTED TOMATOES

BALSAMIC CHICKEN WITH ROASTED TOMATOES

This entree is a fantastic way to savor fresh tomatoes, especially during warm summer months. The sweet, tangy glaze is so good.
—Karen Gehrig, Concord, NC

Takes: 25 min. • **Makes:** 4 servings

- 2 **Tbsp. honey**
- 2 **Tbsp. olive oil, divided**
- 2 **cups grape tomatoes**
- 4 **boneless skinless chicken breast halves (6 oz. each)**

- ½ **tsp. salt**
- ½ **tsp. pepper**
- 2 **Tbsp. balsamic glaze**

1. Preheat oven to 400°. In a small bowl, mix honey and 1 Tbsp. oil. Add tomatoes and toss to coat. Transfer to a greased 15x10x1-in. baking pan. Bake 5-7 minutes or until softened.
2. Pound the chicken breasts with a meat mallet to ½-in. thickness; sprinkle with salt and pepper. In a large skillet, heat remaining oil over medium heat. Add the chicken; cook 5-6 minutes on each side or until no longer pink. Serve with the roasted tomatoes; drizzle with glaze.

1 chicken breast half with ½ cup tomatoes and 1½ tsp. glaze: 306 cal., 11g fat (2g sat. fat), 94mg chol., 384mg sod., 16g carb. (14g sugars, 1g fiber), 35g pro. **Diabetic exchanges:** 5 lean meat, 1½ fat, 1 starch.
Note: To make your own balsamic glaze, bring ½ cup balsamic vinegar to a boil in a small saucepan. Reduce the heat to medium; simmer for 10-12 minutes or until thickened to a glaze consistency. Makes about 2 Tbsp.

OVEN-FRIED FISH NUGGETS

THAI SALMON BROWN RICE BOWLS

Here's a quick and nourishing meal. The store-bought sesame ginger dressing saves time and adds extra flavor to the salmon.
—Naylet LaRochelle, Miami, FL

- -

Takes: 15 min. • **Makes:** 4 servings

4	salmon fillets (4 oz. each)
½	cup sesame ginger salad dressing, divided
3	cups hot cooked brown rice
½	cup chopped fresh cilantro
¼	tsp. salt
1	cup julienned carrot Thinly sliced red cabbage, optional

1. Preheat oven to 400°. Place the salmon in a foil-lined 15x10x1-in. pan; brush with ¼ cup dressing. Bake until fish just begins to flake easily with a fork, 8-10 minutes. Meanwhile, toss rice with cilantro and salt.
2. To serve, divide rice mixture among 4 bowls. Top with salmon, carrots and, if desired, cabbage. Drizzle with remaining dressing.
1 serving: 486 cal., 21g fat (4g sat. fat), 57mg chol., 532mg sod., 49g carb. (8g sugars, 3g fiber), 24g pro.

> **TEST KITCHEN TIP**
> Sometimes 4 oz. salmon fillets are hard to find. Another option is to simply buy a 1 lb. fillet and cut it into 4 portions. Also, people seem to love or hate cilantro. If it's not your favorite, omit the cilantro and add some chopped fresh parsley instead.

OVEN-FRIED FISH NUGGETS

My husband and I love fried fish, but we're trying to cut back on dietary fat. I came up with this oven-baked version. He likes it as much as deep-fried fish, so I know it's a winner.
—LaDonna Reed, Ponca City, OK

- -

Takes: 25 min. • **Makes:** 4 servings

⅓	cup seasoned bread crumbs
⅓	cup crushed cornflakes
3	Tbsp. grated Parmesan cheese
½	tsp. salt
¼	tsp. pepper
1½	lbs. cod fillets, cut into 1-in. cubes Butter-flavored cooking spray

1. In a shallow bowl, combine the bread crumbs, cornflakes, Parmesan cheese, salt and pepper. Coat fish with butter-flavored spray, then roll in crumb mixture.
2. Place on a baking sheet coated with cooking spray. Bake at 375° for 15-20 minutes or until the fish flakes easily with a fork.
Freeze option: Cover and freeze unbaked fish nuggets on a waxed paper-lined baking sheet until firm. Transfer to a resealable freezer container; return to freezer. To use, preheat oven to 375°. Bake nuggets on a rack on a greased baking sheet 15-20 minutes or until fish flakes easily with a fork.
9 pieces: 171 cal., 2g fat (1g sat. fat), 66mg chol., 415mg sod., 7g carb. (1g sugars, 0 fiber), 29g pro.
Diabetic exchanges: 5 lean meat, ½ starch.

THAI SALMON
BROWN RICE
BOWLS

SPINACH STEAK PINWHEELS

SPINACH STEAK PINWHEELS

Bacon and spinach bring plenty of flavor to these sirloin steak spirals. It's an easy dish to make and perfect for backyard grilling. I always get lots of compliments.
—Helen Vail, Glenside, PA

- -

Takes: 25 min. • **Makes:** 6 servings

1½ lbs. beef top sirloin steak
8 bacon strips, cooked
1 pkg. (10 oz.) frozen chopped spinach, thawed and squeezed dry
¼ cup grated Parmesan cheese
½ tsp. salt
⅛ tsp. cayenne pepper

1. Lightly score steak by making shallow diagonal cuts into top of steak at 1-in. intervals; repeat cuts in opposite direction. Cover steak with plastic wrap; pound with a meat mallet to ½-in. thickness. Remove plastic.

2. Place bacon widthwise at center of steak. In a bowl, mix remaining ingredients; spoon over bacon. Starting at a short side, roll up steak jelly-roll style; secure with toothpicks. Cut into 6 slices.

3. Place on an oiled grill rack. Grill pinwheels, covered, over medium heat until beef reaches desired doneness (for medium-rare, a thermometer should read 135°; medium, 140°), 5-6 minutes on each side. Discard toothpicks before serving.

1 pinwheel: 227 cal., 10g fat (4g sat. fat), 60mg chol., 536mg sod., 3g carb. (0 sugars, 1g fiber), 31g pro.
Diabetic exchanges: 4 lean meat, 1 fat.

SPAGHETTI WITH FRESH TOMATO SAUCE

When my mom made this spaghetti sauce, the house smelled so good that I opened the windows to torture the neighbors. It tastes even more wonderful the next day, when the flavors have really melded.
—Vera Schulze, Holbrook, NY

Prep: 15 min. • **Cook:** 30 min.
Makes: 4 servings

- 2 **Tbsp. olive oil**
- 1 **large onion, finely chopped**
- 2 **lbs. plum tomatoes, chopped (about 5 cups)**
- 1 **tsp. salt**
- ¼ **tsp. pepper**
- 8 **oz. uncooked spaghetti**
- ¼ **cup thinly sliced fresh basil**
- 1 **tsp. sugar, optional**
  Grated Romano cheese
  Additional basil

1. In a 6-qt. stockpot, heat the oil over medium heat; saute onion until tender, 4-6 minutes. Stir in the tomatoes, salt and pepper; bring to a boil. Reduce the heat; simmer, uncovered, until thickened, 20-25 minutes. Meanwhile, cook spaghetti according to package directions; drain.

2. Stir ¼ cup basil and, if desired, sugar into sauce. Serve over the spaghetti. Top with cheese and additional basil.

SPAGHETTI WITH FRESH TOMATO SAUCE

Freeze option: Freeze cooled sauce in freezer containers. To use, partially thaw in the refrigerator overnight. Heat through in a saucepan, stirring occasionally.

1 cup spaghetti with ¾ cup sauce: 327 cal., 8g fat (1g sat. fat), 0 chol., 607mg sod., 55g carb. (9g sugars, 5g fiber), 10g pro.

SESAME-ORANGE SALMON

We're always looking for new and interesting ways to prepare salmon. This Asian-inspired butter will be a favorite for citrus lovers. Using reduced-fat butter saves 40 calories and 4 grams of fat per serving but still adds a generous coating to the salmon.
—*Taste of Home* Test Kitchen

Takes: 15 min. • **Makes:** 2 servings

- 2 **salmon fillets (4 oz. each)**
- 5 **tsp. reduced-fat butter, melted**
- 1½ **tsp. reduced-sodium soy sauce**
- ¾ **tsp. grated orange zest**
- ½ **tsp. sesame seeds**

Place salmon skin side down on a broiler pan. Combine butter, soy sauce, orange zest and sesame seeds. Brush a third of mixture over salmon. Broil 3-4 in. from the heat until fish flakes easily with a fork, 7-9 minutes, basting occasionally with remaining butter mixture.

1 fillet: 225 cal., 16g fat (5g sat. fat), 69mg chol., 288mg sod., 1g carb. (0 sugars, 0 fiber), 20g pro.
Diabetic exchanges: 3 lean meat, 1½ fat.

SALMON
WITH HONEY
PECAN SAUCE

SALMON WITH HONEY PECAN SAUCE

I love the explosion of sweet and buttery flavors in every bite of this dish. In the summer, I make sauteed zucchini for a perfect side dish.

—Alice Stanko, Warren, MI

- -

Takes: 30 min. • **Makes:** 4 servings

- 4 **salmon fillets (4 oz. each)**
- ½ **tsp. seasoned salt**
- ¼ **tsp. pepper**
- ¼ **cup finely chopped pecans, toasted**
- ¼ **cup honey**
- 3 **Tbsp. reduced-fat butter**

1. Sprinkle salmon with seasoned salt and pepper. Place fish on an oiled grill rack, skin side down. Grill, covered, over medium-high heat or broil 4 in. from heat until fish just begins to flake easily with a fork, 6-8 minutes.

2. Meanwhile, in a small saucepan, cook the pecans, honey and butter over medium heat until bubbly, 5-7 minutes. Serve with salmon.

1 fillet with 2 Tbsp. sauce: 330 cal., 20g fat (5g sat. fat), 68mg chol., 319mg sod., 19g carb. (18g sugars, 1g fiber), 20g pro. **Diabetic exchanges:** 3 lean meat, 2½ fat, 1 starch.

ITALIAN PORK & POTATO CASSEROLE

ITALIAN PORK & POTATO CASSEROLE

This dish's aroma when baking brings back fond memories of home. My mother created the recipe years ago, using the ingredients she had on hand.

—Theresa Kreyche, Tustin, CA

- -

Prep: 10 min. • **Bake:** 45 min.
Makes: 6 servings

- 6 **cups sliced red potatoes**
- 3 **Tbsp. water**
- 1 **garlic clove, minced**
- ½ **tsp. salt**
- ⅛ **tsp. pepper**
- 6 **boneless pork loin chops (6 oz. each)**
- 1 **jar (24 oz.) marinara sauce**
- ¼ **cup shredded Parmesan cheese**

1. Place potatoes and water in a microwave-safe dish. Cover and microwave on high for 5 minutes or until almost tender; drain.

2. Place the potatoes in a 13x9-in. baking dish coated with cooking spray. Sprinkle with garlic, salt and pepper. Top with pork chops and marinara sauce. Cover and bake at 350° until a thermometer inserted in pork reads 145° and potatoes are tender, 40-45 minutes.

3. Sprinkle with the cheese. Bake, uncovered, until cheese is melted, 3-5 minutes longer. Let stand 5 minutes before serving.

1 pork chop with 1 cup potatoes and ½ cup sauce: 412 cal., 11g fat (4g sat. fat), 84mg chol., 506mg sod., 38g carb. (10g sugars, 4g fiber), 39g pro. **Diabetic exchanges:** 5 lean meat, 2½ starch.

TURKEY VERDE LETTUCE WRAPS

I love these wraps because they're a clever pairing of low-fat food with high-end flavor. They will satisfy your cravings for a spicy, fun, quick-to-prepare dish.
—Stephanie Barron, Lake Orion, MI

- -

Takes: 25 min. • **Makes:** 6 servings

2	pkg. (17.6 oz. each) turkey breast cutlets, cut into 1-in. strips
4	tsp. olive oil
1	tsp. garlic salt
¼	tsp. pepper
1	cup salsa verde
12	romaine leaves

In a large bowl, combine turkey, oil, garlic salt and pepper. Heat a large skillet over medium-high heat. Add the turkey mixture in batches; cook and stir 2-4 minutes or until no longer pink. Return all the turkey to pan. Stir in salsa; heat through. Serve in romaine.

2 lettuce wraps: 229 cal., 4g fat (1g sat. fat), 103mg chol., 617mg sod., 3g carb. (1g sugars, 1g fiber), 42g pro. **Diabetic exchanges:** 5 lean meat, ½ fat.

SWEET POTATO & BEAN QUESADILLAS

This recipe is one of my favorites because it's healthy, easy, fast, fun and delicious!
—Brittany Hubbard, St. Paul, MN

- -

Takes: 30 min. • **Makes:** 4 servings

2	medium sweet potatoes
4	whole wheat tortillas (8 in.)
¾	cup canned black beans, rinsed and drained
½	cup shredded pepper jack cheese
¾	cup salsa

1. Scrub sweet potatoes; pierce several times with a fork. Place on a microwave-safe plate. Microwave, uncovered, on high, turning once, until very tender, 7-9 minutes.

2. When cool enough to handle, cut each potato lengthwise in half. Scoop out pulp. Spread onto half of each tortilla; top with beans and cheese. Fold other half of tortilla over filling.

3. Heat a cast-iron skillet or griddle over medium heat. Cook quesadillas until golden brown and cheese is melted, 2-3 minutes on each side. Serve with salsa.

1 quesadilla with 3 Tbsp. salsa: 306 cal., 8g fat (3g sat. fat), 15mg chol., 531mg sod., 46g carb. (9g sugars, 6g fiber), 11g pro.

SWEET POTATO & BEAN QUESADILLAS

PINEAPPLE-GLAZED PORK ROAST

PINEAPPLE-GLAZED PORK ROAST

Some recipes are so versatile that you can serve them for both family dinners and for company. This is the one that gets the most oohs and aahs.
—Nancy Whitford, Edwards, NY

- -

Prep: 10 min.
Bake: 50 min. + standing
Makes: 10 servings

- 1 boneless pork loin roast (2½ lbs.)
- ¾ tsp. salt
- ¼ tsp. pepper
- ⅓ cup pineapple preserves
- 2 Tbsp. stone-ground mustard
- ¼ tsp. dried basil
- 1 can (20 oz.) unsweetened pineapple tidbits, drained

1. Preheat oven to 350°. Place roast on a rack in a shallow roasting pan, fat side up. Sprinkle with salt and pepper. Roast 25 minutes.
2. Meanwhile, for glaze, in a small bowl, whisk preserves, mustard and basil; brush half the mixture over the roast. Add pineapple to roasting pan. Roast 25-35 minutes longer or until a thermometer reads 145°.
3. Remove the roast from the oven and brush with the remaining glaze; tent loosely with foil. Let stand for 10 minutes before slicing. Using a slotted spoon, serve the pineapple with the pork.

3 oz. cooked pork with 1 Tbsp. pineapple: 195 cal., 5g fat (2g sat. fat), 56mg chol., 271mg sod., 14g carb. (12g sugars, 1g fiber), 22g pro.
Diabetic exchanges: 3 lean meat, ½ starch.

MEDITERRANEAN CHICKEN

LEMON-GARLIC TURKEY BREAST

Here is a delightful main dish that easily morphs into tender slices of sandwich meat for lunch the next day. This turkey breast is hearty, healthy and easy to make.
—Sandra Hall, Decatur, TX

- -

Prep: 15 min.
Cook: 5 hours. + standing
Makes: 12 servings

- 2 **medium lemons, sliced**
- 1 **bone-in turkey breast (6 to 7 lbs.), skin removed**
- ¼ **cup minced fresh parsley**
- 8 **garlic cloves, minced**
- 4 **tsp. grated lemon zest**
- 2 **tsp. salt-free lemon-pepper seasoning**
- 1½ **tsp. salt**

1. Line bottom of a greased 6-qt. slow cooker with three-fourths of the lemon slices. Place turkey over lemons, breast side up. Mix parsley, garlic, lemon zest, pepper seasoning and salt; rub over turkey. Top with the remaining lemon slices. Cook, covered, on low until the turkey is tender, 5-6 hours.
2. Remove turkey from slow cooker; tent with foil. Let stand 15 minutes before carving. If desired, skim fat and thicken pan drippings for sauce; serve with turkey.

6 oz. cooked turkey: 197 cal., 1g fat (0 sat. fat), 117mg chol., 371mg sod., 2g carb. (0 sugars, 0 fiber), 43g pro.
Diabetic exchanges: 6 lean meat.

MEDITERRANEAN CHICKEN

This flavorful skillet creation is dressed in tomatoes, olives and capers. It's a knockout main dish at my house.
—Mary Relyea, Canastota, NY

- -

Takes: 25 min. • **Makes:** 4 servings

- 4 **boneless skinless chicken breast halves (6 oz. each)**
- ¼ **tsp. salt**
- ¼ **tsp. pepper**
- 3 **Tbsp. olive oil**
- 1 **pint grape tomatoes**
- 16 **pitted Greek or ripe olives, sliced**
- 3 **Tbsp. capers, drained**

Sprinkle the chicken with salt and pepper. In a large ovenproof skillet, cook the chicken in oil over medium heat until golden brown, 2-3 minutes on each side. Add the tomatoes, olives and capers. Bake, uncovered, at 475° until a thermometer reads 170°, 10-14 minutes.
1 serving: 336 cal., 18g fat (3g sat. fat), 94mg chol., 631mg sod., 6g carb. (3g sugars, 2g fiber), 36g pro.

LEMON-GARLIC TURKEY
BREAST

CHICKEN PESTO ROLL-UPS

CHICKEN PESTO ROLL-UPS

One night I looked in the fridge and pondered what I could make with chicken, cheese, mushrooms and pesto. These pretty roll-ups were the result. Add crusty Italian bread and a fruit salad, and you have a meal!

—Melissa Nordmann, Mobile, AL

- -

Prep: 15 min. • **Bake:** 30 min.
Makes: 4 servings

- **4** boneless skinless chicken breast halves (6 oz. each)
- **½** cup prepared pesto, divided
- **1** lb. medium fresh mushrooms, sliced
- **4** slices reduced-fat provolone cheese, halved

1. Preheat oven to 350°. Pound the chicken breasts with a meat mallet to ¼-in. thickness. Spread ¼ cup pesto over chicken breasts.

2. Coarsely chop half the sliced mushrooms; scatter the remaining sliced mushrooms in a 15x10x1-in. baking pan coated with cooking spray. Top each chicken breast with a fourth of the chopped mushrooms and a halved cheese slice. Roll up chicken from a short side; secure with toothpicks. Place the seam side down on top of the sliced mushrooms.

3. Bake, covered, until chicken is no longer pink, 25-30 minutes. Preheat broiler; top chicken with remaining pesto and remaining cheese. Broil until cheese is melted and browned, 3-5 minutes longer. Discard the toothpicks.

1 stuffed chicken breast half:
374 cal., 17g fat (5g sat. fat), 104mg chol., 582mg sod., 7g carb. (1g sugars, 1g fiber), 44g pro.
Diabetic exchanges: 5 lean meat, 2 fat.

HONEY-GARLIC PORK CHOPS

These chops are so simple to get ready yet taste divine. Honey, lemon and garlic form a classic combination that fits perfectly with grilled pork. I like that I can marinade the chops the night before or even in the morning. Then in the evening, I just start up the grill and dinner is ready in no time.
—Helen Carpenter, Albuquerque, NM

- -

Prep: 5 min. + marinating
Grill: 15 min. • **Makes:** 4 servings

- ¼ cup lemon juice
- ¼ cup honey
- 2 Tbsp. soy sauce
- 2 garlic cloves, minced
- 4 boneless pork loin chops (6 oz. each and 1¼ to 1½ in. thick)

1. In a bowl or shallow dish, combine the lemon juice, honey, soy sauce and garlic. Add the pork chops and turn to coat. Cover and refrigerate for 4-8 hours. Drain pork, discarding the marinade.

2. Grill, covered, over medium heat for 6-8 minutes on each side or until a thermometer reads 145°. Let meat stand for 5 minutes before serving.

1 pork chop: 271 cal., 10g fat (4g sat. fat), 82mg chol., 324mg sod., 11g carb. (11g sugars, 0 fiber), 33g pro.
Diabetic exchanges: 5 lean meat, ½ starch.

SPINACH PIZZA QUESADILLAS

I treasure this dinner because my daughter and I created it together. You can make variations with other veggies you have at home. It's a smart way to get kids to eat healthier.
—Tanna Mancini, Gulfport, FL

- -

Takes: 20 min. • **Makes:** 6 servings

- 6 whole wheat tortillas (8 in.)
- 3 cups shredded part-skim mozzarella cheese
- 3 cups chopped fresh spinach
- 1 can (8 oz.) pizza sauce

1. Preheat oven to 400°. On half of each tortilla, layer ½ cup cheese, ½ cup spinach and about 2 Tbsp. sauce. Fold other half over filling. Place on baking sheets coated with cooking spray.

2. Bake until the cheese is melted, 10-12 minutes.

1 quesadilla: 301 cal., 13g fat (7g sat. fat), 36mg chol., 650mg sod., 29g carb. (3g sugars, 4g fiber), 19g pro.
Diabetic exchanges: 2 starch, 2 medium-fat meat.

HONEY-GARLIC PORK CHOPS

MEDITERRANEAN
TILAPIA

MEDITERRANEAN TILAPIA

I recently became a fan of tilapia. Its mild taste makes it easy to top with my favorite ingredients. Plus, it's low in calories and fat. What's not to love?
—Robin Brenneman, Hilliard, OH

- -

Takes: 20 min. • **Makes:** 6 servings

- 6 **tilapia fillets (6 oz. each)**
- 1 **cup canned Italian diced tomatoes**
- ½ **cup water-packed artichoke hearts, chopped**
- ½ **cup sliced ripe olives**
- ½ **cup crumbled feta cheese**

Preheat oven to 400°. Place fillets in a 15x10x1-in. baking pan coated with cooking spray. Top with tomatoes, artichoke hearts, olives and cheese. Bake, uncovered, until fish flakes easily with a fork, 15-20 minutes.
1 fillet: 197 cal., 4g fat (2g sat. fat), 88mg chol., 446mg sod., 5g carb. (2g sugars, 1g fiber), 34g pro.
Diabetic exchanges: 5 lean meat, ½ fat.

> **TEST KITCHEN TIP**
> Tilapia, catfish, haddock and other lean types of fish may be frozen for up to 6 months. Oily fish, such as mackerel and grouper, shouldn't be frozen for more than 3 months.

CARIBBEAN CHICKEN STIR-FRY

CARIBBEAN CHICKEN STIR-FRY

Fruit cocktail in stir-fry? You might be surprised at how good this dish is. It's a promising go-to option when time is tight.
—Jeanne Holt, Mendota Heights, MN

- -

Takes: 25 min. • **Makes:** 4 servings

- 2 **tsp. cornstarch**
- ¼ **cup water**
- 1 **lb. boneless skinless chicken breasts, cut into ½-in. strips**
- 2 **tsp. Caribbean jerk seasoning**
- 1 **can (15 oz.) mixed tropical fruit, drained and coarsely chopped**
- 2 **pkg. (8.8 oz. each) ready-to-serve brown rice**

1. In a small bowl, mix cornstarch and water until smooth.
2. Coat a large skillet with cooking spray; heat over medium-high heat. Add the chicken; sprinkle with jerk seasoning. Stir-fry 3-5 minutes or until no longer pink. Stir cornstarch mixture and add to pan. Add the fruit. Bring to a boil; cook and stir 1-2 minutes or until the sauce is thickened.
3. Meanwhile, heat rice according to package directions. Serve with the chicken.
½ cup stir-fry with ½ cup rice: 432 cal., 5g fat (1g sat. fat), 63mg chol., 210mg sod., 60g carb. (0 sugars, 3g fiber), 28g pro.

SPICY CATFISH WITH TOMATOES

I came up with this recipe after trying something similar at a catfish house in the mountains of northern Georgia. My husband and I both appreciate this healthy, flavor-packed dish.

—Marla Anthony, Loganville, GA

- -

Takes: 20 min. • **Makes:** 2 servings

- 1 catfish fillet (about ½ lb.)
- ¼ tsp. salt
- ⅛ tsp. pepper
  Dash to ⅛ tsp. cayenne pepper
- 1 cup canned Mexican diced tomatoes with juice
- 1 to 2 green onions, thinly sliced
  Hot cooked white or brown rice, optional

1. Sprinkle fish with salt, pepper and cayenne. In a nonstick skillet, cook the fish over medium for about 3 minutes on each side or until lightly browned. Top with tomatoes and sprinkle with green onions. Bring to a boil. Reduce heat; simmer, uncovered, for about 2 minutes.

2. Cover the skillet and simmer 2-3 minutes longer or until liquid is reduced and fish flakes easily with a fork. Serve with rice if desired.

½ fillet with about ½ cup tomato mixture: 139 cal., 3g fat (0 sat. fat), 52mg chol., 552mg sod., 7g carb. (0 sugars, 2g fiber), 21g pro. **Diabetic exchanges:** 3 lean meat, ½ starch.

GRILLED LEMON-DILL SHRIMP

This grilled shrimp is one of my most-loved recipes. Add veggies if desired, but grill them separately.

—Jane Whittaker, Pensacola, FL

- -

Takes: 30 min. • **Makes:** 4 servings

- ¼ cup olive oil
- 1 Tbsp. lemon juice
- 2 tsp. dill weed
- 2 garlic cloves, minced
- ¾ tsp. salt
- ½ tsp. pepper
- 1 lb. uncooked shrimp (31-40 per lb.), peeled and deveined

1. In a large bowl, whisk the first 6 ingredients until blended. Reserve 3 Tbsp. marinade for basting. Add the shrimp to remaining marinade; toss to coat. Refrigerate, covered, 15 minutes.

2. Drain the shrimp, discarding any remaining marinade. Thread shrimp onto 4 or 8 metal or soaked wooden skewers. Grill, covered, over medium heat or broil 4 in. from the heat for 2-4 minutes on each side, basting with reserved marinade during the last minute of cooking.

1 serving: 221 cal., 15g fat (2g sat. fat), 138mg chol., 578mg sod., 2g carb. (0 sugars, 0 fiber), 19g pro. **Diabetic exchanges:** 3 lean meat, 3 fat.

GRILLED LEMON-DILL SHRIMP

GLAZED PORK CHOPS

GLAZED PORK CHOPS

When I was a new mom, I needed tasty, wholesome meals I could whip up in a jiffy. These juicy chops that are cooked on the stovetop won me over. My family loves them, too. And since this is a one-pan dish, cleanup is always a breeze.
—Kristin Tanis, Hatfield, PA

- -

Takes: 30 min. • **Makes:** 4 servings

4   **bone-in pork loin chops (¾ in. thick and 7 oz. each)**
⅓   **cup plus 1 Tbsp. cider vinegar, divided**
3   **Tbsp. soy sauce**
3   **garlic cloves, minced**
1½   **tsp. cornstarch**

1. In a large nonstick skillet, brown the pork chops over medium heat, about 2 minutes per side. Mix ⅓ cup vinegar, soy sauce and garlic; pour the sauce over the pork chops. Bring to a boil. Reduce the heat; simmer, covered, until a thermometer inserted in the pork reads 145°, about 7-9 minutes.

2. Mix cornstarch and the remaining vinegar until smooth; stir into pan. Bring to a boil; cook and stir until sauce is thickened, about 1 minute.

1 pork chop with 2 Tbsp. sauce: 224 cal., 8g fat (3g sat. fat), 86mg chol., 754mg sod., 2g carb. (0 sugars, 0 fiber), 32g pro. **Diabetic exchanges:** 4 lean meat.

**MOM'S
SLOPPY TACOS**

GRILLED SALMON
WITH NECTARINES

*My family liked this recipe so
much one evening that I made
it for a potluck the next day.
Everyone raved about it there,
too—even people who are not
particularly fond of fish.*
—Kerin Benjamin,
Citrus Heights, CA

- -

Takes: 15 min. • **Makes:** 4 servings

  4   **salmon fillets (4 oz. each)**
  ½ **tsp. salt, divided**
  ⅛ **tsp. pepper**
  1   **Tbsp. honey**
  1   **Tbsp. lemon juice**
  1   **Tbsp. olive oil**
  3   **medium nectarines,
      thinly sliced**
  1   **Tbsp. minced fresh basil**

1. Sprinkle salmon with ¼ tsp. salt
and the pepper. Place on an oiled
grill rack, skin side down. Grill,
covered, over medium heat until
fish just begins to flakes easily with
a fork, 8-10 minutes.
2. Meanwhile, in a bowl, mix honey,
lemon juice, oil and remaining salt.
Stir in nectarines and basil. Serve
with salmon.

1 fillet with ⅓ cup nectarines:
307 cal., 16g fat (3g sat. fat), 67mg
chol., 507mg sod., 17g carb. (13g
sugars, 2g fiber), 23g pro.
Diabetic exchanges: 3 lean meat,
1½ fat, 1 fruit.

MOM'S
SLOPPY TACOS

*No matter how hectic the day,
there's always time to serve your
family a healthy meal. This easy
recipe makes it possible!*
—Kami Jones, Avondale, AZ

- -

Takes: 30 min. • **Makes:** 6 servings

1½ **lbs. extra-lean ground beef
     (95% lean)**
  1   **can (15 oz.) tomato sauce**
  ¾ **tsp. garlic powder**
  ½ **tsp. salt**
  ¼ **tsp. pepper**
  ¼ **tsp. cayenne pepper**

12 **taco shells, warmed**
     **Optional toppings: Shredded
     lettuce and cheese, chopped
     tomatoes, avocado and olives**

1. In a large skillet, cook and crumble
the beef over medium heat until no
longer pink. Stir in the sauce, garlic
powder, salt, pepper and cayenne.
Bring to a boil. Reduce heat; simmer,
uncovered, for 10 minutes.
2. Fill each taco shell with ¼ cup beef
mixture and toppings of your choice.
2 tacos: 264 cal., 10g fat (4g sat. fat),
65mg chol., 669mg sod., 17g carb.
(1g sugars, 1g fiber), 25g pro.
Diabetic exchanges: 3 lean meat,
1 starch, 1 fat.

**GRILLED SALMON
WITH NECTARINES**

GRILLED CHICKEN & MANGO SKEWERS

GRILLED CHICKEN & MANGO SKEWERS

The inspiration for this recipe came from the charbroiled chicken skewers I used to enjoy while strolling along Calle Ocho in Miami on Sunday afternoons. Garnish with sesame seeds or spritz with fresh lime juice.
—Wolfgang Hanau,
West Palm Beach, FL

- - - - - - - - - - - - - - - - - - - -

Takes: 30 min. • **Makes:** 4 servings

3	medium ears sweet corn
1	Tbsp. butter
⅓	cup plus 3 Tbsp. sliced green onions, divided
1	lb. boneless skinless chicken breasts, cut into 1-in. cubes
½	tsp. salt
¼	tsp. pepper
1	medium mango, peeled and cut into 1-in. cubes
1	Tbsp. extra virgin olive oil Lime wedges, optional

1. Cut the corn from cobs. In a large skillet, heat butter over medium-high heat; saute the cut corn until crisp-tender, about 5 minutes. Stir in ⅓ cup green onions. Keep corn mixture warm.

2. Toss chicken with salt and pepper. Alternately thread chicken cubes and mango cubes onto 4 metal or soaked wooden skewers. Brush with oil.

3. Grill, covered, over medium heat or broil 4 in. from heat until chicken is no longer pink, 10-12 minutes, turning occasionally. Serve with the corn mixture; sprinkle with the remaining green onions. If desired, serve with lime wedges.

1 skewer with ½ cup corn mixture: 297 cal., 10g fat (3g sat. fat), 70mg chol., 387mg sod., 28g carb. (16g sugars, 3g fiber), 26g pro.
Diabetic exchanges: 3 lean meat, 2 starch, 1½ fat.

PEPPER-CRUSTED SIRLOIN ROAST

Dinner guests will be surprised to hear this entree calls for only five ingredients. It's an ideal choice for a large group.
—Mary Ann Griffin, Bowling Green, KY

- -

Prep: 15 min.
Bake: 2 hours + standing
Makes: 16 servings

2 Tbsp. Dijon mustard
1 Tbsp. coarsely ground pepper
1 Tbsp. minced fresh mint or 1 tsp. dried mint
1 Tbsp. minced fresh rosemary or 1 tsp. dried rosemary, crushed
1 beef sirloin tip roast (4 lbs.)

1. Preheat oven to 350°. Mix the first 4 ingredients.
2. Place the roast on a rack in a roasting pan; spread with the mustard mixture. Roast until desired doneness (a thermometer should read 135° for medium-rare, 140° for medium and 145° for medium-well), about 2 hours.
3. Remove from oven; tent with foil. Let stand 15 minutes before slicing.
3 oz. cooked beef: 146 cal., 5g fat (2g sat. fat), 72mg chol., 78mg sod., 1g carb. (0 sugars, 0 fiber), 23g pro.
Diabetic exchanges: 3 lean meat.

SLOW-COOKER TURKEY BREAST

Here's an easy recipe to try if you're craving turkey. It uses pantry ingredients, which is handy when you don't have time to make a trip to the supermarket.
—Maria Juco, Milwaukee, WI

- -

Prep: 10 min. • **Cook:** 5 hours
Makes: 14 servings

1 bone-in turkey breast (6 to 7 lbs.), skin removed
1 Tbsp. olive oil
1 tsp. dried minced garlic
1 tsp. seasoned salt
1 tsp. paprika
1 tsp. Italian seasoning
1 tsp. pepper
½ cup water

Brush turkey with oil. Combine the garlic, seasoned salt, paprika, Italian seasoning and pepper; rub over the turkey. Transfer to a 6-qt. slow cooker; add water. Cover and cook on low for 5-6 hours or until tender.
4 oz. cooked turkey: 174 cal., 2g fat (0 sat. fat), 101mg chol., 172mg sod., 0 carb. (0 sugars, 0 fiber), 37g pro.
Diabetic exchanges: 4 lean meat.

PEPPER-CRUSTED SIRLOIN ROAST

BBQ PORK & PEPPERS

BBQ PORK & PEPPERS

This is the first recipe my husband taught me to make, and it is also the first recipe I ever made in a slow cooker. I usually pair this with white rice and a salad.
—Rachael Hughes, Southampton, PA

- -

Prep: 10 min. • **Cook:** 8 hours
Makes: 4 servings

- 4 **bone-in pork loin chops (7 oz. each)**
- 1 **large onion, chopped**
- 1 **large sweet red pepper, chopped**
- 1 **large green pepper, chopped**
- 1 **cup barbecue sauce**
  Chopped fresh parsley, optional

Place chops in a 4-qt. slow cooker coated with cooking spray. Top with onion, peppers and barbecue sauce. Cover and cook on low 8-10 hours or until pork is tender. If desired, top with chopped fresh parsley.

1 pork chop with ¾ cup sauce:
291 cal., 10g fat (3g sat. fat), 86mg chol., 638mg sod., 17g carb. (12g sugars, 3g fiber), 33g pro.
Diabetic exchanges: 4 lean meat, 1 vegetable, ½ starch.

LEMON FETA CHICKEN

LEMON FETA CHICKEN

This Greek-inspired chicken is a busy-day lifesaver! My husband and I prepare the dish often, and it's a hit every time.
—Ann Cain, Morrill, NE

- -

Takes: 25 min. • **Makes:** 4 servings

- 4 **boneless skinless chicken breast halves (4 oz. each)**
- 2 **to 3 Tbsp. lemon juice**
- ¼ **cup crumbled feta cheese**
- 1 **tsp. dried oregano**
- ¼ **to ½ tsp. pepper**

1. Place chicken in a 13x9-in. baking dish coated with cooking spray. Pour lemon juice over the chicken; sprinkle with the feta cheese, oregano and pepper.

2. Bake chicken, uncovered, at 400° for 20-25 minutes or until a thermometer reads 165°.

1 chicken breast half: 143 cal., 4g fat (1g sat. fat), 66mg chol., 122mg sod., 1g carb. (0 sugars, 0 fiber), 24g pro.
Diabetic exchanges: 3 lean meat.

TEST KITCHEN TIP
A weeknight dinner party is easy with this chicken dinner that's special enough for company. Pair it with roasted potatoes and steamed broccoli with fresh herbs to satisfy all your guests (even those who eat gluten free).

GOLDEN APRICOT-GLAZED TURKEY BREAST

Basted with a simple glaze, this tender turkey breast bakes to a lovely golden brown. Make it the centerpiece of your holiday table or enjoy it any time you have a taste for turkey.

—Greg Fontenot, The Woodlands, TX

Prep: 10 min.
Bake: 1½ hours + standing
Makes: 15 servings

- ½ cup apricot preserves
- ¼ cup balsamic vinegar
- ¼ tsp. pepper
  Dash salt
- 1 bone-in turkey breast (5 lbs.)

1. Preheat oven to 325°. Combine preserves, vinegar, pepper and salt. Place turkey breast on a rack in a large shallow roasting pan.

2. Bake, uncovered, 1½-2 hours or until a thermometer reads 170°, basting every 30 minutes with the apricot mixture. (Cover loosely with foil if the turkey browns too quickly.) Cover and let stand 15 minutes before slicing.

4 oz. cooked turkey: 236 cal., 8g fat (2g sat. fat), 81mg chol., 84mg sod., 8g carb. (5g sugars, 0 fiber), 32g pro.
Diabetic exchanges: 4 lean meat, ½ starch.

SMOKY SPANISH CHICKEN

After enjoying a similar dish at a Spanish tapas restaurant, my husband and I were eager to make our own version at home. Make it extra-healthy by removing the chicken skin after browning.

—Ryan Haley, San Diego, California

Takes: 30 min. • **Makes:** 4 servings

- 3 tsp. smoked paprika
- ½ tsp. salt
- ¼ tsp. pepper
- 1 Tbsp. water
- 4 bone-in chicken thighs
- 1½ cups baby portobello mushrooms, quartered
- 1 cup chopped green onions, divided
- 1 can (14-½ ounces) fire-roasted diced tomatoes, undrained

1. Mix the first 4 ingredients; rub over chicken.

2. Place a large skillet over medium heat. Add chicken, skin side down. Cook until browned, 4-5 minutes per side; remove from the pan. Remove all but 1 tablespoon drippings from the pan.

3. In drippings, saute mushrooms and ½ cup green onions over medium heat until the vegetables are tender, 1-2 minutes. Stir in the tomatoes. Add chicken; bring to a boil. Reduce heat; simmer, covered, until a thermometer inserted in chicken reads 170°, 10-12 minutes. Top with remaining green onions.

1 serving: 272 cal., 15g fat (4g sat. fat), 81mg chol., 646mg sod., 10g carb. (4g sugars, 2g fiber), 25g pro.

SMOKY SPANISH CHICKEN

ITALIAN CRUMB-CRUSTED BEEF ROAST

ITALIAN CRUMB-CRUSTED BEEF ROAST

Italian-style panko bread crumbs and the seasoning give this classic roast beef a special touch. It's an effortless weeknight meal so you can put your energy into relaxing.
—Maria Regakis, Saugus, MA

- -

Prep: 10 min.
Bake: 1¾ hours + standing
Makes: 8 servings

- 1   **beef sirloin tip roast (3 lbs.)**
- ¼   **tsp. salt**
- ¾   **cup Italian-style panko bread crumbs**
- ¼   **cup mayonnaise**
- 3   **Tbsp. dried minced onion**
- ½   **tsp. Italian seasoning**
- ¼   **tsp. pepper**

1. Preheat oven to 325°. Place roast on a rack in a shallow roasting pan; sprinkle with salt. In a small bowl, mix bread crumbs, mayonnaise, minced onion, Italian seasoning and pepper; press onto top and sides of roast.
2. Roast until the meat reaches desired doneness (for medium-rare, a thermometer should read 135°; medium, 140°; medium well, 145°), 1¾-2¼ hours. Remove roast from oven; tent with foil. Let roast stand 10 minutes before slicing.

5 oz. cooked beef: 319 cal., 15g fat (3g sat. fat), 111mg chol., 311mg sod., 7g carb. (0 sugars, 0 fiber), 35g pro. **Diabetic exchanges:** 5 lean meat, 1 fat, ½ starch.

**HEARTY
BEANS & RICE**

MAPLE MUSTARD CHICKEN

My husband loves this tasty chicken dish. It calls for only five ingredients, and we try to have them all on hand for a delicious and cozy dinner anytime.
—Jennifer Seidel, Midland, MI

Prep: 5 min. • **Cook:** 3 hours
Makes: 6 servings

6 boneless skinless chicken breast halves (6 oz. each)
½ cup maple syrup
⅓ cup stone-ground mustard
2 Tbsp. quick-cooking tapioca
Hot cooked brown rice

Place chicken in a 3-qt. slow cooker. In a small bowl, combine the syrup, mustard and tapioca; pour over chicken. Cover and cook on low for 3-4 hours or until tender. Serve chicken with rice.

Freeze option: Cool chicken in sauce. Freeze in freezer containers. To use, partially thaw in the refrigerator overnight. Heat through slowly in a covered skillet until a thermometer inserted in the chicken reads 165°, stirring occasionally; add broth or water if necessary.

1 chicken breast half: 289 cal., 4g fat (1g sat. fat), 94mg chol., 296mg sod., 24g carb. (17g sugars, 2g fiber), 35g pro.

HEARTY BEANS & RICE

Filling and fast, this dish is a favorite in my family. It could be served as a side or as a main dish.
—Barbara Musgrove,
Fort Atkinson, WI

Prep: 10 min. • **Cook:** 25 min.
Makes: 5 servings

1 lb. lean ground beef (90% lean)
1 can (15 oz.) black beans, rinsed and drained
1 can (14½ oz.) diced tomatoes with mild green chiles, undrained
1⅓ cups frozen corn, thawed
1 cup water
¼ tsp. salt
1½ cups instant brown rice

In a large saucepan, cook beef over medium heat until no longer pink, breaking into crumbles; drain. Stir in the beans, tomatoes, corn, water and salt. Bring to a boil. Stir in rice; return to a boil. Reduce the heat; cover and simmer for 5 minutes. Remove from the heat; let stand, covered, for 5 minutes.

1¼ cups: 376 cal., 9g fat (3g sat. fat), 56mg chol., 647mg sod., 47g carb. (6g sugars, 7g fiber), 26g pro. **Diabetic exchanges:** 3 starch, 3 lean meat, 1 vegetable.

MAPLE MUSTARD CHICKEN

SALMON SALAD WITH GLAZED WALNUTS

This main-dish salad was inspired by a dish I ate while on a trip. The glazed walnuts give it something special. I've also topped the salad with grilled chicken or portobello mushrooms with amazing results.
—Joanna Kobernik, Berkley, MI

- -

Takes: 15 min. • **Makes:** 2 servings

- **2** salmon fillets (4 oz. each)
- **6** Tbsp. reduced-fat balsamic vinaigrette, divided
- **⅛** tsp. pepper
- **4** cups spring mix salad greens
- **¼** cup glazed walnuts
- **2** Tbsp. crumbled blue cheese

1. Brush the salmon with 2 Tbsp. vinaigrette; sprinkle with pepper. On a greased grill rack, cook salmon, covered, over medium heat or broil 4 in. from heat just until the fish begins to flake easily with a fork, 3-4 minutes on each side.

2. In a bowl, toss the salad greens with the remaining vinaigrette. Divide between 2 plates; sprinkle with walnuts and cheese. Top with the salmon.

1 serving: 374 cal., 25g fat (5g sat. fat), 64mg chol., 607mg sod., 13g carb. (8g sugars, 4g fiber), 24g pro. **Diabetic exchanges:** 3 lean meat, 3 fat, ½ starch.

SALSA SKILLET PORK CHOPS

There's nothing better than a quick skillet supper that pleases the whole family on a busy night.
—Deanna Ellett, Boynton Beach, FL

- -

Takes: 30 min. • **Makes:** 6 servings

- 6 boneless pork loin chops (6 oz. each)
- ½ tsp. salt
- ¼ tsp. pepper
- 2 cups fresh whole kernel corn
- 1 can (15 oz.) pinto beans, rinsed and drained
- 1¼ cups chunky salsa
- 2 Tbsp. water
- 1 tsp. ground cumin

1. Sprinkle the pork chops with salt and pepper. Heat a large nonstick skillet coated with cooking spray over medium heat. Brown chops on both sides in batches.

2. Return all chops to pan. Add remaining ingredients; bring to a boil. Reduce heat; simmer, covered, 6-8 minutes or until thermometer inserted in pork reads 145°. Let stand 5 minutes before serving.

1 pork chop with ½ cup corn mixture: 366 cal., 11g fat (4g sat. fat), 82mg chol., 548mg sod., 29g carb. (5g sugars, 4g fiber), 38g pro

HAMBURGER CASSEROLE

This family recipe has traveled all over the country. My mom first made it in Pennsylvania. I brought it to Texas when I got married, and I'm still making it today in California. Now my daughter serves it in Colorado.
—Helen Carmichall, Santee, CA

- -

Prep: 20 min. • **Cook:** 45 min.
Makes: 10 servings

- 2 lbs. lean ground beef (90% lean)
- 4 lbs. potatoes, peeled and sliced ¼ in. thick
- 1 large onion, sliced
- 1 tsp. salt
- ½ tsp. pepper
- 1 tsp. beef bouillon granules
- 1 cup boiling water
- 1 can (28 oz.) diced tomatoes, undrained
  Minced fresh parsley, optional

In a Dutch oven, layer half each of the meat, potatoes and onion. Sprinkle with half each of the salt and pepper. Repeat layers. Dissolve the bouillon in the water; pour over all. Top with the tomatoes. Cover and cook over medium heat until the potatoes are tender, 45-50 minutes. If desired, garnish with parsley.

1 cup: 270 cal., 8g fat (3g sat. fat), 57mg chol., 493mg sod., 30g carb. (5g sugars, 3g fiber), 21g pro.
Diabetic exchanges: 3 lean meat, 2 starch.

SALSA SKILLET PORK CHOPS

ASIAN
SALMON TACOS

ASIAN SALMON TACOS

This Asian-Mexican fusion dinner is ready in minutes—perfect for an on-the-run meal! If the salmon begins to stick in the skillet, add 2-3 Tbsp. of water and continue cooking through.
—Marisa Raponi, Vaughan, ON

- -

Takes: 20 min. • **Makes:** 4 servings

- 1   **lb. salmon fillet, skin removed, cut into 1-in. cubes**
- 2   **Tbsp. hoisin sauce**
- 1   **Tbsp. olive oil**
     Shredded lettuce
- 8   **corn tortillas (6 in.), warmed**
- 1½ **tsp. black sesame seeds**
     Mango salsa, optional

1. Toss salmon with hoisin sauce. In a large nonstick skillet, heat oil over medium-high heat. Cook the salmon until it begins to flake easily with a fork, 3-5 minutes, turning gently to brown all sides.

2. Serve the salmon and lettuce in tortillas; sprinkle with sesame seeds. If desired, top with salsa.

2 tacos: 335 cal., 16g fat (3g sat. fat), 57mg chol., 208mg sod., 25g carb. (3g sugars, 3g fiber), 22g pro.
Diabetic exchanges: 3 lean meat, 2 starch, 1 fat.

RED PEPPER & PARMESAN TILAPIA

RED PEPPER & PARMESAN TILAPIA

My husband and I are always looking for light fish recipes because of the health benefits. This one's a hit! We've tried it for dinner parties, too.
—Michelle Martin, Durham, NC

- -

Takes: 20 min. • **Makes:** 4 servings

- 1   **large egg, lightly beaten**
- ½   **cup grated Parmesan cheese**
- 1   **tsp. Italian seasoning**
- ½   **to 1 tsp. crushed red pepper flakes**
- ½   **tsp. pepper**
- 4   **tilapia fillets (6 oz. each)**

1. Preheat oven to 425°. Place egg in a shallow bowl. In another shallow bowl, combine the cheese, Italian seasoning, pepper flakes and pepper. Dip the fillets in the egg and then in the cheese mixture.

2. Place fillets in a 15x10x1-in. baking pan coated with cooking spray. Bake until fish just begins to flake easily with a fork, 10-15 minutes.

1 fillet: 179 cal., 4g fat (2g sat. fat), 89mg chol., 191mg sod., 1g carb. (0 sugars, 0 fiber), 35g pro.
Diabetic exchanges: 5 very lean meat, ½ fat.

ROASTED TARRAGON TURKEY BREAST

If you like the flavors of tarragon and lemon pepper, consider this wet rub from our Test Kitchen professionals. It's perfect for turkey or chicken.
—*Taste of Home* Test Kitchen

- -

Prep: 10 min.
Bake: 1¾ hours + standing
Makes: 12 servings

- ¼ cup minced fresh tarragon
- 2 Tbsp. olive oil
- 1 tsp. lemon-pepper seasoning
- ½ tsp. seasoned salt
- 1 bone-in turkey breast (4 lbs.)

1. Preheat oven to 325°. Mix the first 4 ingredients. With fingers, carefully loosen skin from turkey breast; rub half the herb mixture under the skin. Secure skin to the underside of the breast with toothpicks. Rub outside of turkey with remaining mixture.
2. Place turkey on a rack in a roasting pan. Roast until a thermometer reads 170°, 1¾-2 hours. Remove from oven; tent with foil. Let stand 15 minutes. Remove and discard turkey skin and the toothpicks before carving.

4 oz. cooked turkey: 147 cal., 3g fat (1g sat. fat), 78mg chol., 139mg sod., 0 carb. (0 sugars, 0 fiber), 28g pro. **Diabetic exchanges:** 4 lean meat, ½ fat.

PISTACHIO SALMON

This simple salmon gets its crunch from crushed pistachios, panko bread crumbs and Parmesan cheese. Add rice and steamed veggies for a complete meal.
—Anthony Oraczewski,
Port St. Lucie, FL

- -

Takes: 25 min. • **Makes:** 4 servings

- ⅓ cup pistachios, finely chopped
- ¼ cup panko bread crumbs
- ¼ cup grated Parmesan cheese
- 1 salmon fillet (1 lb.)
- ½ tsp. salt
- ¼ tsp. pepper

1. Preheat oven to 400°. In a shallow bowl, toss the pistachios with bread crumbs and cheese.

2. Place the salmon on a greased foil-lined 15x10x1-in. pan, skin side down; sprinkle with salt and pepper. Top with pistachio mixture, pressing to adhere. Bake, uncovered, until fish just begins to flake easily with a fork, 15-20 minutes.

3 oz. cooked fish: 269 cal., 17g fat (3g sat. fat), 61mg chol., 497mg sod., 6g carb. (1g sugars, 1g fiber), 23g pro. **Diabetic exchanges:** 3 lean meat, 1 fat, ½ starch.

TEST KITCHEN TIP
If you have any leftover pistachios, enjoy them as a snack. A serving (about 50 nuts) packs 6 grams of protein, 3 grams of fiber and over 10% of the B6, thiamine and copper we need daily.

PISTACHIO SALMON

PERSONAL MARGHERITA PIZZAS

PERSONAL MARGHERITA PIZZAS

This family-friendly supper is simplicity at its finest. Delectable fresh mozzarella and a sprinkling of sliced basil give these mini pies a savory Italian flair.

—Jerry Gulley, Pleasant Prairie, WI

- -

Takes: 25 min. • **Makes:** 3 servings

- 1 **pkg. (6½ oz.) pizza crust mix**
- ½ **tsp. dried oregano**
- ¾ **cup pizza sauce**
- 6 **oz. fresh mozzarella cheese, thinly sliced**
- ¼ **cup thinly sliced fresh basil leaves**

1. Preheat oven to 425°. Prepare pizza dough according to package directions, adding oregano before mixing. Divide into 3 portions.

2. Pat each portion of dough into an 8-in. circle on greased baking sheets. Bake until edges are lightly browned, 8-10 minutes.

3. Spread each crust with ¼ cup pizza sauce to within ½ in. of edge.

Top with the cheese. Bake until the crust is golden and cheese is melted, 5-10 minutes longer. Sprinkle with fresh basil.

1 pizza: 407 cal., 15g fat (8g sat. fat), 45mg chol., 675mg sod., 48g carb. (7g sugars, 3g fiber), 18g pro.

APPLE-DIJON PORK ROAST

This cold-weather favorite takes less than five minutes to assemble and is incredibly delicious. I serve the roast with rice, then use the tangy sauce as a gravy for both.
—Cindy Steffen, Cedarburg, WI

- -

Prep: 15 min. • **Cook:** 4 hours
Makes: 8 servings

- 1 boneless pork loin roast (2 to 3 lbs.)
- 1 can (14½ oz.) chicken broth
- 1 cup unsweetened apple juice
- ½ cup Dijon mustard
- 6 Tbsp. cornstarch
- 6 Tbsp. cold water
  Coarsely ground pepper, optional

1. Place roast in a 5-qt. slow cooker. In a small bowl, combine the broth, apple juice and mustard; pour over roast. Cover and cook on low for 4-5 hours or until tender. Remove roast and keep warm.
2. For gravy, strain cooking juices and skim fat. Pour juices into a small saucepan. Combine cornstarch and water until smooth; gradually stir into juices. Bring to a boil; cook and stir for 2 minutes or until thickened. Serve with pork. If desired, top with coarsely ground pepper.

4 oz. cooked pork: 197 cal., 7g fat (2g sat. fat), 56mg chol., 413mg sod., 11g carb. (3g sugars, 0 fiber), 23g pro. **Diabetic exchanges:** 3 lean meat, ½ starch.

COD WITH BACON & BALSAMIC TOMATOES

COD WITH BACON & BALSAMIC TOMATOES

Let's face it, everything is better with bacon. I fry it, add cod fillets to the pan and finish it all with a big, tomato-y pop.
—Maureen McClanahan, St. Louis, MO

- -

Takes: 30 min. • **Makes:** 4 servings

- 4 center-cut bacon strips, chopped
- 4 cod fillets (5 oz. each)
- ½ tsp. salt
- ¼ tsp. pepper
- 2 cups grape tomatoes, halved
- 2 Tbsp. balsamic vinegar

1. In a large skillet, cook bacon over medium heat until crisp, stirring occasionally. Remove with a slotted spoon; drain on paper towels.
2. Sprinkle the fillets with salt and pepper. Add fillets to the bacon drippings; cook over medium-high heat until fish just begins to flake easily with a fork, 4-6 minutes on each side. Remove and keep warm.
3. Add tomatoes to skillet; cook and stir until softened, 2-4 minutes. Stir in vinegar; reduce heat to medium-low. Cook until sauce is thickened, 1-2 minutes longer. Serve cod with tomato mixture and bacon.

1 fillet with ¼ cup tomato mixture and 1 Tbsp. bacon: 178 cal., 6g fat (2g sat. fat), 64mg chol., 485mg sod., 5g carb. (4g sugars, 1g fiber), 26g pro. **Diabetic exchanges:** 4 lean meat, 1 vegetable.

APPLE-DIJON PORK ROAST

LAMB MARSALA

LAMB MARSALA

Lamb was a special treat for my family when I was growing up. I've had this recipe for more than 30 years. I hope it becomes a favorite for your family, too.
—Bonnie Silverstein, Denver, CO

- -

Prep: 10 min. • **Bake:** 1 hour
Makes: 6 servings

¾   **cup Marsala wine or
½ cup chicken broth,
¼ cup white grape juice and
1 Tbsp. white wine vinegar**
1   **garlic clove, minced**
1   **Tbsp. dried oregano**
1   **Tbsp. olive oil**

1   **boneless leg of lamb
(2½ lbs.), rolled and tied**
½   **tsp. salt**
¼   **tsp. pepper**
1   **lb. fresh mushrooms,
quartered**

1. In a small bowl, combine the wine, garlic and oregano; set aside. Rub oil over lamb, then sprinkle with salt and pepper. Place roast on a rack in a shallow roasting pan; spoon some wine mixture over roast. Set aside remaining wine mixture.

2. Bake, uncovered, at 325° for 1-1½ hours or until the meat reaches desired doneness (for medium-rare, a thermometer should read 135°; medium, 140°; medium-well, 145°), basting occasionally with some reserved wine mixture. Remove from the oven; cover loosely with foil for 10-15 minutes.

3. Meanwhile, pour pan drippings into a measuring cup; skim fat. In a large skillet coated with cooking spray, saute the mushrooms until tender. Add pan drippings and any remaining wine mixture; heat through. Slice lamb and serve with the mushroom sauce.

1 serving: 330 cal., 13g fat (5g sat. fat), 114mg chol., 296mg sod., 7g carb. (4g sugars, 1g fiber), 38g pro.
Diabetic exchanges: 5 lean meat, 1 vegetable.

CRISPY DILL TILAPIA

Every week I try to serve a new fish dish. With its fresh dill and delicious panko bread crumb herb crust, this is a winner.
—Tamara Huron, New Market, AL

- -

Takes: 20 min. • **Makes:** 4 servings

- 1   cup panko bread crumbs
- 2   Tbsp. olive oil
- 2   Tbsp. snipped fresh dill
- ¼   tsp. salt
- ⅛   tsp. pepper
- 4   tilapia fillets (6 oz. each)
- 1   Tbsp. lemon juice
     Lemon wedges

1. Preheat oven to 400°. Toss together the first 5 ingredients.
2. Place tilapia in a 15x10x1-in. baking pan coated with cooking spray; brush with lemon juice. Top with the crumb mixture, patting to help adhere.
3. Bake, uncovered, on an upper oven rack for 12-15 minutes or until the fish just begins to flake easily with a fork. Serve with the lemon wedges.
1 fillet: 256 cal., 9g fat (2g sat. fat), 83mg chol., 251mg sod., 10g carb. (1g sugars, 1g fiber), 34g pro. **Diabetic exchanges:** 5 lean meat, 1½ fat, ½ starch.

CREAMY HAM PENNE

Think pasta can't be healthy? Give this lightened-up version a try.
—Barbara Pletzke, Herndon, VA

- -

Takes: 30 min. • **Makes:** 4 servings

- 2   cups uncooked whole wheat penne pasta
- 2   cups fresh broccoli florets
- 1   cup fat-free milk
- 1   pkg. (6½ oz.) reduced-fat garlic-herb spreadable cheese
- 1   cup cubed fully cooked ham
- ¼   tsp. pepper

1. In a large saucepan, cook penne according to package directions, adding the broccoli during the last 5 minutes of cooking; drain. Remove and set aside.
2. In the same pan, combine the milk and spreadable cheese. Cook and stir over medium heat for 3-5 minutes or until the cheese is melted. Add the ham, pepper and penne mixture; heat through.
1¼ cups: 371 cal., 8g fat (5g sat. fat), 47mg chol., 672mg sod., 49g carb. (5g sugars, 7g fiber), 25g pro.

CRISPY DILL TILAPIA

PARMESAN BAKED COD

PARMESAN BAKED COD

This is a goof-proof way to keep oven-baked cod moist and flavorful. My mom shared this recipe with me years ago and I've been loving it ever since.
—Mary Jo Hoppe, Pewaukee, WI

Takes: 25 min. • **Makes:** 4 servings

- 4 cod fillets (4 oz. each)
- ⅔ cup mayonnaise
- 4 green onions, chopped
- ¼ cup grated Parmesan cheese
- 1 tsp. Worcestershire sauce

1. Preheat oven to 400°. Place cod in an 8-in. square baking dish coated with cooking spray. Mix remaining ingredients; spread over fillets.
2. Bake, uncovered, until fish just begins to flake easily with a fork, 15-20 minutes.

1 fillet: 247 cal., 15g fat (2g sat. fat), 57mg chol., 500mg sod., 7g carb. (2g sugars, 0 fiber), 20g pro.
Diabetic exchanges: 3 lean meat, 3 fat.

TOMATO-BASIL BAKED FISH

TOMATO-BASIL BAKED FISH

This recipe can be made with different kinds of fish as desired, and I usually have the rest of the ingredients on hand. Baked fish is wonderful, and I fix this tasty dish often.
—Annie Hicks, Zephyrhills, FL

Takes: 15 min. • **Makes:** 2 servings

- 1 Tbsp. lemon juice
- 1 tsp. olive oil
- 8 oz. red snapper, cod or haddock fillets
- ¼ tsp. dried basil
- ⅛ tsp. salt
- ⅛ tsp. pepper
- 2 plum tomatoes, thinly sliced
- 2 tsp. grated Parmesan cheese

1. In a shallow bowl, combine the lemon juice and oil. Add fish fillets; turn to coat. Place in a greased 9-in. pie plate. Sprinkle with half each of the basil, salt and pepper. Arrange tomatoes over top; sprinkle with cheese and remaining seasonings.
2. Cover and bake at 400° for 10-12 minutes or until fish flakes easily with a fork.

1 serving: 121 cal., 4g fat (1g sat. fat), 24mg chol., 256mg sod., 4g carb. (2g sugars, 1g fiber), 18g pro.
Diabetic exchanges: 3 lean meat, 1 vegetable, ½ fat.

CITRUS-SPICED ROAST CHICKEN

My famous chipotle citrus roast turkey has designated me the Thanksgiving host in my family. Even finicky eaters love it. And I use the same recipe for chicken so we can enjoy the delicious flavors year-round.
—Robin Haas, Cranston, RI

Prep: 20 min.
Bake: 1 hour + standing
Makes: 6 servings

3 Tbsp. orange marmalade
4½ tsp. chopped chipotle
    peppers in adobo sauce
3 garlic cloves, minced
¾ tsp. salt, divided
½ tsp. ground cumin
1 broiler/fryer chicken (4 lbs.)

1. Preheat oven to 350°. Mix the marmalade, chipotle peppers, garlic, ½ tsp. salt and cumin. With fingers, carefully loosen skin from chicken; rub mixture under the skin.
2. Place chicken on a rack in a shallow roasting pan, breast side up. Tuck wings under chicken; tie drumsticks together. Rub skin with remaining salt. Roast 1-1¼ hours or until a thermometer inserted in thickest part of the thigh reads 170°-175°, covering with foil halfway through cooking to prevent overbrowning.
3. Remove chicken from oven; let stand, loosely covered, 15 minutes before carving. Remove and discard skin before serving.
4 oz. cooked chicken (skin removed): 239 cal., 8g fat (2g sat. fat), 98mg chol., 409mg sod., 8g carb. (6g sugars, 0 fiber), 32g pro.
Diabetic exchanges: 4 lean meat.

COD & ASPARAGUS BAKE

Lemon is the star in this flavorful and healthy dish. You can also use grated Parmesan cheese instead of Romano.
—Thomas Faglon, Somerset, NJ

Takes: 30 min. • **Makes:** 4 servings

4 cod fillets (4 oz. each)
1 lb. fresh thin asparagus,
   trimmed
1 pint cherry tomatoes, halved
2 Tbsp. lemon juice
1½ tsp. grated lemon zest
¼ cup grated Romano cheese

1. Preheat oven to 375°. Place cod and asparagus in a 15x10x1-in. baking pan brushed with oil. Add tomatoes, cut sides down. Brush the fish with lemon juice; sprinkle with lemon zest. Sprinkle fish and vegetables with Romano cheese. Bake until fish just begins to flake easily with a fork, about 12 minutes.
2. Remove pan from oven; preheat broiler. Broil the cod mixture 3-4 in. from heat until vegetables are lightly browned, 2-3 minutes.
1 serving: 141 cal., 3g fat (2g sat. fat), 45mg chol., 184mg sod., 6g carb. (3g sugars, 2g fiber), 23g pro.
Diabetic exchanges: 3 lean meat, 1 vegetable.

TEST KITCHEN TIP
If fresh asparagus is not in season, fresh green beans make a fine substitute and will cook in about the same amount of time. We tested cod fillets that were about ¾ in. thick. You'll need to adjust the bake time up or down if your fillets are thicker or thinner.

COD & ASPARAGUS BAKE

**SAVORY BEER
PORK CHOPS**

SAVORY BEER PORK CHOPS

These tender chops cooked in a savory sauce are perfect for a hectic night because they're so easy to prep. Try them with hot buttery noodles.

—Jana Christian, Farson, WY

- -

Takes: 20 min. • **Makes:** 4 servings

- 4 **boneless pork loin chops (4 oz. each)**
- ½ **tsp. salt**
- ½ **tsp. pepper**
- 1 **Tbsp. canola oil**
- 3 **Tbsp. ketchup**
- 2 **Tbsp. brown sugar**
- ¾ **cup beer or nonalcoholic beer**

1. Sprinkle the pork chops with salt and pepper. In a large skillet, heat oil over medium heat; brown chops on both sides.

2. Mix ketchup, brown sugar and beer; pour over chops. Bring to a boil. Reduce the heat; simmer, uncovered, until a thermometer inserted in the pork reads 145°, 4-6 minutes. Let stand 5 minutes before serving.

Freeze option: Place pork chops in freezer containers; top with sauce. Cool and freeze. To use, partially thaw in the refrigerator overnight. Heat through in a covered saucepan, gently stirring sauce; add a little water if necessary.

1 pork chop: 239 cal., 10g fat (3g sat. fat), 55mg chol., 472mg sod., 11g carb. (11g sugars, 0 fiber), 22g pro.
Diabetic exchanges: 3 lean meat, 1 fat, ½ starch.

SLOW-COOKED
SWISS STEAK

ORANGE POMEGRANATE SALMON

Salmon makes an impressive addition to your menu—and it is as delicious as it is beautiful. I serve this with roasted baby potatoes and fresh asparagus for a show-stopping holiday meal.
—Thomas Faglon, Somerset, NJ

Prep: 10 min. • **Bake:** 25 min.
Makes: 4 servings

- 1 small red onion, thinly sliced
- 1 skinned salmon fillet (about 2 lbs.)
- ½ tsp. salt
- 1 medium navel orange, thinly sliced
- 1 cup pomegranate seeds
- 2 Tbsp. olive oil
- 1 Tbsp. minced fresh dill

1. Preheat oven to 375°. Place a 28x18-in. piece of heavy-duty foil in a 15x10x1-in. baking pan. Place onion slices in a single layer on foil. Top with salmon; sprinkle with salt. Arrange the orange slices over top. Sprinkle with pomegranate seeds; drizzle with oil. Top with a second piece of foil. Bring the edges of foil together on all sides and crimp to seal, forming a large packet.

2. Bake until fish just begins to flake easily with a fork, 25-30 minutes. Be careful of escaping steam when opening packet. Remove to a serving platter; sprinkle with dill.

4 oz. cooked salmon: 307 cal., 19g fat (3g sat. fat), 76mg chol., 274mg sod., 8g carb. (6g sugars, 1g fiber), 26g pro. **Diabetic exchanges:** 4 lean meat, 1½ fat, ½ fruit.

SLOW-COOKED SWISS STEAK

This is one of my favorites recipes because I can flour and season the steaks the night before and refrigerate them overnight. The next morning, I just put all the ingredients in the slow cooker, and then I have a hot, delicious dinner waiting when I arrive home from work.
—Sarah Burks, Wathena, KS

Prep: 10 min. • **Cook:** 6 hours
Makes: 6 servings

- 2 Tbsp. all-purpose flour
- ½ tsp. salt
- ¼ tsp. pepper
- 1½ lbs. beef round steak, cut into 6 pieces
- 1 medium onion, cut into ¼-in. slices
- 1 celery rib, cut into ½-in. slices
- 2 cans (8 oz. each) tomato sauce

1. In a bowl or shallow dish, combine the flour, salt and pepper. Add the steak and turn to coat.

2. Place the onion in a greased 3-qt. slow cooker. Top with the steak, celery and tomato sauce. Cover and cook on low for 6-8 hours or until meat is tender.

1 serving: 171 cal., 4g fat (1g sat. fat), 64mg chol., 409mg sod., 6g carb. (2g sugars, 1g fiber), 27g pro.
Diabetic exchanges: 3 lean meat, 1 vegetable.

**ORANGE
POMEGRANATE
SALMON**

SAUSAGE-STUFFED
BUTTERNUT SQUASH

SAUSAGE-STUFFED BUTTERNUT SQUASH

Load butternut squash shells with a turkey sausage mixture for a quick, easy meal. As an added bonus, it's low in calories.
—Katia Slinger, West Jordan, UT

Takes: 30 min. • **Makes:** 4 servings

- 1 **medium butternut squash (about 3 lbs.)**
- 1 **lb. Italian turkey sausage links, casings removed**
- 1 **medium onion, finely chopped**
- 4 **garlic cloves, minced**
- ½ **cup shredded Italian cheese blend**
  Crushed red pepper flakes, optional

1. Preheat broiler. Cut the squash lengthwise in half; discard seeds. Place squash in a large microwave-safe dish, cut side down; add ½ in. of water. Microwave, covered, on high until soft, 20-25 minutes. Cool slightly.

2. Meanwhile, in a large nonstick skillet, cook and crumble sausage with onion over medium-high heat until no longer pink, 5-7 minutes.

Add garlic; cook and stir 1 minute.

3. Leaving ½-in.-thick shells, scoop flesh from squash and stir it into sausage mixture. Place squash shells on a baking sheet; fill with sausage mixture. Sprinkle with cheese.

4. Broil 4-5 in. from heat until the cheese is melted, 1-2 minutes. If desired, sprinkle with the pepper flakes. To serve, cut each half into 2 portions.

1 serving: 325 cal., 10g fat (4g sat. fat), 52mg chol., 587mg sod., 44g carb. (10g sugars, 12g fiber), 19g pro. **Diabetic exchanges:** 3 starch, 3 lean meat.

GRILLED SIRLOIN KABOBS WITH PEACH SALSA

Peaches three ways—fresh, as preserves and in salsa—star in these beef kabobs with a blend of hot and sweet flavors. I love that it's a fun new way to cook with salsa.

—Beth Royals, Richmond, VA

Takes: 25 min. • **Makes:** 6 servings

- 3 **Tbsp. peach preserves**
- 1 **Tbsp. finely chopped seeded jalapeno pepper**
- 1 **beef top sirloin steak (1½ lbs.), cut into 1-in. cubes**
- ½ **tsp. salt**
- ¼ **tsp. pepper**
- 3 **medium peaches, each cut into 6 slices**
- 1½ **cups peach salsa**

1. In a small bowl, mix preserves and jalapeno. Season beef with salt and pepper. Alternately thread beef and peaches onto 6 metal or soaked wooden skewers.

2. Place the kabobs on greased grill rack. Grill the kabobs, covered, over medium heat or broil 4 in. from heat for 6-8 minutes or until the beef reaches desired doneness, turning occasionally. Remove from the grill; brush with the preserves mixture. Serve with salsa.

1 kabob with ¼ cup salsa: 219 cal., 5g fat (2g sat. fat), 46mg chol., 427mg sod., 17g carb. (16g sugars, 3g fiber), 25g pro. **Diabetic exchanges:** 3 lean meat, ½ starch, ½ fruit.

GRILLED SIRLOIN KABOBS WITH PEACH SALSA

CHICKEN SAUSAGES WITH PEPPERS

Chicken sausage is lower in calories compared to its pork counterpart, but it doesn't skimp on the bold, savory flavors you love. Try it with sweet, crunchy bell peppers for a fast and healthy weeknight dinner.

—Deborah Schaefer, Durand, MI

Takes: 30 min. • **Makes:** 4 servings

- 1 **small onion, halved and sliced**
- 1 **small sweet orange pepper, julienned**
- 1 **small sweet red pepper, julienned**
- 1 **Tbsp. olive oil**
- 1 **garlic clove, minced**
- 1 **pkg. (12 oz.) fully cooked apple chicken sausage links or flavor of your choice, cut into 1-in. pieces**

In a large nonstick skillet, saute onion and peppers in oil until crisp-tender. Add garlic; cook 1 minute longer. Stir in sausages; heat through.

1 cup: 208 cal., 11g fat (2g sat. fat), 60mg chol., 483mg sod., 14g carb. (11g sugars, 1g fiber), 15g pro. **Diabetic exchanges:** 2 lean meat, 1 vegetable, ½ starch, ½ fat.

**CRUNCHY ONION
BARBECUE CHICKEN**

CRUNCHY ONION BARBECUE CHICKEN

I threw this easy dish together and was thrilled with how tasty it turned out. The crispy fried onions and baked-on barbecue sauce add flavor and texture to regular chicken breasts.

—Jane Holey, Clayton, MI

Prep: 10 min. • **Bake:** 25 min.
Makes: 4 servings

- ½ **cup barbecue sauce**
- 1⅓ **cups french-fried onions, crushed**
- ¼ **cup grated Parmesan cheese**
- ½ **tsp. pepper**
- 4 **boneless skinless chicken breast halves (6 oz. each)**

1. Preheat oven to 440°. Place the barbecue sauce in a shallow bowl. In another shallow bowl, combine the onions, cheese and pepper. Dip both sides of chicken in barbecue sauce, then 1 side in onion mixture.
2. Place chicken, crumb side up, on a greased baking sheet. Bake until a thermometer reads 165°, 22-27 minutes.
1 chicken breast half: 327 cal., 11g fat (3g sat. fat), 97mg chol., 582mg sod., 19g carb. (11g sugars, 0 fiber), 35g pro.

SKILLET CHICKEN WITH OLIVES

SKILLET CHICKEN WITH OLIVES

My cousin Lilliana made this chicken for lunch one day while I was visiting her in Italy. Now it's a family favorite stateside, too.

—Rosemarie Pisano, Revere, MA

Takes: 20 min. • **Makes:** 4 servings

- 4 **boneless skinless chicken thighs (about 1 lb.)**
- 1 **tsp. dried rosemary, crushed**
- ½ **tsp. pepper**
- ¼ **tsp. salt**
- 1 **Tbsp. olive oil**
- ½ **cup pimiento-stuffed olives, coarsely chopped**
- ¼ **cup white wine or chicken broth**
- 1 **Tbsp. drained capers, optional**

1. Sprinkle chicken with rosemary, pepper and salt. In a large skillet, heat oil over medium-high heat. Brown chicken on both sides.
2. Add olives, wine and, if desired, capers. Reduce heat; simmer, covered, 2-3 minutes or until a thermometer inserted in chicken reads 170°.
1 serving: 237 cal., 15g fat (3g sat. fat), 76mg chol., 571mg sod., 2g carb. (0 sugars, 0 fiber), 21g pro.
Diabetic exchanges: 3 lean meat, 2 fat.

SIDES, SALADS & BREADS

WATERMELON–
BLUEBERRY
SALAD
P. 162

1

2

3

4

5

ROUNDING OUT YOUR MENUS IS EASY WITH
THESE QUICK SIDES, SALADS AND BREADS.
THEY'RE GOOD FOR YOU, TOO, SO GO
AHEAD AND PILE YOUR PLATE HIGH!

**JICAMA
CITRUS SALAD**

ROASTED ASPARAGUS

Since asparagus is so abundant in spring, I like to put it to use with this tasty recipe. Not only does it come together quickly, but it calls for just a handful of items. We all look forward to this side dish each year.

—Vikki Rebholz, West Chester, OH

- -

Takes: 25 min. • **Makes:** 12 servings

4   lbs. fresh asparagus, trimmed
¼   cup olive oil
½   tsp. salt
¼   tsp. pepper
¼   cup sesame seeds, toasted

Preheat oven to 400°. Arrange the asparagus in a single layer in 2 foil-lined 15x10x1-in. baking pans. Drizzle with oil. Sprinkle with the salt and pepper. Bake, uncovered, until crisp-tender, 12-15 minutes, turning once. Sprinkle with the sesame seeds.

1 serving: 73 cal., 6g fat (1g sat. fat), 0 chol., 122mg sod., 4g carb. (1g sugars, 2g fiber), 2g pro. **Diabetic exchanges:** 1 vegetable, 1 fat.

JICAMA CITRUS SALAD

Never tried jicama? It is a crunchy Mexican turnip, and I love to use it in this super easy salad. The jicama is ideal alongside the vibrant flavors of the tangerines and shallots. Between the sweet and sour flavors in this salad and its crunchy texture, it's all delish!

—Crystal Jo Bruns, Iliff, CO

- -

Takes: 15 min. • **Makes:** 10 servings

8   tangerines, peeled, quartered and sliced
1   lb. medium jicama, peeled and cubed
2   shallots, thinly sliced
2   Tbsp. lemon or lime juice
¼   cup chopped fresh cilantro
½   tsp. salt
½   tsp. pepper

Combine all ingredients; refrigerate until serving.

¾ cup: 76 cal., 0 fat (0 sat. fat), 0 chol., 123mg sod., 19g carb. (11g sugars, 4g fiber), 1g pro. **Diabetic exchanges:** 1 vegetable, ½ fruit.

ROASTED ASPARAGUS

WHOLE WHEAT PIZZA DOUGH

Pizza, stromboli, egg pockets—this make-ahead dough has endless potential for quick and impressive breakfasts, lunches or dinners. Store it in the freezer for busy nights.

—*Taste of Home* Test Kitchen

- -

Prep: 25 min. + standing
Makes: 3 lbs. (enough for 3 pizzas)

- 3 pkg. (¼ oz. each) quick-rise yeast
- 2 Tbsp. sugar
- 1½ tsp. salt
- 2¼ cups whole wheat flour
- 2½ cups water
- 3 Tbsp. olive oil
- 3 to 3½ cups white whole wheat flour

1. In a large bowl, combine the yeast, sugar, salt and whole wheat flour; set aside. In a small saucepan, heat water and oil to 120°-130°; stir into the dry ingredients. Stir in enough white whole wheat flour to form a soft dough (dough will be sticky).
2. Turn onto a floured surface; knead the dough until smooth and elastic, about 6-8 minutes. Cover with plastic wrap and let rest 10 minutes. Punch down the dough; divide it into 3 portions. Use the dough immediately, refrigerate overnight or freeze for up to 1 month.

4 oz. uncooked dough: 229 cal., 4g fat (1g sat. fat), 0 chol., 297mg sod., 43g carb. (2g sugars, 7g fiber), 8g pro.

TOMATO & BASIL COUSCOUS SALAD

It's hard to believe that tossing a few pantry ingredients with summer's best herbs and veggies can yield such a lovely salad. Pair it with grilled lemon chicken for a delightful dinner.

—Sonya Labbe,
West Hollywood, CA

- -

Prep: 20 min. + chilling
Makes: 8 servings

- 1½ cups water
- 1½ cups uncooked couscous
- 2 medium tomatoes, seeded and chopped
- ¼ cup fresh basil leaves, thinly sliced
- ½ cup olive oil
- ¼ cup balsamic vinegar
- ½ tsp. salt
- ¼ tsp. pepper

1. In a small saucepan, bring water to a boil. Stir in couscous. Remove from the heat; cover and let stand for 5-10 minutes or until water is absorbed. Fluff with a fork; cool.
2. In a large bowl, combine the couscous, tomatoes and basil. In a small bowl, whisk the oil, vinegar, salt and pepper. Pour over salad; toss to coat. Refrigerate until chilled.

¾ cup: 255 cal., 14g fat (2g sat. fat), 0 chol., 155mg sod., 29g carb. (3g sugars, 2g fiber), 5g pro.
Diabetic exchanges: 2 starch, 2 fat.

TOMATO & BASIL COUSCOUS SALAD

SAUTEED SQUASH WITH TOMATOES & ONIONS

SAUTEED SQUASH WITH TOMATOES & ONIONS

This zucchini dish with tomatoes is like a scaled-down ratatouille. My family loves it.

—Adan Franco, Milwaukee, WI

- -

Takes: 20 min. • **Makes:** 8 servings

- 2 **Tbsp. olive oil**
- 1 **medium onion,
  finely chopped**
- 4 **medium zucchini, chopped**
- 2 **large tomatoes,
  finely chopped**
- 1 **tsp. salt**
- ¼ **tsp. pepper**

1. In a skillet, heat oil over medium-high heat. Add the onion; cook and stir until tender, 2-4 minutes. Add zucchini; cook and stir 3 minutes.

2. Stir in tomatoes, salt and pepper; cook and stir until squash is tender, 4-6 minutes longer. Serve with a slotted spoon.

¾ cup: 60 cal., 4g fat (1g sat. fat), 0 chol., 306mg sod., 6g carb. (4g sugars, 2g fiber), 2g pro.
Diabetic exchanges: 1 vegetable, ½ fat.

TEST KITCHEN TIP
Transform this side dish into an entree by adding cooked and cubed chicken. It's also delightful topped with tender slices of last night's steak dinner and then rolled up in a flour tortilla for a hearty wrap.

SLOW-COOKER
BAKED
POTATOES

SLOW-COOKER BAKED POTATOES

This baked potato recipe is so easy—just add your favorite toppings. Save any extra potatoes to make baked potato soup the next day.

—Teresa Emrick, Tipp City, OH

Prep: 10 min. • **Cook:** 8 hours
Makes: 6 potatoes

- 6 medium russet potatoes
- 3 Tbsp. butter, softened
- 3 garlic cloves, minced
- 1 cup water
  Salt and pepper to taste
  Optional: Sour cream, butter, crumbled bacon, minced chives, guacamole, shredded cheddar cheese and minced fresh cilantro

1. Scrub the potatoes; pierce each several times with a fork. In a small bowl, mix butter and garlic. Rub the potatoes with butter mixture. Wrap each tightly with a piece of foil.
2. Pour the water into a 6-qt. slow cooker; add the potatoes. Cook, covered, on low 8-10 hours or until tender. Season and top as desired.

1 potato: 217 cal., 6g fat (4g sat. fat), 15mg chol., 59mg sod., 38g carb. (2g sugars, 5g fiber), 5g pro.

> **TEST KITCHEN TIP**
> Serve the potatoes right in the foil packets to get the most out of the incredible garlic butter.

ROASTED ROSEMARY CAULIFLOWER

ROASTED ROSEMARY CAULIFLOWER

Roasting the cauliflower really brings out its flavor in this side dish. Even folks who aren't cauliflower lovers like it this way.

—Joann Fritzler, Belen, NM

Takes: 30 min. • **Makes:** 6 servings

- 1 medium head cauliflower (about 2½ lbs.), broken into florets
- 2 Tbsp. olive oil
- 2 tsp. minced fresh rosemary or ¾ tsp. dried rosemary, crushed
- ½ tsp. salt

Preheat oven to 450°. Toss together all ingredients; spread in a greased 15x10x1-in. pan. Roast until tender and lightly browned, 20-25 minutes, stirring occasionally.

¾ cup: 65 cal., 5g fat (1g sat. fat), 0 chol., 226mg sod., 5g carb. (2g sugars, 2g fiber), 2g pro.
Diabetic exchanges: 1 vegetable, 1 fat.

SOUR CREAM CUCUMBERS

SOUR CREAM CUCUMBERS

We have a tradition at our house to serve this dish with the other Hungarian specialties my mom learned to make from the women at church. It's especially good during the summer when the cucumbers are freshly picked from the garden.

—Pamela Eaton, Monclova, OH

- -

Prep: 15 min. + chilling
Makes: 8 servings

½ cup sour cream
3 Tbsp. white vinegar
1 Tbsp. sugar
   Pepper to taste

4 medium cucumbers, peeled if desired and thinly sliced
1 small sweet onion, thinly sliced and separated into rings

In a large bowl, whisk the sour cream, vinegar, sugar and pepper until blended. Add the cucumbers and onion; toss to coat. Refrigerate, covered, at least 4 hours. Serve with a slotted spoon.

¾ cup: 62 cal., 3g fat (2g sat. fat), 10mg chol., 5mg sod., 7g carb. (5g sugars, 2g fiber), 2g pro. **Diabetic exchanges:** 1 vegetable, ½ fat.

TEST KITCHEN TIP
Many grocery store cucumbers are coated with protective wax to prolong freshness. They should be peeled before eating. There's no need to peel English cucumbers, however, as those are wrapped in plastic instead. Ditto for cukes from the farmers market or your own garden.

SOFT OATMEAL BREAD

My husband loves to make this bread. With its mild oat flavor and soft, lovely texture, it's sure to be a hit with the whole family. Slices are a real treat toasted for breakfast, too.

—Nancy Montgomery, Plainwell, MI

Prep: 10 min. • **Bake:** 3 hours
Makes: 1 loaf (2 lbs., 20 slices)

1½ cups water (70° to 80°)
¼ cup canola oil
1 tsp. lemon juice
¼ cup sugar
2 tsp. salt
3 cups all-purpose flour
1½ cups quick-cooking oats
2½ tsp. active dry yeast

1. In bread machine pan, place all ingredients in order suggested by manufacturer. Select basic bread setting. Choose crust color and loaf size if available.

2. Bake according to the bread machine directions (check the dough after 5 minutes of mixing; add 1-2 Tbsp. of water or flour if needed).

Freeze option: Securely wrap cooled loaf in foil and then freeze. To use, thaw at room temperature.

1 slice: 127 cal., 3g fat (0 sat. fat), 0 chol., 237mg sod., 21g carb. (3g sugars, 1g fiber), 3g pro.

FROZEN FRUIT SALAD

I use this recipe to add a healthy twist to brown-bag lunches. I'm always in a hurry in the morning, so having a ready-made salad in the freezer is a huge help.

—Virginia Powell, Eureka, KS

Prep: 20 min. + freezing
Makes: 24 servings

1 can (16 oz.) apricot halves, drained
1 container (16 oz.) frozen sweetened sliced strawberries, thawed and drained
3 medium bananas, sliced
¾ cup pineapple tidbits
1 can (6 oz.) frozen orange juice concentrate, thawed
1 juice can of water

1. In a food processor, chop the apricots. In a bowl, combine the apricots, strawberries, bananas, pineapple, orange juice and water. Ladle into muffin cups that have been sprayed with cooking spray. Freeze the cups.

2. When frozen, quickly remove salads to tightly covered storage containers. When packing a lunch, place a salad in an individual storage container in a thermal lunch bag and it will thaw by lunchtime.

½ cup: 62 cal., 0 fat (0 sat. fat), 0 chol., 2mg sod., 16g carb. (14g sugars, 1g fiber), 1g pro.

SOFT OATMEAL BREAD

BROWN SUGAR-GLAZED BABY CARROTS

Here's an easy dressing that is perfect for Thanksgiving get-togethers. Once it's in the slow cooker, you're free to turn your attention to the other side dishes on your menu.

—Rita Nodland, Bismarck, ND

Prep: 15 min. • **Cook:** 3 hours
Makes: 8 servings

2 Tbsp. olive oil
1 medium celery rib, chopped
1 small onion, chopped
8 cups unseasoned stuffing cubes
1 tsp. poultry seasoning
¼ tsp. salt
¼ tsp. pepper
2 cups reduced-sodium chicken broth

1. In a large skillet, heat the oil over medium-high heat; saute celery and onion until tender. Place the stuffing cubes, celery mixture and seasonings in a large bowl; toss to combine. Gradually stir in broth.

2. Transfer to a greased 5-qt. slow cooker. Cook, covered, on low until heated through, 3-4 hours.

½ cup: 226 cal., 5g fat (0 sat. fat), 0 chol., 635mg sod., 40g carb. (3g sugars, 3g fiber), 8g pro.

BROWN SUGAR-GLAZED BABY CARROTS

These delicious glazed carrots come to the rescue when I'm serving a special meal. They cook while I prepare the other dishes, and the slow-cooker simmering saves me precious oven space. Plus, they're so easy, and the pretty orange color brightens any table or buffet.

—Anndrea Bailey, Huntington Beach, CA

Prep: 10 min. • **Cook:** 6 hours
Makes: 6 servings

2 lbs. fresh baby carrots
1 celery rib, finely chopped
1 small onion, finely chopped
¼ cup packed brown sugar
3 Tbsp. butter, cubed
½ tsp. salt
½ tsp. pepper

In a 3-qt. slow cooker, combine all ingredients. Cover and cook on low until carrots are tender, 6-8 hours.
¾ cup: 144 cal., 6g fat (4g sat. fat), 15mg chol., 364mg sod., 23g carb. (17g sugars, 3g fiber), 1g pro.

SLOW-COOKER
DRESSING

GINGER ORANGE SQUASH

Bursting with citrus flavor, this tender side dish complements dinner parties and weeknight suppers alike. Our Test Kitchen home economists developed the five-ingredient recipe—which is low in fat and sodium—so you can spend less time in the kitchen and more time with family.
—*Taste of Home* Test Kitchen

- -

Prep: 15 min. • **Bake:** 50 min.
Makes: 10 servings

- 2 **butternut squash (2 lbs. each), peeled and cut into 1½-in. cubes**
- 1 **cup thawed orange juice concentrate**
- 3 **Tbsp. coarsely chopped fresh gingerroot**
- ½ **tsp. pepper**
- 4 **tsp. butter, melted**

1. Line a 15x10x1-in. baking pan with foil and coat with cooking spray; set aside. In a large bowl, toss the squash, orange juice concentrate, ginger and pepper. Arrange in a single layer in prepared pan.
2. Bake at 375° for 50-55 minutes or until squash is tender, stirring twice. Stir in butter before serving.
½ cup: 129 cal., 2g fat (1g sat. fat), 4mg chol., 23mg sod., 29g carb. (15g sugars, 5g fiber), 2g pro.
Diabetic exchanges: 1 starch, 1 fruit, ½ fat.

ORANGE POMEGRANATE SALAD WITH HONEY

I discovered this fragrant salad in a cooking class. If you can, try to find orange flower water (also called orange blossom water), which really perks up the orange segments. But orange juice adds a nice zip, too!
—Carol Richardson Marty, Lynwood, WA

- -

Takes: 15 min. • **Makes:** 6 servings

- 5 **medium oranges or 10 clementines**
- ½ **cup pomegranate seeds**
- 2 **Tbsp. honey**
- 1 **to 2 tsp. orange flower water or orange juice**

1. Cut a thin slice from the top and bottom of each orange; stand orange upright on a cutting board. With a knife, remove peel and outer membrane from the oranges. Cut crosswise into ½-in. slices.
2. Arrange orange slices on a serving platter; sprinkle with pomegranate seeds. In a small bowl, mix the honey and orange flower water; drizzle over fruit.
⅔ cup: 62 cal., 0 fat (0 sat. fat), 0 chol., 2mg sod., 15g carb. (14g sugars, 0 fiber), 1g pro.
Diabetic exchanges: 1 fruit.

ORANGE POMEGRANATE SALAD WITH HONEY

ROASTED
BROCCOLI &
CAULIFLOWER

ROASTED BROCCOLI & CAULIFLOWER

Whenever we make an entree that takes a lot of time, we also prepare this quick side. The veggies are a good fit when you're watching calories.
—Debra Tolbert, Deville, LA

Takes: 25 min. • **Makes:** 8 servings

- 4 cups fresh cauliflowerets
- 4 cups fresh broccoli florets
- 10 garlic cloves, peeled and halved
- 2 Tbsp. olive oil
- ½ tsp. salt
- ½ tsp. pepper

Preheat oven to 425°. In a large bowl, combine all ingredients; toss to coat. Transfer to 2 greased 15x10x1-in. baking pans. Roast 15-20 minutes or until tender.

¾ cup: 58 cal., 4g fat (1g sat. fat), 0 chol., 173mg sod., 6g carb. (2g sugars, 2g fiber), 2g pro.
Diabetic exchanges: 1 vegetable, ½ fat.

PEAR COTTAGE CHEESE SALAD

Perfect anytime, this quick-fix salad makes a terrific snack, too!
—Jeannie Thomas, Dry Ridge, KY

Takes: 10 min. • **Makes:** 6 servings

- 2 cups 2% cottage cheese
- 2 medium pears, chopped
- 2 celery ribs, chopped
- ⅓ cup chopped pecans
- ½ tsp. ground ginger

In a large bowl, combine all ingredients. Chill until serving.
⅔ cup: 135 cal., 6g fat (1g sat. fat), 9mg chol., 255mg sod., 14g carb. (8g sugars, 3g fiber), 8g pro.
Diabetic exchanges: 1 lean meat, 1 fat, ½ fruit.

CARROT RAISIN
SALAD

CARROT RAISIN SALAD

This colorful traditional salad is one of my mother-in-law's favorites. It's fun to eat because of its crunchy texture, and the raisins give it a slightly sweet flavor. Plus, the dish is easy to prepare.
—Denise Baumert, Dalhart, TX

- -

Takes: 10 min. • **Makes:** 8 servings

- 4 **cups shredded carrots**
- ¾ **to 1½ cups raisins**
- ¼ **cup mayonnaise**
- 2 **Tbsp. sugar**
- 2 **to 3 Tbsp. 2% milk**

Mix the first 4 ingredients. Stir in enough milk to reach desired consistency. Refrigerate until serving.

½ cup: 122 cal., 5g fat (1g sat. fat), 1mg chol., 76mg sod., 19g carb. (14g sugars, 2g fiber), 1g pro. **Diabetic exchanges:** 1 fat, ½ starch, ½ fruit.

BALSAMIC-GLAZED ZUCCHINI

BALSAMIC-GLAZED ZUCCHINI

I'm a member of a community-supported agriculture farm. I once received the most delicious garlic and garden-fresh zucchini in a seasonal box. That's when I came up with this fabulous recipe.
—Joe Cherry, Metuchen, NJ

- -

Takes: 15 min. • **Makes:** 4 servings

- 1 **Tbsp. olive oil**
- 3 **medium zucchini, cut into ½-in. slices**
- 2 **garlic cloves, minced**
- ¼ **tsp. salt**
- ¼ **cup balsamic vinegar**

1. In a large enamel-coated cast-iron or other heavy skillet, heat the oil over medium-high heat. Add the zucchini; cook and stir until tender, 5-7 minutes. Add garlic and salt; cook 1 minute longer. Remove from pan.

2. Add vinegar to same pan; bring to a boil. Cook until reduced by half. Add zucchini; toss to coat.

⅔ cup: 65 cal., 4g fat (1g sat. fat), 0 chol., 166mg sod., 8g carb. (5g sugars, 2g fiber), 2g pro. **Diabetic exchanges:** 1 vegetable, 1 fat.

**BROCCOLI
MUSHROOM SALAD**

BROCCOLI MUSHROOM SALAD

Pretty and packed with broccoli, mushrooms, bacon and cheese, this salad makes a perfect partner for summer entrees.

—Deborah Williams, Peoria, AZ

- -

Takes: 20 min. • **Makes:** 8 servings

7	cups fresh broccoli florets
1	cup sliced fresh mushrooms
½	cup shredded cheddar cheese
⅓	cup prepared honey Dijon salad dressing
4	bacon strips, cooked and crumbled

1. In a large saucepan, bring 3 cups water to a boil. Add broccoli; cover and cook for 2-3 minutes or until crisp-tender. Drain and immediately place broccoli in ice water. Drain and pat dry.

2. Transfer broccoli to a large bowl; toss with remaining ingredients.

¾ cup: 98 cal., 7g fat (2g sat. fat), 11mg chol., 203mg sod., 6g carb. (3g sugars, 2g fiber), 5g pro. **Diabetic exchanges:** 1 vegetable, 1 fat.

WATERMELON- BLUEBERRY SALAD

(PICTURED ON P. 146)

People just love the unique combination of flavors in the dressing that tops this salad's fresh fruit.

—Jenni Sharp, Milwaukee, WI

- -

Takes: 5 min. • **Makes:** 2 servings

1	Tbsp. honey
¾	tsp. lemon juice
½	tsp. minced fresh mint
1	cup seeded chopped watermelon
½	cup fresh blueberries

In a small bowl, combine honey, lemon juice and mint. Add the watermelon and blueberries; toss gently to coat. Chill until serving.

¾ cup: 78 cal., 0 fat (0 sat. fat), 0 chol., 2mg sod., 20g carb. (17g sugars, 1g fiber), 1g pro. **Diabetic exchanges:** 1 fruit, ½ starch.

OREGANO GREEN BEANS WITH TOASTED PINE NUTS

This super easy side dish is a wonderful picnic or potluck recipe. It's a beautiful, surprising mix that leaves guests and family raving. Substitute any kind of nut for the pine nuts or even replace them with fresh berries.
—Wolfgang Hanau, West Palm Beach, FL

- -

Prep: 15 min. • **Cook:** 5 hours
Makes: 8 servings

- 2 lbs. fresh thin french-style green beans, cut into 2-in. pieces
- ½ cup water
- 2 Tbsp. minced fresh oregano
- ½ tsp. onion powder
- ½ tsp. salt
- ¼ tsp. celery salt
- ¼ tsp. pepper
- ½ cup pine nuts or sliced almonds, toasted

In a 6-qt. slow cooker, combine all ingredients except pine nuts. Cook, covered, on low until the beans are tender, 5-6 hours. Remove with a slotted spoon. Top with pine nuts.

1 cup: 94 cal., 6g fat (0 sat. fat), 0 chol., 191mg sod., 10g carb. (3g sugars, 4g fiber), 3g pro. **Diabetic exchanges:** 1 vegetable, 1 fat.

POPOVERS FOR TWO

This recipe has been handed down through my family, and I've had it for almost 50 years. My husband and I especially enjoy these popovers for a late breakfast or brunch, and they're tasty with soup or salad. Simply served with butter and honey, they're delicious anytime.
—Alpha Wilson, Roswell, NM

- -

Prep: 10 min. + standing
Bake: 30 min. • **Makes:** 4 popovers

- ½ cup 2% milk
- 1 large egg
- ½ cup all-purpose flour
- ¼ tsp. salt
- ¼ tsp. poultry seasoning, optional

Let the milk and egg stand at room temperature for 30 minutes. Combine all ingredients in a bowl; beat just until smooth. Pour into 4 greased 6-oz. custard cups; place on a baking sheet. Bake at 425° for 15 minutes. Reduce heat to 350° (do not open door). Bake 15-20 minutes longer or until popovers are deep golden brown (do not underbake). Serve warm.

2 popovers: 180 cal., 4g fat (2g sat. fat), 98mg chol., 360mg sod., 27g carb. (3g sugars, 1g fiber), 8g pro. **Diabetic exchanges:** 2 starch.

OREGANO GREEN BEANS WITH TOASTED PINE NUTS

ROASTED SWEET POTATOES WITH DIJON & ROSEMARY

ROASTED ITALIAN GREEN BEANS & TOMATOES

When you roast green beans and tomatoes, their flavors really shine through. The vibrant colors light up a table. What a perfect side dish for the holidays!
—Brittany Allyn, Mesa, AZ

Takes: 25 min. • **Makes:** 8 servings

1½ lbs. fresh green beans, trimmed and halved
1 Tbsp. olive oil
1 tsp. Italian seasoning
½ tsp. salt
2 cups grape tomatoes, halved
½ cup grated Parmesan cheese

1. Preheat oven to 425°. Place green beans in a 15x10x1-in. baking pan coated with cooking spray. Mix oil, Italian seasoning and salt; drizzle over the beans. Toss to coat. Roast 10 minutes, stirring once.
2. Add tomatoes to pan. Roast until the beans are crisp-tender and the tomatoes are softened, 4-6 minutes longer. Sprinkle with cheese.
¾ cup: 70 cal., 3g fat (1g sat. fat), 4mg chol., 231mg sod., 8g carb. (3g sugars, 3g fiber), 4g pro.
Diabetic exchanges: 1 vegetable, ½ fat.

ROASTED SWEET POTATOES WITH DIJON & ROSEMARY

After moving to Alabama, I found out my friends and co-workers love sweet potatoes. I roast these potatoes with Dijon, fresh rosemary and a touch of honey for a heartwarming side.
—Tamara Huron, New Market, AL

Prep: 10 min. • **Bake:** 25 min.
Makes: 4 servings

2 medium sweet potatoes (about 1½ lbs.)
2 Tbsp. olive oil
2 tsp. Dijon mustard
2 tsp. honey
1 tsp. minced fresh rosemary or ¼ tsp. dried rosemary, crushed
¼ tsp. salt
¼ tsp. pepper

Preheat oven to 400°. Peel and cut each sweet potato lengthwise into ½-in.-thick wedges; place in a large bowl. Mix the remaining ingredients; drizzle over potatoes and toss to coat. Transfer to a greased 15x10x1-in. baking pan. Roast 25-30 minutes or until tender, stirring occasionally.
1 serving: 170 cal., 7g fat (1g sat. fat), 0 chol., 217mg sod., 26g carb. (12g sugars, 3g fiber), 2g pro.
Diabetic exchanges: 2 starch, 1½ fat.

ROASTED
ITALIAN GREEN BEANS
& TOMATOES

PROSCIUTTO BREADSTICKS

Pair these breadsticks with your favorite pasta or egg dish. They are a tasty brunch substitute for bacon and toast.
—Maria Regakis, Saugus, MA

- -

Takes: 30 min. • **Makes:** 1 dozen

- 6   thin slices prosciutto or deli ham
- 1   tube (11 oz.) refrigerated breadsticks
- 1   large egg, lightly beaten
- ¼   tsp. fennel seed, crushed
- ¼   tsp. pepper

1. Preheat oven to 375°. Cut each slice of prosciutto into 4 thin strips. Unroll the dough; separate into breadsticks. Top each with 2 strips of the prosciutto, pressing gently to adhere. Twist each breadstick; place on ungreased baking sheet, pressing ends down firmly. Brush with the beaten egg.

2. Combine the fennel and pepper; sprinkle over the breadsticks. Bake 10-13 minutes or until golden brown.

1 breadstick: 86 cal., 2g fat (1g sat. fat), 8mg chol., 323mg sod., 13g carb. (2g sugars, 0 fiber), 4g pro. **Diabetic exchanges:** 1 starch.

SOCCA

Socca is a traditional flatbread from Nice, France. It's a common street food, cooked on a grill and served in a paper cone, usually chopped and sprinkled with salt, pepper, herbs or other delicious toppings. Bonus: It's gluten free.
—*Taste of Home* Test Kitchen

- -

Prep: 5 min. + standing
Cook: 5 minutes • **Makes:** 6 servings

- 1   cup chickpea flour
- 1   cup water
- 2   Tbsp. extra virgin olive oil, divided
- ¾   tsp. salt
  Optional toppings: Za'atar seasoning, sea salt flakes, coarsely ground pepper, pesto and additional extra virgin olive oil

1. In a small bowl, whisk the chickpea flour, water, 1 Tbsp. oil and salt until smooth. Let stand 30 minutes.

2. Meanwhile, preheat broiler. Place a 10-in. cast-iron skillet in oven until hot, about 5 minutes. Add remaining 1 Tbsp. oil to the pan; swirl to coat. Pour bater into the hot pan and tilt to coat evenly.

3. Broil 6 in. from heat until edges are crisp and browned and center just begins to brown, 5-7 minutes. Cut into wedges. If desired, top with optional ingredients.

1 wedge: 113 cal., 6g fat (1g sat. fat), 0 chol., 298mg sod., 12g carb. (2g sugars, 3g fiber), 4g pro. **Diabetic exchanges:** 1 fat, ½ starch.

SOCCA

EASY PEASY SLAW

EASY PEASY SLAW

I get so many compliments when I bring out this slaw. Brightened up with peas, peanuts and poppy seed dressing, it's fresh, colorful and crunchy.
—Sue Ort, Des Moines, IA

Takes: 5 min. • **Makes:** 12 servings

- 4 cups frozen peas (about 16 oz.), thawed
- 1 pkg. (14 oz.) coleslaw mix
- 4 green onions, chopped
- 1 cup poppy seed salad dressing
- 1 cup sweet and crunchy peanuts or honey-roasted peanuts

Place peas, coleslaw mix and green onions in a large bowl. Pour dressing over salad and toss to coat. Stir in peanuts just before serving.

⅔ cup: 202 cal., 12g fat (2g sat. fat), 7mg chol., 178mg sod., 20g carb. (14g sugars, 4g fiber), 4g pro.
Diabetic exchanges: 2 fat, 1 starch, 1 vegetable.

ORANGE YOGURT DRESSING

Honey brings a hint of sweetness to this creamy homemade salad dressing. The citrus flavor is a refreshing complement to salad greens or spinach. It's also terrific served over fresh fruit.
—Beverly Florence, Midwest City, OK

Prep: 10 min. + chilling
Makes: ⅔ cup

- ½ cup reduced-fat mayonnaise
- ⅓ cup fat-free plain yogurt
- 2 Tbsp. orange juice
- 2 tsp. honey
- 1 tsp. grated orange zest
- ¼ tsp. salt
  Dash white pepper, optional

In a small bowl, whisk together all ingredients, including white pepper if desired. Cover and refrigerate for at least 1 hour.

2 Tbsp: 57 cal., 4g fat (1g sat. fat), 4mg chol., 220mg sod., 5g carb. (0 sugars, 0 fiber), 1g pro.
Diabetic exchanges: 1 fat.

NECTARINE
& BEET SALAD

NECTARINE & BEET SALAD

Beets, nectarines and feta cheese make for scrumptious additions to mixed greens. While the combination of ingredients may seem unlikely, I guarantee it will become a favorite salad on your home menu.
—Nicole Werner, Ann Arbor, MI

Takes: 10 min. • **Makes:** 8 servings

- 2 pkg. (5 oz. each) spring mix salad greens
- 2 medium nectarines, sliced
- ½ cup balsamic vinaigrette
- 1 can (14½ oz.) sliced beets, drained
- ½ cup crumbled feta cheese

In a serving dish, toss greens and nectarines with vinaigrette. Top with beets and cheese; serve immediately.

1 cup: 84 cal., 4g fat (1g sat. fat), 4mg chol., 371mg sod., 10g carb. (6g sugars, 3g fiber), 3g pro. **Diabetic exchanges:** 2 vegetable, ½ fat.

CARROT PUREE

CARROT PUREE

Carrots pair beautifully with anything from roasted meat to grilled fish. Cook the carrots fully to ensure a velvety smooth puree.
—Gina Myers, Spokane, WA

Prep: 20 min. • **Cook:** 40 min.
Makes: 4 servings

- 2 Tbsp. olive oil
- 2 lbs. carrots, peeled and chopped
- 2 shallots, chopped
- 4 garlic cloves, minced
- 1 tsp. fresh thyme leaves
- ½ tsp. salt
- ¼ tsp. pepper

1. In a Dutch oven, heat the oil over medium heat. Add the carrots and shallots; cook and stir 12-15 minutes or until carrots are crisp-tender. Stir in garlic and thyme; cook 1 minute longer. Add water to cover carrots; bring to a boil. Reduce heat; simmer, uncovered, 20-25 minutes or until carrots are very tender.

2. Drain; cool slightly. Place carrot mixture, salt and pepper in a food processor; process until smooth.

⅔ cup: 172 cal., 7g fat (1g sat. fat), 0 chol., 455mg sod., 26g carb. (11g sugars, 7g fiber), 3g pro.

STEAMED KALE

With this good-for-you steamed kale, it's easy to eat healthy and get out of the kitchen quick. A wonderful accompaniment to most any entree, it is packed with vitamins and is a snap to prepare. I use garlic, red pepper and balsamic vinegar for this side dish that keeps my family coming back for seconds. Try it tonight with chicken or fish.

—Mary Bilyeu, Ann Arbor, MI

- -

Prep: 15 min. • **Cook:** 25 min.
Makes: 4 servings

1 **bunch kale**
1 **Tbsp. olive oil**
3 **garlic cloves, minced**
⅔ **cup water**
¼ **tsp. salt**
⅛ **tsp. crushed red pepper flakes**
1 **Tbsp. balsamic vinegar**

1. Trim the kale, discarding the thick ribs and stems. Chop the leaves. In a Dutch oven, saute kale leaves in oil until wilted. Add the garlic; cook 1 minute longer.

2. Stir in the water, salt and pepper flakes. Bring to a boil. Reduce heat; cover and simmer for 20-25 minutes or until kale is tender. Remove from the heat; stir in vinegar.

¾ cup: 61 cal., 4g fat (1g sat. fat), 0 chol., 171mg sod., 6g carb. (1g sugars, 1g fiber), 2g pro.
Diabetic exchanges: 1 vegetable, ½ fat.

OVEN FRIES

I jazz up my french fries with a little paprika and garlic powder. This combo of spices packs a punch! The leftovers are even good cold.
—Heather Byers, Pittsburgh, PA

- -

Prep: 10 min. • **Bake:** 40 min.
Makes: 4 servings

- 4 medium potatoes
- 1 Tbsp. olive oil
- 2½ tsp. paprika
- ¾ tsp. salt
- ¾ tsp. garlic powder

1. Preheat oven to 400°. Cut each potato into 12 wedges. In a large bowl, combine oil, paprika, salt and garlic powder. Add the potatoes; toss to coat.
2. Transfer to a greased 15x10x1-in. baking pan. Bake until tender, for 40-45 minutes, turning once.
12 pieces: 200 cal., 4g fat (1g sat. fat), 0 chol., 457mg sod., 38g carb. (2g sugars, 5g fiber), 5g pro.
Cajun Oven Fries: Omit paprika, salt and garlic powder. Combine oil with 2-3 tsp. Cajun seasoning.
Chili Oven Fries: Omit paprika. Combine the oil with salt, garlic powder and 1 Tbsp. chili powder
Herbed Oven Fries: Omit paprika and garlic powder. Combine oil with salt, ⅓ cup grated Parmesan, 4 tsp. dried basil and ¾ tsp. pepper.

PARTY TORTELLINI SALAD

Here's a fast and colorful salad that has plenty of crowd-pleasing flavor. It's a wonderful addition to cookouts and picnics with its light vinaigrette dressing.
—Mary Wilt, Ipswich, MA

- -

Takes: 25 min. • **Makes:** 10 servings

- 1 pkg. (19 oz.) frozen cheese tortellini
- 2 cups fresh broccoli florets
- 1 medium sweet red pepper, chopped
- ½ cup pimiento-stuffed olives, halved
- ¾ cup reduced-fat red wine vinaigrette
- ½ tsp. salt

1. Cook the tortellini according to package directions; drain and rinse in cold water.
2. In a large bowl, combine the tortellini, broccoli, red pepper and olives. Drizzle with the dressing and sprinkle with the salt; toss to coat. Cover and refrigerate until serving.
¾ cup: 156 cal., 7g fat (2g sat. fat), 8mg chol., 596mg sod., 19g carb. (3g sugars, 1g fiber), 6g pro.
Diabetic exchanges: 1 starch, 1 lean meat, ½ fat.

OVEN FRIES

CHEDDAR BASIL CAULIFLOWER

CALIFORNIA AVOCADO SALAD

Spread a little sunshine with this easy salad. Just four ingredients drizzled with a homemade citrus dressing and you have a light lunch or a pretty side to serve with dinner.
—James Schend, Pleasant Prairie, WI

Takes: 20 min. • **Makes:** 8 servings

- 3 medium oranges, peeled and sectioned
- 2 medium ripe avocados, peeled and sliced
- ¼ cup toasted pine nuts
- 2 tsp. minced fresh rosemary
  Orange Yogurt Dressing (see recipe on p. 167) or dressing of your choice

Arrange the oranges and avocados on a platter; sprinkle with pine nuts and rosemary. Drizzle dressing over salad. Serve immediately.
½ cup: 135 cal., 11g fat (1g sat. fat), 3mg chol., 129mg sod., 10g carb. (5g sugars, 3g fiber), 2g pro.

CHEDDAR BASIL CAULIFLOWER

If you grow your own basil or simply like to keep it on hand, you'll want to save some for a side of flavorful, versatile cauliflower. The dish will also warm you up during winter.
—David Harper, Clackamas, OR

Takes: 20 min. • **Makes:** 2 servings

- 2½ cups small fresh cauliflowerets
- 1 Tbsp. white wine or water
- 1½ tsp. minced fresh basil or ½ tsp. dried basil
- 1 tsp. water
- 1 tsp. canola oil
- ½ tsp. sugar
- ¼ tsp. salt
- ⅓ cup shredded cheddar cheese

In a small saucepan, combine the first 7 ingredients. Cover and cook over medium heat until cauliflower is tender, 10-12 minutes, stirring once. Transfer to a small serving bowl; sprinkle with cheese.
¾ cup: 128 cal., 8g fat (4g sat. fat), 20mg chol., 446mg sod., 8g carb. (4g sugars, 3g fiber), 6g pro.
Diabetic exchanges: 1 vegetable, 1 fat, ½ fat-free milk.

CALIFORNIA
AVOCADO SALAD

SESAME FLATBREADS

Turn everyday dinner roll dough into an elegant gourmet flatbread with this quick and easy trick.
—*Taste of Home* Test Kitchen

Takes: 20 min. • **Makes:** 2 servings

> 2 frozen Texas-size whole wheat dinner rolls, thawed
> Cooking spray
> ⅛ tsp. garlic powder
> ½ tsp. sesame seeds

On a baking sheet coated with cooking spray, press the dough to ¼-in. thickness. Spritz with cooking spray. Sprinkle with garlic powder and sesame seeds. Bake at 425° for 7-9 minutes or until lightly browned.
1 flatbread: 146 cal., 4g fat (0 sat. fat), 0 chol., 210mg sod., 24g carb. (3g sugars, 3g fiber), 6g pro. **Diabetic exchanges:** 1½ starch, ½ fat.

MINT WATERMELON SALAD

I invented this refreshing fruit salad one sultry afternoon while my friends were gathered around my pool. It was simple to prepare and disappeared from their plates even quicker than it took me to make it. Even the kids loved it!
—Antoinette DuBeck, Huntingdon Valley, PA

Takes: 20 min. • **Makes:** 8 servings

> 6 cups cubed seedless watermelon
> 2 Tbsp. minced fresh mint
> 1 Tbsp. lemon juice
> 1 Tbsp. olive oil
> 2 tsp. sugar

Place watermelon and mint in a large bowl. In a small bowl, whisk lemon juice, oil and sugar until sugar is dissolved. Drizzle over salad; toss gently to combine.
¾ cup: 56 cal., 2g fat (0 sat. fat), 0 chol., 2mg sod., 9g carb. (9g sugars, 1g fiber), 1g pro. **Diabetic exchanges:** ½ fruit.

MINT WATERMELON SALAD

ONE-DISH
NO-KNEAD BREAD

ONE-DISH NO-KNEAD BREAD

Here's an almost effortless way to have homemade bread for dinner. Don't worry if you are new to baking. Anyone who can stir can make this a success!
—Heather Chambers, Largo, FL

- -

Prep: 15 min. + rising • **Bake:** 40 min.
Makes: 1 loaf (12 slices)

1	tsp. active dry yeast
1½	cups warm water (110° to 115°)
2¾	cups all-purpose flour
2	Tbsp. sugar
2	Tbsp. olive oil
1½	tsp. salt

1. In a large bowl, dissolve the yeast in warm water. Stir in the remaining ingredients to form a wet dough; transfer to a greased 2½-qt. baking dish. Cover; let stand in a warm place 1 hour.

2. Stir down dough. Cover; let stand 1 hour. Preheat oven to 425°.

3. Bake 20 minutes. Reduce the oven setting to 350°. Bake until the top is golden brown and a thermometer reads 210°, about 20 minutes longer.

4. Remove bread from baking dish to a wire rack to cool. Serve warm.

1 slice: 133 cal., 3g fat (0 sat. fat), 0 chol., 296mg sod., 24g carb. (2g sugars, 1g fiber), 3g pro. **Diabetic exchanges:** 1½ starch, ½ fat.

TEST KITCHEN TIP
Salt plays many roles in yeast bread. It slows the yeast's growth, allowing the dough to develop more complex flavors and a stronger structure. Salt also contributes to the finished bread's flavor and shelf life.

SPINACH WITH PINE NUTS & RAISINS

SPINACH WITH PINE NUTS & RAISINS

A nice side for winter meals, this bright and flavorful dish is a delicious way to get greens onto any table. The simple list of ingredients makes it easy to put together any night of the week.
—Gretchen Whelan, San Francisco, CA

- -

Prep: 25 min. • **Cook:** 10 min.
Makes: 6 servings

⅓ cup golden raisins
⅓ cup pine nuts
3 garlic cloves, minced
¼ cup olive oil
2 pkg. (10 oz. each) fresh spinach, torn
¼ tsp. salt
⅛ tsp. pepper

1. Place the raisins in a small bowl. Cover with boiling water; let stand for 5 minutes. Drain and set aside.
2. In a Dutch oven, cook pine nuts and garlic in oil over medium heat for 2 minutes. Stir in raisins; cook 1 minute longer. Stir in the spinach, salt and pepper; cook just until tender, 4-5 minutes. Serve with a slotted spoon.

½ cup: 171 cal., 13g fat (2g sat. fat), 0 chol., 175mg sod., 11g carb. (6g sugars, 3g fiber), 5g pro. **Diabetic exchanges:** 2 fat, 1 vegetable, ½ fruit.

LEMONY ZUCCHINI RIBBONS

LEMONY ZUCCHINI RIBBONS

Yum! Fresh zucchini gets a shave and a drizzle of lemony goodness in this fabulous salad. Sprinkle goat cheese or feta on top.
—Ellie Martin Cliffe, Milwaukee, WI

- -

Takes: 15 min. • **Makes:** 4 servings

1 Tbsp. olive oil
½ tsp. grated lemon zest
1 Tbsp. lemon juice
½ tsp. salt
¼ tsp. pepper
3 medium zucchini
⅓ cup crumbled goat or feta cheese

1. For dressing, in a small bowl, mix the first 5 ingredients. Using a vegetable peeler, shave zucchini lengthwise into very thin slices; arrange on a serving plate.
2. To serve, drizzle with dressing and toss lightly to coat. Top with cheese.

¾ cup: 83 cal., 6g fat (2g sat. fat), 12mg chol., 352mg sod., 5g carb. (3g sugars, 2g fiber), 3g pro. **Diabetic exchanges:** 1 vegetable, 1 fat.

DID YOU KNOW?
Making this colorful salad with zucchini instead of spaghetti saves roughly 130 calories per serving.

OVERNIGHT HONEY-WHEAT ROLLS

OVERNIGHT HONEY-WHEAT ROLLS

These yeast rolls don't require kneading, and the make-ahead dough saves you time on the day of your meal. But the best part is the hint of honey flavor.

—Lisa Varner, El Paso, TX

Prep: 30 min. + chilling
Bake: 10 min. • **Makes:** 1½ dozen

 1   pkg. (¼ oz.) active dry yeast
1¼ cups warm water
     (110° to 115°), divided
 2   large egg whites
⅓   cup honey
¼   cup canola oil
 1   tsp. salt
1½ cups whole wheat flour
2½ cups all-purpose flour
     Melted butter, optional

1. In a small bowl, dissolve yeast in ¼ cup warm water. In a large bowl, beat egg whites until foamy. Add the yeast mixture, honey, oil, salt, whole wheat flour and remaining water. Beat on medium speed for roughly 3 minutes. Beat until smooth. Stir in enough all-purpose flour to form a soft dough (dough will be sticky). Cover and refrigerate overnight.

2. Punch dough down. Turn onto a floured surface; divide in half. Shape each portion into 9 balls. To form knots, roll each ball into a 10-in. rope; tie into a knot. Tuck the ends under.

3. Place rolls 2 in. apart on greased baking sheets. Cover and let rise until doubled, about 50 minutes.

4. Bake at 375° for 10-12 minutes or until golden brown. Brush with melted butter if desired.

1 roll: 147 cal., 3g fat (0 sat. fat), 0 chol., 139mg sod., 26g carb. (6g sugars, 2g fiber), 4g pro.
Diabetic exchanges: 1½ starch, ½ fat.

BROCCOLI WITH GARLIC, BACON & PARMESAN

My approach to this broccoli is to cook it slowly in the seasonings so the garlic blends with smoky bacon. A few simple ingredients make the broccoli irresistible.
—Erin Chilcoat, Central Islip, NY

Takes: 30 min. • **Makes:** 8 servings

- 1 tsp. salt
- 2 bunches broccoli (about 3 lbs.), stems removed, cut into florets
- 6 thick-sliced bacon strips, chopped
- 2 Tbsp. olive oil
- 6 to 8 garlic cloves, thinly sliced
- ½ tsp. crushed red pepper flakes
- ¼ cup shredded Parmesan cheese

1. Fill a 6-qt. stockpot two-thirds full with water; add salt and bring to a boil over high heat. In batches, add broccoli and cook 2-3 minutes or until broccoli turns bright green; remove with a slotted spoon.
2. In a large skillet, cook bacon over medium heat until crisp, stirring occasionally. Remove with a slotted spoon; drain on paper towels. Discard drippings, reserving 1 Tbsp. in pan.
3. Add oil to drippings; heat over medium heat. Add the garlic and red pepper flakes; cook and stir 2-3 minutes or until the garlic is fragrant (do not allow to brown). Add broccoli; cook until broccoli is tender, stirring occasionally. Stir in bacon; sprinkle with cheese.

¾ cup: 155 cal., 10g fat (3g sat. fat), 11mg chol., 371mg sod., 11g carb. (3g sugars, 4g fiber), 8g pro. **Diabetic exchanges:** 2 fat, 1 vegetable.

OAT BREAD

I love making bread in my bread machine. This loaf has a slightly sweet flavor from molasses and a nice tender texture from oats.
—Ruth Andrewson, Leavenworth, Washington

Prep: 10 min. • **Bake:** 3 hours
Makes: 1 loaf

- 1 cup warm water (70° to 80°)
- ½ cup molasses
- 1 Tbsp. canola oil
- 1 tsp. salt
- 3 cups bread flour
- 1 cup quick-cooking oats
- 1 pkg. (¼ ounce) active dry yeast

In a bread machine pan, place all ingredients in order suggested by manufacturer. Select basic bread setting. Choose crust color and loaf size if available. Check the dough after 5 minutes of mixing; add 1-2 Tbsp. of water or flour if needed. Bake according to manufacturer's directions.

1 slice: 105 cal., 1g fat (0 sat. fat), 0 chol., 121mg sod., 22g carb. (4g sugars, 1g fiber), 3g pro. **Diabetic exchanges:** 1½ starch.

BROCCOLI WITH GARLIC, BACON & PARMESAN

ROASTED BRUSSELS SPROUTS WITH CRANBERRIES

OLIVE OIL MASHED POTATOES WITH PANCETTA

Classic American mashed potatoes take a trip to Italy with the flavors of olive oil, garlic and savory pancetta.
—Bryan Kennedy, Kaneohe, HI

Prep: 20 min. • **Cook:** 20 min.
Makes: 8 servings

- 3 lbs. Yukon Gold potatoes, peeled and cubed
- 3 slices pancetta or bacon, chopped
- 1 Tbsp. plus ¼ cup olive oil, divided
- 4 garlic cloves, minced
- ⅓ cup minced fresh parsley
- ½ tsp. salt
- ½ tsp. pepper

1. Place potatoes in a large saucepan and cover with water. Bring to a boil. Reduce heat; cover and simmer until tender, 15-20 minutes.
2. Meanwhile, in a large skillet, cook pancetta in 1 Tbsp. oil over medium heat until crisp. Add garlic; cook for 1 minute longer. Remove from heat.
3. Drain potatoes and transfer to a large bowl. Mash potatoes with remaining oil. Stir in the parsley, pancetta mixture, salt and pepper.
⅔ cup: 206 cal., 11g fat (2g sat. fat), 7mg chol., 313mg sod., 23g carb. (2g sugars, 2g fiber), 4g pro.
Diabetic exchanges: 2 fat, 1½ starch.

ROASTED BRUSSELS SPROUTS WITH CRANBERRIES

There's nothing to this recipe— the preparation and cooking times are so quick. I toss in some dried cranberries, but you can let your imagination take over. Add a handful of raisins or walnuts at the end, or even sliced oranges. If your Brussels sprouts are large, cut them in half.
—Ellen Ruzinsky,
Yorktown Heights, NY

Prep: 15 min. • **Bake:** 20 min.
Makes: 12 servings

- 3 lbs. fresh Brussels sprouts, trimmed and halved
- 3 Tbsp. olive oil
- 1 tsp. kosher salt
- ½ tsp. pepper
- ½ cup dried cranberries

Preheat oven to 425°. Divide the Brussels sprouts between 2 greased 15x10x1-in. baking pans. Drizzle with oil; sprinkle with the salt and pepper. Toss to coat. Roast until tender, stirring occasionally, 20-25 minutes. Transfer to a large bowl; stir in the cranberries.
½ cup: 94 cal., 4g fat (1g sat. fat), 0 chol., 185mg sod., 14g carb. (6g sugars, 5g fiber), 4g pro.
Diabetic exchanges: 1 vegetable, 1 fat.

OLIVE OIL
MASHED POTATOES
WITH PANCETTA

LEMONY GREEN BEANS

You can throw together this dish in minutes using ingredients you probably already have on hand. That's the beauty of it.

—Jennifer Capoano, Carlstadt, NJ

Takes: 20 min. • **Makes:** 6 servings

- ¼ cup chicken broth
- 2 Tbsp. olive oil
- 1½ lbs. fresh green beans, trimmed
- ¾ tsp. lemon-pepper seasoning
  Lemon wedges

In a large skillet, heat chicken broth and oil over medium-high heat. Add the green beans; cook and stir until crisp-tender. Sprinkle with lemon pepper. Serve with lemon wedges.

1 serving: 76 cal., 5g fat (1g sat. fat), 0 chol., 88mg sod., 8g carb. (3g sugars, 4g fiber), 2g pro.
Diabetic exchanges: 1 vegetable, 1 fat.

WARM FAVA BEAN & PEA SALAD

I know that when the favas are at the market, I can always find this refreshing and tasty salad in my mom's fridge! She's been making it for years. You can use fresh or frozen beans.

—Francesca Ferenczi, New York, NY

Prep: 55 min. • **Cook:** 25 min.
Makes: 12 servings

- 3 cups shelled fresh fava beans (about 4 lbs. unshelled) or 1 pkg. (28 oz.) frozen fava beans, thawed
- 8 cups shelled fresh peas (about 8 lbs. unshelled) or 8 cups frozen peas (about 32 oz.)
- 3 Tbsp. olive oil, divided
- 4 oz. diced pancetta
- 8 shallots, thinly sliced
- ½ tsp. salt
- ¼ tsp. pepper

1. For fresh fava beans, add beans to a large pot of boiling water; return to a boil. Cook, uncovered, until tender, 4-5 minutes. Using a strainer, remove beans to a bowl of ice water to cool. Drain cooled beans; squeeze gently to remove skins. (If using frozen fava beans, prepare according to the package directions.)
2. For fresh peas, add the peas to boiling water; return to a boil. Cook, uncovered, just until tender, 2-4 minutes. Drain well; place in a large bowl. (If using frozen peas, cook according to the package directions.)
3. In a large skillet, heat 1 Tbsp. oil over medium heat. Add pancetta; cook and stir until crisp, about 5 minutes. Drain on paper towels, reserving drippings.
4. In same pan, heat the remaining oil and reserved drippings over medium heat. Add the shallots; cook and stir until tender and lightly browned, 5-6 minutes. Stir in the fava beans and heat through. Add to the peas; stir in salt, pepper and pancetta. Serve warm.
¾ cup: 293 cal., 7g fat (2g sat. fat), 8mg chol., 282mg sod., 49g carb. (35g sugars, 8g fiber), 10g pro.

WARM FAVA BEAN & PEA SALAD

CHILI POTATO WEDGES

CHILI POTATO WEDGES

These potato wedges make a perfect side any time you're looking for full-flavored fries. I think they go well with burgers.

—Peggy Key, Grant, AL

- -

Takes: 30 min. • **Makes:** 2 servings

- 1 tsp. chili powder
- ¼ tsp. garlic powder
- ⅛ tsp. salt
- 1 large baking potato
  Cooking spray

1. In a small bowl, combine the chili powder, garlic powder and salt. Cut potato lengthwise into 8 wedges.

Spray wedges with cooking spray, then coat with seasoning mixture.

2. Place in a single layer on a baking sheet coated with cooking spray. Bake wedges, uncovered, at 450° for 25-30 minutes or until golden brown.

4 wedges: 158 cal., 1g fat (0 sat. fat), 0 chol., 172mg sod., 34g carb. (3g sugars, 3g fiber), 4g pro. **Diabetic exchanges:** 2 starch.

ROASTED ASPARAGUS WITH FETA

This delectable side dish is delicious right out of the oven.

—Phyllis Schmalz, Kansas City, KS

- -

Takes: 25 min. • **Makes:** 6 servings

- 2 lbs. fresh asparagus, trimmed
- 1 Tbsp. olive oil
  Kosher salt to taste
- 2 medium tomatoes, seeded and chopped
- ½ cup crumbled feta cheese

1. Arrange the asparagus in an ungreased 13x9-in. baking dish. Drizzle with oil and sprinkle with salt.

2. Bake, uncovered, at 400° for 15-20 minutes or until tender. Transfer to a serving dish; sprinkle with tomatoes and feta cheese. Serve immediately.

1 serving: 72 cal., 4g fat (1g sat. fat), 5mg chol., 103mg sod., 6g carb. (3g sugars, 2g fiber), 4g pro. **Diabetic exchanges:** 1 vegetable, 1 fat.

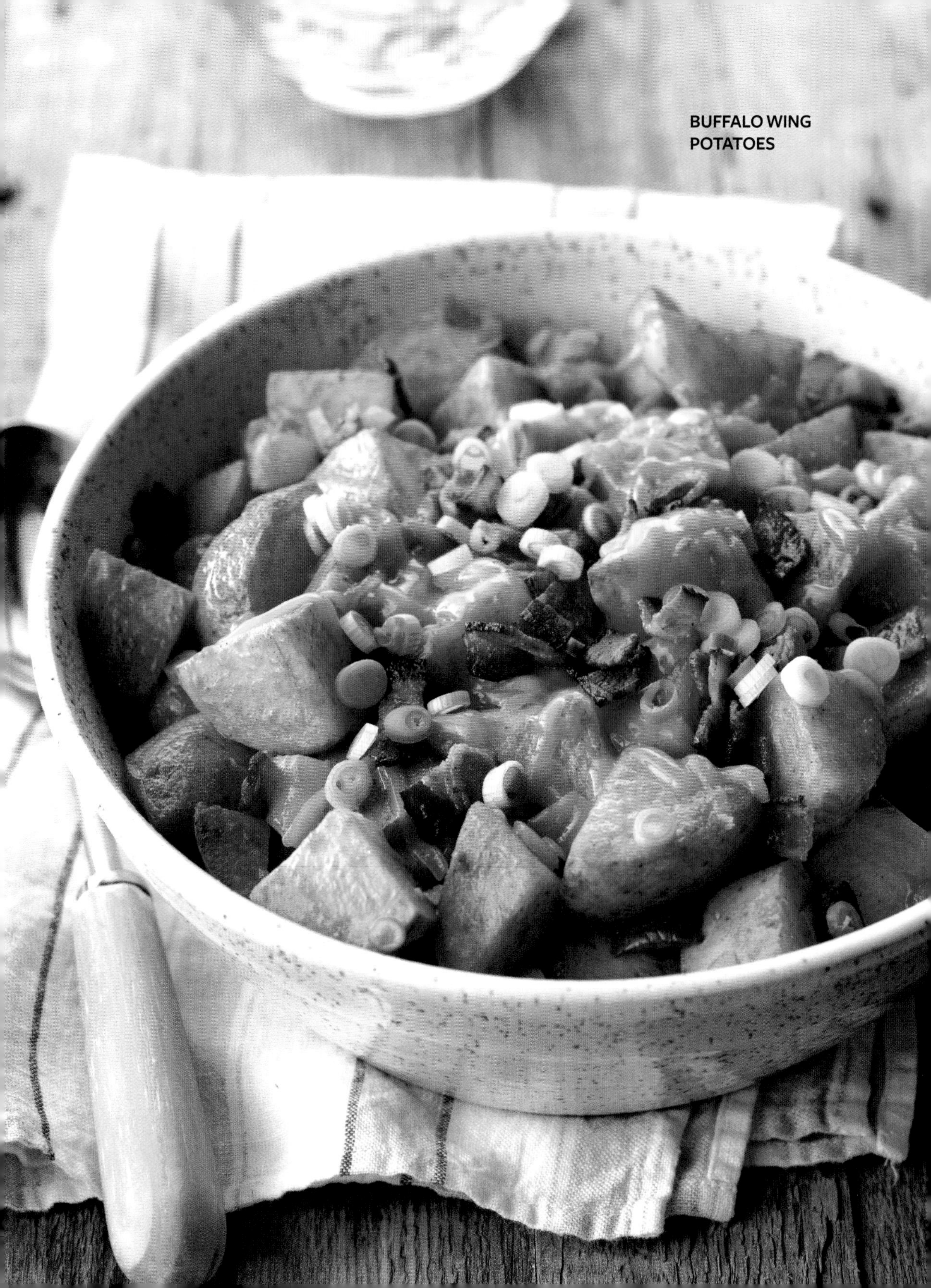

BUFFALO WING
POTATOES

BUFFALO WING POTATOES

I was getting tired of mashed and baked potatoes, so I decided to create something new. This potluck-ready recipe is an easy and delicious twist on the usual potato dish.
—Summer Feaker, Ankeny, IA

- -

Prep: 15 min. • **Cook:** 6¼ hours
Makes: 12 servings

- 4 **lbs. large Yukon Gold potatoes, cut into 1-in. cubes**
- 1 **medium sweet yellow pepper, chopped**
- 1 **small red onion, chopped**
- ½ **cup Buffalo wing sauce**
- 1 **cup shredded cheddar cheese**
  Optional toppings: Crumbled cooked bacon, sliced green onions and sour cream

STRAWBERRY ORANGE VINEGAR

1. Place potatoes, yellow pepper and red onion in a 6-qt. slow cooker. Add the Buffalo wing sauce; stir to coat. Cook, covered, on low 6 hours or until the potatoes are tender, stirring halfway through. Stir the potato mixture; sprinkle with cheese. Cover and cook until the cheese is melted, about 15 minutes.
2. Transfer to a serving bowl. If desired, top with the bacon, green onions and sour cream.
¾ cup: 182 cal., 4g fat (2g sat. fat), 9mg chol., 382mg sod., 32g carb. (3g sugars, 3g fiber), 6g pro.
Diabetic exchanges: 2 starch, ½ fat.

STRAWBERRY ORANGE VINEGAR

Top your next salad with this lovely homemade dressing. Use your favorite salad greens or a ready-to-serve package to keep things simple.
—*Taste of Home* Test Kitchen

- -

Prep: 10 min.
Cook: 10 min. + standing
Makes: 1⅔ cups

- 1 **medium orange**
- 2 **cups white wine vinegar**
- 2 **Tbsp. sugar**
- 2 **cups sliced fresh strawberries**

1. Using a citrus zester, peel rind from orange in long narrow strips (being careful not to remove pith). In a large saucepan, heat vinegar and sugar to just below the boiling point.
2. Place the strawberries in a warm sterilized quart jar; add the heated vinegar mixture and orange peel. Cover and let stand in a cool dark place 10 days.
3. Strain the mixture through a cheesecloth; discard the pulp and orange rind. Pour into a sterilized pint jar. Seal tightly. Store in the refrigerator up to 6 months.
1 Tbsp.: 15 cal., 0 fat (0 sat. fat), 0 chol., 0 sod., 4g carb. (2g sugars, 0 fiber), 0 pro.

CHAPATI BREADS

COLESLAW WITH POPPY SEED DRESSING

I love this salad because I can keep it in the fridge for a couple of days and it just gets better. It packs lots of crunch and flavor for very little effort. If you prefer raisins or even dried cranberries, feel free to toss in a few.

—Trisha Kruse, Eagle, ID

- -

Prep: 20 min. + chilling
Makes: 12 servings

½	medium head cabbage, shredded (about 4½ cups)
6	large carrots, shredded (about 4½ cups)
8	green onions, chopped (about 1 cup)
1	cup fat-free poppy seed salad dressing
⅓	cup sunflower kernels

In a large bowl, combine cabbage, carrots and green onions. Drizzle with the dressing; toss to coat. Refrigerate, covered, at least 1 hour. Just before serving, top with sunflower kernels.

¾ cup: 83 cal., 2g fat (0 sat. fat), 3mg chol., 102mg sod., 15g carb. (3g sugars, 3g fiber), 2g pro.
Diabetic exchanges: 1 vegetable, ½ starch, ½ fat.

CHAPATI BREADS

My daughter and I prepare this Indian flatbread frequently. It is so fun to make and goes well with any spiced dish. We use the extras to make sandwich wraps.

—Joyce McCarthy, Sussex, WI

- -

Prep: 20 min. • **Cook:** 5 min./batch
Makes: 10 servings

1½	cups all-purpose flour
½	cup whole wheat flour
1	tsp. salt
¼	tsp. garlic powder, optional
¾	cup hot water (140°)
2	Tbsp. olive oil

In a large bowl, combine the flours, salt and, if desired, garlic powder. Stir in water and oil. Turn onto a floured surface; knead until smooth and elastic, 8-10 minutes. Cover and let rest for 30 minutes. Divide dough into 10 portions. On a lightly floured surface, roll each portion into a 6-in. circle. In a large cast-iron or other heavy skillet, cook the breads over medium heat until lightly browned, 1 minute on each side. Keep warm.

1 bread: 113 cal., 3g fat (0 sat. fat), 0 chol., 237mg sod., 19g carb. (0 sugars, 1g fiber), 3g pro. **Diabetic exchanges:** 1 starch, ½ fat.

COLESLAW
WITH
POPPY SEED DRESSING

PARTY FOODS

CAPRESE SALAD KABOBS
P. 193

1

2

3

4

FILIPPO
BERIO
OLIVE OIL

5

BALSAMIC
VINEGAR
OF MODENA

THESE EASY PARTY PLEASERS MAY BE
LOWER IN CALORIES, FAT AND SODIUM, BUT
THEY ARE BIG ON FLAVOR AND WILL HAVE
EVERYONE COMING BACK FOR MORE!

BASIL CITRUS COCKTAIL

EASY BUFFALO CHICKEN DIP

Everyone will devour this savory and delicious dip with shredded chicken throughout. The spicy kick makes it perfect football-watching food, and the recipe always brings raves.
—Janice Foltz, Hershey, PA

- -

Takes: 30 min.
Makes: 21 servings (4 cups)

- 1   **pkg. (8 oz.) reduced-fat cream cheese**
- 1   **cup reduced-fat sour cream**
- ½   **cup Louisiana-style hot sauce**
- 3   **cups shredded cooked chicken breast**
     Assorted crackers

1. Preheat oven to 350°. In a large bowl, beat the cream cheese, sour cream and hot sauce until smooth; stir in chicken.
2. Transfer to an 8-in. square baking dish coated with cooking spray. Cover and bake 18-22 minutes or until heated through. Serve warm with crackers.
3 Tbsp.: 77 cal., 4g fat (2g sat. fat), 28mg chol., 71mg sod., 1g carb. (1g sugars, 0 fiber), 8g pro.

BASIL CITRUS COCKTAIL

This irresistible cocktail is fruity, fantastic and low in calories!
—*Taste of Home* Test Kitchen

- -

Takes: 10 min. • **Makes:** 1 serving

- 6   **fresh basil leaves**
- 1½ to 2 **cups ice cubes**
- 2   **oz. white grapefruit juice**
- 2   **oz. mandarin orange juice**
- ¾   **oz. gin**
- ½   **oz. Domaine de Canton ginger liqueur**

1. In a shaker, muddle basil leaves.
2. Fill shaker three-fourths full with ice. Add the juices, gin and ginger liqueur; cover and shake until condensation forms on outside of shaker, 10-15 seconds. Strain into a chilled cocktail glass.
1 serving: 136 cal., 0 fat (0 sat. fat), 0 chol., 0 sod., 14g carb. (7g sugars, 0 fiber), 1g pro.

EASY
BUFFALO
CHICKEN
DIP

GRILLED LEEK DIP

Smoky leeks from the grill add a punch of flavor to this chunky dip.
—Ramona Parris, Canton, GA

- -

Prep: 10 min. • **Grill:** 10 min. + chilling
Makes: 2½ cups

2	**medium leeks**
2	**tsp. olive oil**
½	**tsp. salt, divided**
¼	**tsp. pepper**
2	**cups reduced-fat sour cream**
2	**Tbsp. Worcestershire sauce**
	Assorted fresh vegetables

1. Trim and discard the dark green portions of leeks. Brush the leeks with oil; sprinkle with ¼ tsp. salt and the pepper. Grill leeks, covered, over medium-high heat until lightly charred and tender, 8-10 minutes, turning occasionally. Cool slightly; chop leeks.

2. In a small bowl, combine the sour cream, Worcestershire sauce and the remaining salt; stir in the leeks. Refrigerate, covered, 2 hours before serving. Serve with vegetables.

2 Tbsp.: 43 cal., 2g fat (1g sat. fat), 8mg chol., 93mg sod., 3g carb. (2g sugars, 0 fiber), 2g pro.

DID YOU KNOW?
Leeks belong to the onion family. They look a bit like oversized scallions, with a white-green tubular base and broad ribbonlike green leaves. Available year-round, leeks bring a light, sweet flavor to foods—milder and more complex than a standard onion. When eaten raw, leeks are crunchy and nutritious. Since the leaves are coarse in texture, many people eat the softer, pale part of the stalk. But the entire leek is edible. Simply saute the leaves for a while for a more tender bite.

GRILLED SHRIMP WITH SPICY-SWEET SAUCE

These shrimp practically fly off the platter at my get-togethers. Play with the amount of Sriracha sauce to get the spice level just the way you like it.

—Susan Harrison, Laurel, MD

- -

Takes: 30 min.
Makes: 15 servings (⅓ cup sauce)

- 3 Tbsp. reduced-fat mayonnaise
- 2 Tbsp. sweet chili sauce
- 1 green onion, thinly sliced
- ¾ tsp. Sriracha chili sauce or ½ tsp. hot pepper sauce
- 45 uncooked large shrimp (about 1½ lbs.), peeled and deveined
- ¼ tsp. salt
- ¼ tsp. pepper

1. In a small bowl, mix mayonnaise, chili sauce, green onion and Sriracha. Sprinkle the shrimp with the salt and pepper. Thread 3 shrimp onto each of 15 metal or soaked wooden skewers.

2. Place the shrimp on an oiled grill rack. Grill the shrimp, covered, over medium heat or broil 4 in. from heat 3-4 minutes on each side or until shrimp turn pink. Serve with sauce.

3 shrimp with 1 tsp. sauce: 56 cal., 2g fat (0 sat. fat), 61mg chol., 156mg sod., 2g carb. (1g sugars, 0 fiber), 8g pro. **Diabetic exchanges:** ½ lean meat.

GRILLED SHRIMP WITH
SPICY-SWEET SAUCE

CAPRESE SALAD KABOBS

(PICTURED ON P. 188)

Trade in the usual veggie platter for these fun kabobs. In addition to preparing these for parties, I make these as snacks for my family. And because assembly is so easy, the kids often ask to help.

—Christine Mitchell, Glendora, CA

- -

Takes: 10 min. • **Makes:** 12 kabobs

- 24 grape tomatoes
- 12 cherry-size fresh mozzarella cheese balls
- 24 fresh basil leaves
- 2 Tbsp. olive oil
- 2 tsp. balsamic vinegar

On each of 12 appetizer skewers, alternately thread 2 tomatoes, 1 cheese ball and 2 basil leaves. Whisk the olive oil and vinegar; drizzle over kabobs.

1 kabob: 44 cal., 4g fat (1g sat. fat), 5mg chol., 10mg sod., 2g carb. (1g sugars, 0 fiber), 1g pro. **Diabetic exchanges:** 1 fat.

SOFT
GIANT
PRETZELS

SOFT GIANT PRETZELS

My husband, friends and family love these soft, chewy pretzels. Let your machine mix the dough; then all you have to do is shape and bake these fun snacks.

—Sherry Peterson, Fort Collins, CO

- -

Prep: 20 min. + rising
Bake: 10 min. • **Makes:** 8 pretzels

- 1 cup plus 2 Tbsp. water (70° to 80°)
- 3 cups all-purpose flour
- 3 Tbsp. brown sugar
- 1½ tsp. active dry yeast
- 2 qt. water
- ½ cup baking soda
- Coarse salt

1. In bread machine pan, place 1 cup water and next 3 ingredients in order suggested by manufacturer. Select the dough setting (check the dough after 5 minutes of mixing; add 1 to 2 Tbsp. water or flour if needed).
2. When cycle is completed, turn dough onto a lightly floured surface. Divide the dough into 8 balls. Roll each into a 20-in. rope; form into pretzel shape.
3. Preheat oven to 425°. In a large saucepan, bring 2 qt. water and the baking soda to a boil. Drop pretzels into boiling water, 2 at a time; boil for 10-15 seconds. Remove with a slotted spoon; drain pretzels on paper towels.
4. Place pretzels on greased baking sheets. Bake until golden brown, 8-10 minutes. Spritz or lightly brush with water. Sprinkle with salt.
1 pretzel: 193 cal., 1g fat (0 sat. fat), 0 chol., 380mg sod., 41g carb. (5g sugars, 1g fiber), 5g pro.

SIMPLE GUACAMOLE

SIMPLE GUACAMOLE

Because avocados can brown quickly, it's best to make this guacamole just before serving. If you have to make it a little in advance, place the avocado pit in the guacamole until ready.

—Heidi Main, Anchorage, AK

- -

Takes: 10 min. • **Makes:** 1½ cups

- 2 medium ripe avocados
- 1 Tbsp. lemon juice
- ¼ cup chunky salsa
- ⅛ to ¼ tsp. salt

Peel and chop avocados; place in a small bowl. Sprinkle with lemon juice. Add salsa and salt; mash coarsely with a fork. Refrigerate until serving.
2 Tbsp.: 53 cal., 5g fat (1g sat. fat), 0 chol., 51mg sod., 3g carb. (0 sugars, 2g fiber), 1g pro.

ASPARAGUS WITH HORSERADISH DIP

This is a terrific dip for party season. Serve asparagus on a decorative platter with lemon wedges on the side for garnish. For flavor variation, use chopped garlic in place of the horseradish.
—Lynn Caruso, Gilroy, CA

- -

Takes: 15 min. • **Makes:** 16 appetizers

- 32 **fresh asparagus spears (about 2 lbs.), trimmed**
- 1 **cup reduced-fat mayonnaise**
- ¼ **cup grated Parmesan cheese**
- 1 **Tbsp. prepared horseradish**
- ½ **tsp. Worcestershire sauce**

1. Place the asparagus in a steamer basket; place in a large saucepan over 1 in. of water. Bring to a boil; cover and steam until crisp-tender, 2-4 minutes. Drain and immediately place in ice water. Drain and pat dry.
2. In a small bowl, combine the remaining ingredients. Serve with the asparagus.
2 asparagus spears with 1 Tbsp. dip: 63 cal., 5g fat (1g sat. fat), 6mg chol., 146mg sod., 3g carb. (1g sugars, 0 fiber), 1g pro. **Diabetic exchanges:** 1 fat.

STRAWBERRY-BASIL REFRESHER

Fresh strawberries and basil blend for a cooler that's pure sunshine. Garnish with basil leaves and sip it in the shade.
—Carolyn Turner, Reno, NV

- -

Takes: 10 min. • **Makes:** 12 servings

- ⅔ **cup lemon juice**
- ½ **cup sugar**
- 1 **cup sliced fresh strawberries**
  Ice cubes
- 1 **to 2 Tbsp. chopped fresh basil**
- 1 **bottle (1 liter) club soda, chilled**

1. Place the lemon juice, sugar, strawberries and 1 cup ice cubes in a blender; cover and process until blended. Add basil; pulse 1 or 2 times to combine.
2. Divide strawberry mixture among 12 cocktail glasses. Fill with ice; top with club soda.
1 serving: 40 cal., 0 fat (0 sat. fat), 0 chol., 18mg sod., 10g carb. (9g sugars, 0 fiber), 0 pro. **Diabetic exchanges:** ½ starch.

STRAWBERRY-BASIL REFRESHER

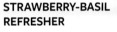

CASHEW CHEESE

CASHEW CHEESE

Spread this vegan cashew cheese on crackers, layer it on a toasted bagel or serve it with fresh veggies. It also makes a delicious, out-of-the-ordinary sandwich spread.
—*Taste of Home* Test Kitchen

- -

Prep: 1 hour + chilling • **Makes:** ¾ cup

- 1 **cup raw cashews**
- ⅓ **cup water**
- 2 **Tbsp. nutritional yeast**
- 2 **tsp. lemon juice**
- ½ **tsp. salt**
- ⅛ **tsp. garlic powder**

Place the cashews in a small bowl. Add enough warm water to cover completely. Soak the cashews for 1-2 hours; drain and discard water. Add cashews and the remaining ingredients to food processor. Cover and process until smooth, 1-2 minutes, scraping down sides occasionally. Transfer to serving dish. Cover and refrigerate for at least 1 hour before serving.

1 Tbsp.: 56 cal., 4g fat (1g sat. fat), 0 chol., 101mg sod., 3g carb. (1g sugars, 0 fiber), 2g pro. **Diabetic exchanges:** 1 fat.

DID YOU KNOW?

Cashew cheese is a non-dairy, vegan substitute for cheese. It is typically made of blended cashews, nutritional yeast, water and a blend of seasonings. You can use cashew cheese for vegan mac and cheese, as a cheese spread for crackers, or even as a substitute for cheesy vegetable soup.

FAST
FRUIT SALSA

POMEGRANATE GINGER SPRITZER

Conveniently, a pitcher of this non-alcoholic beverage can be made hours before holiday guests arrive. Add the club soda just before serving.
—*Taste of Home* Test Kitchen

- -

Prep: 10 min. + chilling
Makes: 7 servings

½   **cup sliced fresh gingerroot**
1   **medium lime, sliced**
3   **cups pomegranate juice**
¾   **cup orange juice**
3   **cups chilled club soda**
     Optional: Lime wedges, pomegranate seeds and ice

1. Place ginger and lime slices in a pitcher; stir in pomegranate and orange juices. Refrigerate overnight.
2. Just before serving, strain and discard ginger and lime. Stir club soda into juice mixture. Garnish as desired.
1 cup: 80 cal., 0 fat (0 sat. fat), 0 chol., 35mg sod., 20g carb. (17g sugars, 0 fiber), 1g pro.

FAST FRUIT SALSA

We enjoy this refreshing, colorful salsa with tortilla chips or even spooned over grilled chicken. For another fruity option, try stirring in some diced cantaloupe or peaches when they're in season.
—Eileen Miller, Woodridge, IL

- -

Takes: 10 min. • **Makes:** 1½ cups

1   **can (8 oz.) unsweetened crushed pineapple, drained**
1   **can (8 oz.) mandarin oranges, drained and chopped**
¼   **cup chopped red onion**
1   **Tbsp. minced fresh cilantro**
     Tortilla chips

In a large bowl, combine pineapple, oranges, red onion and cilantro. Cover and refrigerate until serving. Serve with tortilla chips.
¼ cup: 48 cal., 0 fat (0 sat. fat), 0 chol., 3mg sod., 13g carb. (12g sugars, 1g fiber), 0 pro.

POMEGRANATE
GINGER SPRITZER

STRAWBERRY
TOMATO SALSA

STRAWBERRY TOMATO SALSA

Here's a sweet and tangy salsa that's miles away from the spicy version people expect. Serve it as an appetizer with tortilla chips or use it to garnish your favorite chicken or pork entree.

—Amy Hinkle, Topeka, KS

Takes: 25 min. • **Makes:** 6 cups

2 pints cherry tomatoes, quartered
1 pint fresh strawberries, chopped
8 green onions, chopped
½ cup minced fresh cilantro
6 Tbsp. olive oil
2 Tbsp. balsamic vinegar
½ tsp. salt

In a large bowl, combine tomatoes, berries, green onions and cilantro. In a small bowl, whisk the oil, vinegar and salt; gently stir into the tomato mixture. Refrigerate until serving.

¼ cup: 41 cal., 4g fat (0 sat. fat), 0 chol., 53mg sod., 3g carb. (2g sugars, 1g fiber), 0 pro.

PINEAPPLE ICED TEA

We have a large family, so we go through beverages quickly at our house. This thirst-quenching tea is easy to mix together and has a sparkling citrus flavor we all enjoy.
—K. Kittell, Lenexa, KS

- -

Prep: 10 min. + chilling • **Cook:** 5 min.
Makes: 6 servings

- 4   cups water
- 7   tea bags
- 2   Tbsp. sugar
- 1   cup unsweetened
       pineapple juice
- ⅓   cup lemon juice
       Optional: Pineapple wedges,
       lemon slices and
       fresh mint leaves

1. In a large saucepan, bring water to a boil; remove from heat. Add tea bags; steep, covered, 3-5 minutes according to taste. Discard tea bags. Stir in sugar until dissolved. Transfer to a pitcher; cool slightly. Stir in the fruit juices.

2. Refrigerate, covered, overnight. Serve over ice. Garnish as desired.

1 cup: 51 cal., 0 fat (0 sat. fat), 0 chol., 1mg sod., 13g carb. (0 sugars, 0 fiber), 0 pro.
Diabetic exchanges: 1 fruit.

RASPBERRY-LIME YOGURT DIP FOR FRESH FRUIT

Fresh seasonal fruit is the essence of beauty. This yogurt dipping sauce made with sweet raspberries and tart lime juice makes a good thing even better.
—Clara Coulson Minney, Washington Court House, OH

- -

Takes: 15 min. • **Makes:** 1¾ cups

- 1   cup fresh or
        frozen raspberries,
        thawed and drained
- 1¼   cups reduced-fat
        plain Greek yogurt
- ⅓   cup packed brown sugar
- 1   Tbsp. lime juice
- ½   tsp. grated lime zest
        Assorted fresh fruit

Place raspberries in a blender; cover and process until smooth. Strain and discard seeds. In a large bowl, whisk the yogurt, brown sugar, lime juice, lime zest and raspberry puree until blended. Chill until serving. Serve with fruit.

¼ cup: 78 cal., 1g fat (0 sat. fat), 2mg chol., 23mg sod., 14g carb. (13g sugars, 0 fiber), 4g pro.
Diabetic exchanges: 1 starch.

PINEAPPLE ICED TEA

SHRIMP SALAD APPETIZERS

SHRIMP SALAD APPETIZERS

This refreshing hors d'oeuvre has gained a big following since a friend shared her family recipe with me. My son says it best: The celery and shrimp are so good together!
—Solie Kimble, Kanata, ON

- -

Takes: 15 min. • **Makes:** 2 dozen

- 1 lb. peeled and deveined cooked shrimp, chopped
- 1 can (6 oz.) lump crabmeat, drained
- 2 celery ribs, finely chopped
- ¼ cup Dijon-mayonnaise blend
- 24 Belgian endive leaves (3 to 4 heads) or small Bibb lettuce leaves Chopped fresh parsley, optional

In a large bowl, combine the shrimp, crab and celery. Add mayonnaise blend; toss to coat. To serve, top each leaf with about 2 Tbsp. shrimp mixture. If desired, top with chopped fresh parsley.

1 appetizer: 31 cal., 0 fat (0 sat. fat), 35mg chol., 115mg sod., 1g carb. (0 sugars, 0 fiber), 5g pro.

GOAT CHEESE MUSHROOMS

GOAT CHEESE MUSHROOMS

Baked stuffed mushrooms are superstars in the hot appetizer category. I use baby portobellos and load them with creamy goat cheese and sweet red peppers.
—Mike Bass, Alvin, TX

- -

Takes: 30 min. • **Makes:** 2 dozen

- 24 baby portobello mushrooms (about 1 lb.), stems removed
- ½ cup crumbled goat cheese
- ½ cup chopped drained roasted sweet red peppers
- Pepper to taste
- 4 tsp. olive oil
- Chopped fresh parsley

1. Preheat oven to 375°. Place the mushroom caps in a greased 15x10x1-in. baking pan. Fill each with 1 tsp. cheese; top each with 1 tsp. red pepper. Sprinkle with pepper; drizzle with oil.

2. Bake 15-18 minutes or until the mushrooms are tender. Sprinkle with parsley.

1 stuffed mushroom: 19 cal., 1g fat (0 sat. fat), 3mg chol., 31mg sod., 1g carb. (1g sugars, 0 fiber), 1g pro.

SMOKED SALMON CANAPES

My boyfriend's mother gave me the idea for this classy appetizer that I serve for Sunday brunch and on special occasions like New Year's Eve. The textures and flavors of the dill, cream cheese and smoked salmon are wonderful together. This dish is sure to be the toast of your tasty buffet.
—Tristin Crenshaw, Tucson, AZ

Takes: 15 min. • **Makes:** 12 servings

- 1   **pkg. (8 oz.) reduced-fat cream cheese**
- 1   **tsp. snipped fresh dill or ¼ tsp. dill weed**
- 36   **slices cocktail rye bread**
- 12   **oz. sliced smoked salmon or lox**
- 1   **medium red onion, thinly sliced and separated into rings**
       Fresh dill sprigs, optional

In a small bowl, combine the cream cheese and dill. Spread on rye bread. Top with the salmon and red onion. Garnish with dill sprigs if desired.

3 appetizers: 155 cal., 7g fat (3g sat. fat), 21mg chol., 905mg sod., 15g carb. (0 sugars, 2g fiber), 11g pro. **Diabetic exchanges:** 1 starch, 1 lean meat, ½ fat.

BALSAMIC-GOAT CHEESE GRILLED PLUMS

Make a bold statement with this simple yet elegant starter. Ripe plums are grilled and then dressed with a balsamic reduction glaze and tangy goat cheese.
—Ariana Abelow, Holliston, MA

Takes: 25 min. • **Makes:** 8 servings

- 1   **cup balsamic vinegar**
- 2   **tsp. grated lemon zest**
- 4   **medium firm plums, halved and pitted**
- ½   **cup crumbled goat cheese**

1. For glaze, in a small saucepan, combine vinegar and lemon zest; bring to a boil. Cook 10-12 minutes or until mixture is thickened and reduced to about ⅓ cup (do not overcook).

2. Grill plums, covered, over medium heat 2-3 minutes on each side or until tender. Drizzle with the glaze; top with cheese.

1 plum half with 1 Tbsp. cheese and 2 tsp. glaze: 58 cal., 2g fat (1g sat. fat), 9mg chol., 41mg sod., 9g carb. (8g sugars, 1g fiber), 2g pro. **Diabetic exchanges:** ½ starch, ½ fat.

BALSAMIC-GOAT CHEESE GRILLED PLUMS

TOASTED RAVIOLI PUFFS

TOASTED RAVIOLI PUFFS

Toasted ravioli is a fan favorite. It disappears faster than I can make it. With just five easy ingredients, this is how you start the party.

—Kathy Morgan, Temecula, CA

- -

Takes: 30 min. • **Makes:** 2 dozen

24 **refrigerated cheese ravioli**
1 **Tbsp. reduced-fat Italian salad dressing**
1 **Tbsp. Italian-style panko bread crumbs**
1 **Tbsp. grated Parmesan cheese**
   Warm marinara sauce

1. Preheat oven to 400°. Cook ravioli according to the package directions; drain. Transfer to a greased baking sheet. Brush with salad dressing. In a small bowl, mix bread crumbs and Parmesan cheese; sprinkle mixture over ravioli.

2. Bake 12-15 minutes or until golden brown. Serve with marinara sauce.

1 ravioli: 21 cal., 1g fat (0 sat. fat), 3mg chol., 43mg sod., 3g carb. (0 sugars, 0 fiber), 1g pro.

SLIM ITALIAN DEVILED EGGS

1 stuffed egg half: 49 cal., 4g fat (1g sat. fat), 62mg chol., 72mg sod., 0 carb. (0 sugars, 0 fiber), 3g pro.

SLOW-COOKED SALSA

I love the taste of homemade salsa, but as a busy working mother, I don't have much time to make it. I came up with this slow-cooked version that practically makes itself!
—Toni Menard, Lompoc, CA

- -

Prep: 15 min.
Cook: 2½ hours + cooling
Makes: about 2 cups

10	plum tomatoes
2	garlic cloves
1	small onion, cut into wedges
2	jalapeno peppers
¼	cup cilantro leaves
½	tsp. salt, optional

1. Core tomatoes. Cut a small slit in 2 tomatoes; insert a garlic clove into each slit. Place tomatoes and onion in a 3-qt. slow cooker.
2. Cut stems off jalapenos; remove the seeds if a milder salsa is desired. Place jalapenos in the slow cooker.
3. Cover and cook on high for 2½-3 hours or until vegetables are softened (some may brown slightly); cool.
4. In a blender, combine the tomato mixture, cilantro and, if desired, salt; cover and process until blended. Refrigerate leftovers.
¼ cup: 20 cal., 0 fat (0 sat. fat), 0 chol., 5mg sod., 4g carb. (3g sugars, 1g fiber), 1g pro.
Diabetic exchanges: 1 free food.

SLIM ITALIAN DEVILED EGGS

When you are in the mood for good finger food, try one of these sinfully yummy deviled eggs. They are a cinch to fill and a popular dish for a potluck.
—*Taste of Home* Test Kitchen

- -

Takes: 20 min. • **Makes:** 1 dozen

6	hard-boiled large eggs
3	Tbsp. mayonnaise
¼	tsp. dried basil
¼	tsp. dried oregano
⅛	tsp. salt
⅛	tsp. pepper
	Optional: Shredded Parmesan cheese and fresh oregano leaves

1. Cut the eggs in half lengthwise. Remove yolks; set aside egg whites and 4 yolks (discard remaining yolks or save for another use).
2. In a large bowl, mash the 4 yolks. Stir in mayonnaise, basil, oregano, salt and pepper. Stuff or pipe into the egg whites. If desired, garnish with cheese and fresh oregano leaves. Chill until serving.

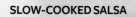
SLOW-COOKED SALSA

ICED HONEYDEW MINT TEA

ICED HONEYDEW MINT TEA

I grow mint in the garden on my balcony. For this tea, I blend two of my favorite beverages—Moroccan mint tea and honeydew agua fresca.
—Sarah Batt Throne, El Cerrito, CA

- -

Takes: 20 min. • **Makes:** 10 servings

  4   **cups water**
 24   **fresh mint leaves**
  8   **green tea bags**
 ⅔   **cup sugar**
  5   **cups diced honeydew melon**
  3   **cups ice cubes**
      Additional ice cubes

1. In a large saucepan, bring water to a boil; remove from heat. Add mint leaves and tea bags; steep, covered, 3-5 minutes according to taste, stirring occasionally. Discard mint and tea bags. Stir in sugar.
2. Place 2½ cups honeydew, 2 cups tea and 1½ cups ice in a blender; cover and process until blended. Serve over additional ice. Repeat with remaining ingredients.

1 cup: 83 cal., 0 fat (0 sat. fat), 0 chol., 15mg sod., 21g carb. (20g sugars, 1g fiber), 0 pro.
Diabetic exchanges: 1 starch, ½ fruit.

MINI ZUCCHINI PIZZAS

This low-carb snack is the perfect way to satisfy your pizza cravings.
—*Taste of Home* Test Kitchen

Takes: 20 min.
Makes: about 2 dozen

- 1 large zucchini (about 11 oz.), cut diagonally into ¼-in. slices
- ⅛ tsp. salt
- ⅛ tsp. pepper
- ⅓ cup pizza sauce
- ¾ cup shredded part-skim mozzarella cheese
- ½ cup miniature pepperoni slices
  Minced fresh basil

1. Preheat broiler. Arrange the zucchini in a single layer on a greased baking sheet. Broil 3-4 in. from heat just until crisp-tender, 1-2 minutes per side.
2. Sprinkle zucchini with salt and pepper; top with sauce, cheese and pepperoni. Broil until cheese is melted, about 1 minute. Sprinkle with basil.

1 appetizer: 29 cal., 2g fat (1g sat. fat), 5mg chol., 108mg sod., 1g carb. (1g sugars, 0 fiber), 2g pro.

MINI ZUCCHINI PIZZAS

THYME-SEA SALT CRACKERS

These homemade crackers are decidedly light and crispy. They are irresistible on their own or pair them with a sharp white cheddar.
—Jessica Wirth, Charlotte, NC

Prep: 25 min. • **Bake:** 10 min./batch
Makes: about 7 dozen

- 2½ cups all-purpose flour
- ½ cup white whole wheat flour
- 1 tsp. salt
- ¾ cup water
- ¼ cup plus 1 Tbsp. olive oil, divided
- 1 to 2 Tbsp. minced fresh thyme
- ¾ tsp. sea or kosher salt

1. Preheat oven to 375°. In a large bowl, whisk flours and salt. Gradually add water and ¼ cup oil, tossing with a fork until the dough holds together when pressed. Divide the dough into 3 portions.
2. On a lightly floured surface, roll each portion of dough to ⅛-in. thickness. Cut with a floured 1½-in. round cookie cutter. Place 1 in. apart on ungreased baking sheets. Prick each cracker with a fork; brush lightly with remaining oil. Mix thyme and sea salt; sprinkle over crackers.
3. Bake 9-11 minutes or until the bottoms are lightly browned.

1 cracker: 23 cal., 1g fat (0 sat. fat), 0 chol., 45mg sod., 3g carb. (0 sugars, 0 fiber), 0 pro.

CRAB
PHYLLO CUPS

CRAB PHYLLO CUPS

I always like a little extra chili sauce on top of these simple snacks. If you don't have any crabmeat on hand, water-packed tuna works well, too.

—Johnna Johnson, Scottsdale, AZ

- -

Takes: 20 min. • **Makes:** 2½ dozen

- ½ cup reduced-fat spreadable garden vegetable cream cheese
- ½ tsp. seafood seasoning
- ¾ cup lump crabmeat, drained
- 2 pkg. (1.9 oz. each) frozen miniature phyllo tart shells
- 5 Tbsp. chili sauce

In a small bowl, mix cream cheese and seafood seasoning; gently stir in crab. Spoon 2 tsp. crab mixture into each tart shell; top with chili sauce.

1 filled phyllo cup: 34 cal., 2g fat (0 sat. fat), 5mg chol., 103mg sod., 3g carb. (1g sugars, 0 fiber), 1g pro.

ORANGE BLOSSOM MINT REFRESHER

I came up with this recipe because I'm not a fan of regular iced tea. This tea has the perfect combo of freshness and sweetness. The orange blossom water gives it a distinctive flavor.

—Juliana Gauss, Centennial, CO

- -

Prep: 10 min. + chilling
Cook: 6 hours • **Makes:** 20 servings

- 20 cups water
- 1 bunch fresh mint (about 1 cup)
- 1 cup sugar
- 1 large navel orange

ORANGE BLOSSOM MINT REFRESHER

- 1 to 2 Tbsp. orange blossom water or 1½ to 2½ tsp. orange extract
- Optional: Orange slices and additional fresh mint

1. Place the water and mint in a 6-qt. slow cooker. Cover and cook on high until heated through, about 6 hours. Strain tea; discard mint.

2. Whisk in sugar until dissolved. Cut the orange crosswise in half; squeeze juice from the orange. Stir in juice and orange blossom water. Transfer to a pitcher. Refrigerate until cold, 4-6 hours. If desired, serve over ice with orange slices and mint.

1 cup: 43 cal., 0 fat (0 sat. fat), 0 chol., 0 sod., 11g carb. (11g sugars, 0 fiber), 0 pro.

TEST KITCHEN TIP
Orange blossom water, also called orange flower water, can be found at most specialty grocery stores or spice shops. If you use orange extract, it will add a hint of orange flavor, but the blossom water adds a unique floral note.

APRICOT-RICOTTA STUFFED CELERY

This healthful protein filling can double as a dip for sliced apples. I make it ahead, so when the kids come home, they can help themselves to a snack.
—Dorothy Reinhold, Malibu, CA

Takes: 15 min.
Makes: about 2 dozen

- 3 **dried apricots**
- ½ **cup part-skim ricotta cheese**
- 2 **tsp. brown sugar**
- ¼ **tsp. grated orange zest**
- ⅛ **tsp. salt**
- 5 **celery ribs,**
  cut into 1½-in. pieces

Place apricots in a food processor. Cover and process until finely chopped. Add the ricotta cheese, brown sugar, orange zest and salt; cover and process until blended. Stuff or pipe into the celery. Chill until serving.

1 piece: 12 cal., 0 fat (0 sat. fat), 2mg chol., 25mg sod., 1g carb. (1g sugars, 0 fiber), 1g pro.

GARLIC-HERB MINI QUICHES

Looking for a little bite to dress up the brunch buffet? These delectable tartlets are divine!
—Josephine Piro, Easton, PA

Takes: 25 min.
Makes: 45 mini quiches

- 1 **pkg. (6½ oz.) reduced-fat garlic-herb spreadable cheese**
- ¼ **cup fat-free milk**
- 2 **large eggs**
- 3 **pkg. (1.9 oz. each) frozen miniature phyllo tart shells**
- 2 **Tbsp. minced fresh parsley**
  Minced chives, optional

1. In a bowl, beat the spreadable cheese, milk and eggs. Place the tart shells on an ungreased baking sheet; fill each with 2 tsp. mixture. Sprinkle with parsley.
2. Bake at 350° for 10-12 minutes or until filling is set and shells are lightly browned. Sprinkle with chives if desired. Serve warm.

1 mini quiche: 31 cal., 2g fat (0 sat. fat), 12mg chol., 32mg sod., 2g carb. (0 sugars, 0 fiber), 1g pro.

GARLIC-HERB MINI QUICHES

GARBANZO-
STUFFED
MINI PEPPERS

GARBANZO-STUFFED MINI PEPPERS

Mini peppers are colorful and the perfect size for a two-bite snack. They have all the crunch of a pita chip without the extra calories.

—Christine Hanover, Lewiston, CA

- -

Takes: 20 min.
Makes: 32 appetizers

1	tsp. cumin seeds
1	can (15 oz.) garbanzo beans or chickpeas, rinsed and drained
¼	cup fresh cilantro leaves
3	Tbsp. water
3	Tbsp. cider vinegar
¼	tsp. salt
16	miniature sweet peppers, halved lengthwise
	Additional fresh cilantro leaves

1. In a dry small skillet, toast the cumin seeds over medium heat until aromatic, 1-2 minutes, stirring frequently. Transfer to a food processor. Add garbanzo beans, cilantro, water, vinegar and salt; pulse until blended.

2. Spoon into pepper halves. Top with additional cilantro. Refrigerate until serving.

1 appetizer: 15 cal., 0 fat (0 sat. fat), 0 chol., 36mg sod., 3g carb. (1g sugars, 1g fiber), 1g pro.

TREATS

WINTER FRUIT WITH PROSECCO SABAYON P. 251

1

2

3

4

5

EATING HEALTHIER DOESN'T MEAN YOU HAVE TO SKIP SWEETS. THESE LIGHT DESSERTS ARE DECADENT AND DELICIOUS BUT EASY ON THE WAISTLINE.

**CHEESECAKE
BERRY PARFAITS**

FLUFFY KEY LIME PIE

*For a taste of paradise, try a light
and creamy confection. It's low
in fat, sugar and fuss. Dessert
doesn't get any better than this!*
—Frances VanFossan, Warren, MI

Prep: 20 min. + chilling
Makes: 8 servings

- ¼ cup boiling water
- 1 pkg. (0.3 oz.) sugar-free
  lime gelatin
- 2 cartons (6 oz. each)
  Key lime yogurt
- 1 carton (8 oz.) frozen fat-free
  whipped topping, thawed
- 1 reduced-fat
  graham cracker crust (8 in.)

1. In a large bowl, add the boiling
water to the gelatin; stir 2 minutes
to completely dissolve. Whisk in
yogurt. Fold in whipped topping.
Pour into crust.
2. Refrigerate, covered, until set,
about 2 hours.
1 piece: 194 cal., 3g fat (1g sat. fat),
2mg chol., 159mg sod., 33g carb.
(18g sugars, 0 fiber), 3g pro.
Diabetic exchanges: 2 starch, ½ fat.

CHEESECAKE
BERRY PARFAITS

*The summer berry season is a
real treat. This is an easy way to
enjoy berries with cheesecake,
which is a refreshing change
from traditional pudding and
fruit parfaits.*
—Patricia Schroedl, Jefferson, WI

Takes: 15 min. • **Makes:** 2 parfaits

- 2 oz. cream cheese, softened
- 4 tsp. sugar
- ⅔ cup whipped topping
- 1½ cups mixed fresh berries
  Additional whipped topping,
  optional

1. In a small bowl, beat cream cheese
and sugar until smooth. Fold in the
whipped topping.
2. In each of 2 parfait glasses, layer
a fourth of the cream cheese mixture
and a fourth of the berries. Repeat
layers. Top with the additional
whipped topping if desired. Chill
until serving.
1 parfait: 146 cal., 4g fat (4g sat. fat),
0 chol., 1mg sod., 25g carb. (21g
sugars, 3g fiber), 1g pro.

FLUFFY KEY LIME PIE

CAMPFIRE PINEAPPLE UPSIDE-DOWN CAKES

We make these fun cakes while camping or sitting in the backyard around a fire. It's a yummy treat for kids and adults alike. But the sandwich iron gets hot, so adults should handle and open it.

—Cheryl Grimes, Whiteland, IN

Prep: 10 min. • **Cook:** 5 min./cake
Makes: 6 servings

- 6 **tsp. butter**
- 6 **Tbsp. brown sugar**
- 6 **canned pineapple slices**
- 6 **maraschino cherries**
- 6 **individual round sponge cakes**

1. Place 1 tsp. butter in 1 side of sandwich iron. Hold over fire to melt; remove from fire. Carefully sprinkle 1 Tbsp. brown sugar over melted butter. Top with pineapple ring; add cherry to center of pineapple. Top with cake (flat side up); close iron. Cook pineapple side down over a hot campfire until brown sugar is melted and cake is heated through, 5-8 minutes. Invert iron to open, and serve cake on an individual plate.

1 cake: 211 cal., 6g fat (3g sat. fat), 38mg chol., 214mg sod., 39g carb. (32g sugars, 1g fiber), 2g pro.

TEST KITCHEN TIP
We tested these mini cakes with both canned and fresh pineapple. Canned was the clear winner. The fresh pineapple took too long to get tender.

CRANBERRY PEAR TART

This homey tart looks and tastes like an apple pie, except it uses pears! Each serving has half the calories of an average pie slice.
—*Taste of Home* Test Kitchen

Prep: 15 min.
Bake: 30 min. + cooling
Makes: 8 servings

- 1 sheet refrigerated pie crust
- 4 cups sliced peeled fresh pears (about 4 medium)
- ⅓ cup dried cranberries
- ⅓ cup thawed apple juice concentrate
- 1 tsp. apple pie spice

1. Press crust onto the bottom and up the sides of an ungreased 9-in. tart pan with removable bottom; trim edges. Generously prick the bottom with a fork; set aside.
2. In a large skillet, cook the pears, cranberries, apple juice concentrate and apple pie spice over medium heat until pears are tender. Pour into crust. Bake at 375° until crust is golden brown, 30-35 minutes. Cool on a wire rack.

1 slice: 203 cal., 7g fat (3g sat. fat), 5mg chol., 104mg sod., 35g carb. (17g sugars, 3g fiber), 1g pro.
Diabetic exchanges: 1½ starch, 1½ fat, ½ fruit.

CRANBERRY PEAR TART

PEANUT BUTTER POPCORN BARS

If you're looking for a fun snack for kids, try these chewy popcorn treats that have a mild peanut butter taste. They're easy to mix and can be pressed into a pan to form bars or shaped into balls.
—Kathy Oswald, Wauzeka, WI

Takes: 30 min. • **Makes:** 2 dozen

- 10 cups popped popcorn
- ½ cup sugar
- ½ cup light corn syrup
- ½ cup creamy peanut butter
- ½ tsp. vanilla extract

1. Place the popcorn in a large bowl; set aside. In a saucepan over medium heat, bring the sugar and corn syrup to a boil, stirring constantly. Boil for 1 minute. Remove from the heat.
2. Stir in peanut butter and vanilla; mix well. Pour over popcorn and stir until well coated. Press into a buttered 13x9-in. pan. Cool slightly before cutting.

1 bar: 90 cal., 4g fat (1g sat. fat), 0 chol., 74mg sod., 13g carb. (8g sugars, 1g fiber), 2g pro.

> **TEST KITCHEN TIP**
> To cut down on sugar, opt for a natural peanut butter. If you prefer fresh popcorn, feel free to pop the kernels yourself on the stove.

BERRIES WITH
VANILLA CUSTARD

BERRIES WITH VANILLA CUSTARD

Here's a simple and delicious way to enjoy fresh raspberries. The homemade custard is also divine with strawberries or peaches.
—Sarah Vasques, Milford, NH

Prep: 20 min. + chilling
Makes: 4 servings

- 1 **cup half-and-half cream**
- 2 **large egg yolks**
- 2 **Tbsp. sugar**
- 2 **tsp. vanilla extract**
- 2 **cups fresh berries**

1. In a small heavy saucepan, mix cream, egg yolks and sugar. Cook and stir over low heat until mixture is just thick enough to coat a metal spoon and a thermometer reads at least 160°. Do not allow to boil.
2. Transfer to a bowl; stir in vanilla. Refrigerate, covered, until cold. Serve over fresh berries.

½ cup berries with ¼ cup sauce: 166 cal., 9g fat (5g sat. fat), 132mg chol., 34mg sod., 16g carb. (11g sugars, 4g fiber), 4g pro. **Diabetic exchanges:** 1½ fat, ½ starch, ½ fruit.

MARBLED MERINGUE HEARTS

Pretty pastel cookies are a fun way to brighten Valentine's Day, a birthday or any special occasion. Feel free to replace the vanilla with another flavor of extract, such as almond or cherry.
—Laurie Herr, Westford, VT

Prep: 25 min.
Bake: 20 min. + cooling
Makes: about 2 dozen

MARBLED MERINGUE HEARTS

- 3 **large egg whites**
- ½ **tsp. vanilla extract**
- ¼ **tsp. cream of tartar**
- ¾ **cup sugar**
  Red food coloring

1. Place egg whites in a large bowl; let stand at room temperature for 30 minutes. Line baking sheets with parchment.
2. Preheat oven to 200°. Add vanilla and cream of tartar to egg whites; beat on medium speed until soft peaks form. Gradually beat in sugar, 1 Tbsp. at a time, on high until stiff peaks form. Remove ¼ cup and tint pink. Lightly swirl pink mixture into remaining meringue. Fill pastry bag with meringue. Pipe 2-in. heart shapes 2 in. apart onto prepared baking sheets.
3. Bake until set and dry, about 20 minutes. Turn oven off; leave meringues in oven until oven has completely cooled. Store in an airtight container.

1 meringue: 27 cal., 0 fat (0 sat. fat), 0 chol., 7mg sod., 6g carb. (6g sugars, 0 fiber), 0 pro.

PEPPERMINT MERINGUES

Peppermint lovers won't be able to get enough of these light and airy delights. They make terrific Christmas gifts or lovely treats to pass around when guests drop in.

—Dixie Terry, Goreville, IL

Prep: 10 min.
Bake: 1½ hours + cooling
Makes: about 1½ dozen

- 2   large egg whites, room temperature
- ⅛   tsp. salt
- ⅛   tsp. cream of tartar
- ½   cup sugar
- 2   peppermint candy canes, crushed

1. In a bowl, beat the egg whites until foamy. Sprinkle with salt and cream of tartar; beat until soft peaks form. Gradually add sugar, beating until stiff peaks form, about 7 minutes. Drop by teaspoonfuls onto ungreased foil or paper-lined baking sheets; sprinkle with the crushed candy.

2. Bake at 225° for 1½ hours. Turn off heat; leave the cookies in the oven with the door ajar until cool, for at least 1 hour. Store in an airtight container.

1 meringue: 32 cal., 0 fat (0 sat. fat), 0 chol., 23mg sod., 8g carb. (7g sugars, 0 fiber), 0 pro. **Diabetic exchanges:** ½ starch.

GRILLED STONE FRUITS WITH BALSAMIC SYRUP

Hot off the grill, this late-summer stone-fruit dessert practically melts in your mouth.

—Sonya Labbe, West Hollywood, CA

Takes: 20 min. • **Makes:** 4 servings

- ½   cup balsamic vinegar
- 2   Tbsp. brown sugar
- 2   medium peaches, peeled and halved
- 2   medium nectarines, peeled and halved
- 2   medium plums, peeled and halved

1. In a small saucepan, combine vinegar and brown sugar. Bring to a boil; cook until liquid is reduced by half.

2. On a lightly oiled grill rack, grill the peaches, nectarines and plums, covered, over medium heat or broil 4 in. from heat until tender, 3-4 minutes on each side.

3. Slice fruits; arrange on a serving plate. Drizzle with sauce.

1 serving: 114 cal., 1g fat (0 sat. fat), 0 chol., 10mg sod., 28g carb. (24g sugars, 2g fiber), 2g pro. **Diabetic exchanges:** 1 starch, 1 fruit.

GRILLED
STONE FRUITS WITH
BALSAMIC SYRUP

CHOCOLATE-AVOCADO MOUSSE

CHOCOLATE-AVOCADO MOUSSE

I have rheumatoid arthritis and follow a special diet to help manage my symptoms. This recipe is simple to make, tastes heavenly and helps to reduce inflammation. I like it frozen, too.
—Kelly Kirby, Mill Bay, BC

- -

Prep: 5 min. + chilling
Makes: 4 servings

¼ cup refrigerated sweetened coconut milk
¼ cup maple syrup
¼ tsp. vanilla extract
2 medium ripe avocados, peeled and pitted
¼ cup baking cocoa

Place all ingredients in a blender; cover and process until smooth. Transfer to 4 dessert dishes. Refrigerate until serving, at least 2 hours.

⅓ cup: 181 cal., 11g fat (1g sat. fat), 0 chol., 8mg sod., 22g carb. (12g sugars, 6g fiber), 2g pro.

TEST KITCHEN TIP
Feel free to swap in honey or agave syrup for the maple syrup. Just don't use granulated sugar or you'll end up with a slightly gritty texture. If you are following a paleo diet, stick with maple syrup or honey for the sweeteners and use unsweetened almond milk. You may need to double the amount of maple syrup, but taste the mousse as you're mixing and add only as much as you want.

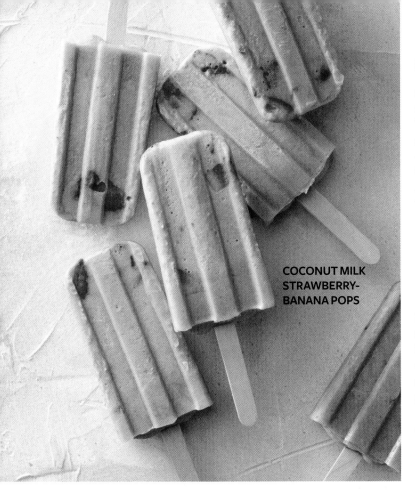

COCONUT MILK STRAWBERRY-BANANA POPS

APPLE YOGURT PARFAITS

Get the morning started right with this super simple parfait. Try it with chunky or flavored applesauce for easy variations.
—Rebekah Radewahn, Wauwatosa, WI

Takes: 10 min. • **Makes:** 4 servings

- 1 cup sweetened applesauce
     Dash ground nutmeg
- ½ cup granola with raisins
- 1⅓ cups vanilla yogurt

In a small bowl, combine applesauce and nutmeg. Spoon 1 Tbsp. granola into each of 4 parfait glasses. Layer each with ⅓ cup yogurt and ¼ cup applesauce; sprinkle with remaining granola. Serve immediately.

1 parfait: 158 cal., 2g fat (1g sat. fat), 4mg chol., 70mg sod., 30g carb. (24g sugars, 1g fiber), 5g pro.

COCONUT MILK STRAWBERRY-BANANA POPS

These four-ingredient freezer pops are a delicious way to use up a pint of fresh strawberries. You'll love the hint of tropical flavor, thanks to the coconut milk.
—*Taste of Home* Test Kitchen

Prep: 10 min. + freezing
Makes: 12 servings

- 1 **can (13.66 oz.) coconut milk**
- 1 **pint fresh strawberries, chopped, divided**
- 1 **medium banana, sliced**
- 2 **Tbsp. maple syrup**
- 12 **freezer pop molds or 12 paper cups (3 oz. each) and wooden pop sticks**

Place the coconut milk, 1½ cups strawberries, banana and syrup in a blender; cover and process until smooth. Divide the remaining strawberries among 12 molds or paper cups. Pour pureed mixture into molds or cups, filling ¾ full. Top molds with holders. If using cups, top with foil and insert sticks through foil. Freeze until firm, at least 4 hours.

1 pop: 51 cal., 3g fat (3g sat. fat), 0 chol., 5mg sod., 7g carb. (5g sugars, 1g fiber), 1g pro.

APPLE
YOGURT
PARFAITS

TREATS

STRAWBERRY-
HAZELNUT
MERINGUE
SHORTCAKES

STRAWBERRY-HAZELNUT MERINGUE SHORTCAKES

In summer the strawberry farms are open for picking. I serve strawberries with a crunchy hazelnut meringue cookie.

—Barbara Estabrook, Appleton, WI

Prep: 25 min.
Bake: 45 min. + cooling
Makes: 8 servings

- 2 **large egg whites**
- ½ **cup sugar**
- ¼ **cup finely chopped hazelnuts**
- 6 **cups fresh strawberries, hulled and sliced**
- 4 **cups low-fat frozen yogurt**

1. Place egg whites in a small bowl; let stand at room temperature for 30 minutes.

2. Preheat oven to 250°. Beat the egg whites on medium speed until foamy. Gradually add sugar, 1 Tbsp. at a time, beating on high after each addition until the sugar is dissolved. Continue beating until stiff glossy peaks form.

3. Using a measuring cup and spatula or an ice cream scoop, drop the meringue into 8 even mounds on a parchment-lined baking sheet. With the back of a spoon, shape into 3-in. cups. Sprinkle with hazelnuts. Bake 45-50 minutes or until set and dry. Turn off oven (do not open the oven door); leave meringues in oven 1 hour. Remove from the oven; cool completely on the baking sheets. Remove meringues from paper.

4. Place 3 cups strawberries in a large bowl; mash slightly. Stir in remaining strawberries. Just before serving, top meringues with frozen yogurt and strawberries.

1 serving: 212 cal., 4g fat (1g sat. fat), 5mg chol., 74mg sod., 40g carb. (36g sugars, 3g fiber), 7g pro.

CHOCOLATY S'MORES BARS

One night my husband had some friends over to play poker and he requested these s'mores bars. They polished off the pan and asked for more! I shared the recipe, and now their families make them, too.

—Rebecca Shipp, Beebe, AR

- -

Prep: 15 min. + cooling
Makes: 1½ dozen

- ¼ cup butter, cubed
- 1 pkg. (10 oz.) large marshmallows
- 1 pkg. (12 oz.) Golden Grahams cereal
- ⅓ cup milk chocolate chips, melted

1. In a large saucepan, melt butter over low heat. Add marshmallows; cook and stir until blended. Remove from heat. Stir in cereal until coated.
2. Press into a greased 13x9-in. pan using a buttered spatula. Drizzle with melted chocolate. Cool completely before cutting. Store in an airtight container.

1 bar: 159 cal., 4g fat (2g sat. fat), 7mg chol., 197mg sod., 30g carb. (17g sugars, 1g fiber), 1g pro.

TEST KITCHEN TIP
There are so many fun ways to enjoy these bars. For a peanuty twist, add ¼ cup of peanut butter to the marshmallow mixture and stir a handful of chopped peanuts into the cereal. Chocolate lovers can drizzle a combo of melted white and milk chocolate on top. Or use one of these bars (halved lengthwise) instead of a graham cracker to make a traditional s'more.

BANANA-PINEAPPLE ICE

My family loves dessert, but we are trying to make healthier food choices. This low-calorie summer treat is always a hit.

—Myra Hughes, Malvern, AR

- -

Prep: 15 min. + freezing
Makes: 10 servings

- 2 cups unsweetened apple juice
- 2 cups mashed ripe bananas
- 1 can (8 oz.) unsweetened crushed pineapple, undrained
- 2 Tbsp. lemon juice
- 1 tsp. vanilla extract

1. In a large bowl, combine all of the ingredients. Pour into an 8-in. square dish. Cover and freeze for 1½-2 hours or until almost firm.
2. Transfer to a large bowl. Beat for 1-2 minutes or until smooth and creamy. Return mixture to dish; freeze until firm. Remove from the freezer 30 minutes before serving.

½ cup: 79 cal., 0 fat (0 sat. fat), 0 chol., 2mg sod., 20g carb. (14g sugars, 1g fiber), 1g pro.

CHOCOLATY S'MORES BARS

**ARCTIC
ORANGE PIE**

ARCTIC ORANGE PIE

Looking for a frosty treat on a warm summer day? This easy pie delivers cool relief. I have tried lemonade, mango and pineapple juice concentrates in place of the orange, and we love each one.
—Marie Przepierski, Erie, PA

- -

Prep: 20 min. + freezing
Makes: 8 servings

- 1 pkg. (8 oz.) fat-free cream cheese
- 1 can (6 oz.) frozen orange juice concentrate, thawed
- 1 carton (8 oz.) frozen reduced-fat whipped topping, thawed
- 1 reduced-fat graham cracker crust (8 in.)
- 1 can (11 oz.) mandarin oranges, drained

In a large bowl, beat cream cheese and orange juice concentrate until smooth. Fold in whipped topping; pour into crust. Cover and freeze for 4 hours or until firm. Remove from the freezer about 10 minutes before cutting. Garnish with the mandarin oranges.
1 piece: 248 cal., 7g fat (4g sat. fat), 3mg chol., 298mg sod., 35g carb. (24g sugars, 0 fiber), 6g pro.

EASY LEMON BERRY TARTLETS

EASY LEMON BERRY TARTLETS

These fruity, flaky tartlets filled with raspberries and topped with a lemon-tinged cream cheese are a sweet ending to any weeknight meal. They are elegant yet easy and come together quickly.
—Elizabeth Dehart, West Jordan, UT

- -

Takes: 15 min. • **Makes:** 15 tartlets

- ⅔ cup frozen unsweetened raspberries, thawed and drained
- 1 tsp. confectioners' sugar
- 1 pkg. (1.9 oz.) frozen miniature phyllo tart shells
- 4 oz. reduced-fat cream cheese
- 2 Tbsp. lemon curd
     Fresh raspberries, optional

1. In a small bowl, combine the raspberries and confectioners' sugar; mash with a fork. Spoon into tart shells.
2. In a small bowl, combine cream cheese and lemon curd. Pipe or spoon over filling. Top with fresh raspberries if desired.
1 tartlet: 51 cal., 3g fat (1g sat. fat), 7mg chol., 43mg sod., 5g carb. (2g sugars, 0 fiber), 1g pro. **Diabetic exchanges:** ½ starch, ½ fat.

WHITE CHOCOLATE CEREAL BARS

A friend shared with me this fresh take on traditional crispy treats. My husband loves them.
—Anne Powers, Munford, AL

- -

Takes: 15 min.
Makes: about 3 dozen

    4   cups miniature
        marshmallows
    8   oz. white baking chips
        (about 1⅓ cups)
    ¼   cup butter, cubed
    6   cups crisp rice cereal

1. In a Dutch oven, combine the marshmallows, baking chips and butter. Cook and stir over medium-low heat until melted. Remove from heat. Add cereal; stir to coat.
2. Transfer to a greased 13x9-in. pan; gently press mixture evenly into pan. Cut into bars.
1 bar: 79 cal., 3g fat (2g sat. fat), 3mg chol., 58mg sod., 13g carb. (8g sugars, 0 fiber), 0 pro.

TEST KITCHEN TIP
To make White Chocolate Cereal Eggs, pack the cereal mixture into egg molds or clean 2-piece plastic eggs to help form the egg shape. If desired, decorate with sprinkles.

PATRIOTIC POPS

My kids love homemade ice pops, and I love knowing that the ones we make are good for them. We whip up a big batch with multiple flavors so they have choices, but these patriotic red, white and blue ones are always a favorite!
—Shannon Carino, Frisco, TX

- -

Prep: 15 min. + freezing
Makes: 1 dozen

    1¾ cups vanilla yogurt, divided
    2   Tbsp. honey, divided
    1¼ cups sliced fresh
        strawberries, divided
    1¼ cups fresh or frozen
        blueberries, thawed, divided
    12 freezer pop molds or
        12 paper cups (3 oz. each)
        and wooden pop sticks

1. Place 2 Tbsp. yogurt, 1 Tbsp. honey and 1 cup strawberries in a blender; cover and process until blended. Remove to a small bowl. Chop remaining strawberries; stir into strawberry mixture.
2. In the blender, process 2 Tbsp. yogurt, the remaining honey and 1 cup blueberries until blended; remove to another bowl. Stir in remaining blueberries.
3. In each mold, layer 1 Tbsp. strawberry mixture, 2 Tbsp. yogurt and 1 Tbsp. blueberry mixture. Top with holders. (If using paper cups, top with foil and insert sticks through the foil.) Freeze until firm.
1 pop: 55 cal., 1g fat (0 sat. fat), 2mg chol., 24mg sod., 11g carb. (10g sugars, 1g fiber), 2g pro.

PATRIOTIC POPS

**BLUEBERRY PIE
WITH GRAHAM
CRACKER CRUST**

BLUEBERRY PIE WITH GRAHAM CRACKER CRUST

We live in blueberry country, and this traditional pie is a perfect way to showcase these luscious berries. A neighbor first made this pie for us when we had a death in the family several years ago. Our whole family enjoys it.
—R. Ricks, Kalamazoo, MI

- -

Prep: 20 min. + chilling
Makes: 8 servings

¾   cup sugar
3   Tbsp. cornstarch
⅛   tsp. salt
¼   cup water
4   cups fresh blueberries, divided
1   graham cracker crust (9 in.)
     Whipped cream

1. In a large saucepan, combine the sugar, cornstarch and salt. Gradually add water, stirring until smooth. Stir in 2 cups of blueberries. Bring to a boil; cook and stir until thickened,

1-2 minutes. Remove from heat; cool to room temperature.
2. Gently stir remaining blueberries into the cooled blueberry mixture. Spoon into the crust. Refrigerate, covered, until chilled, 1-2 hours. Serve with whipped cream.

1 piece: 230 cal., 6g fat (1g sat. fat), 0 chol., 159mg sod., 46g carb. (35g sugars, 2g fiber), 1g pro.

FROSTY WATERMELON ICE

4 serving dishes; freeze, covered, until firm. Remove from freezer 15-20 minutes before serving.

¾ cup: 81 cal., 0 fat (0 sat. fat), 0 chol., 3mg sod., 21g carb. (18g sugars, 1g fiber), 1g pro. **Diabetic exchanges:** 1 fruit, ½ starch.

FRUITY CEREAL BARS

With the dried apples and cranberries, these cereal bars are perfect for snacks or brown-bag lunches.
—Giovanna Kranenberg, Cambridge, MN

Takes: 20 min. • **Makes:** 20 servings

- 3 **Tbsp. butter**
- 1 **pkg. (10 oz.) large marshmallows**
- ½ **cup dried cranberries**
- ½ **cup chopped dried apples**
- 6 **cups Rice Krispies**

1. In a large saucepan, melt butter over low heat. Add marshmallows; cook and stir until blended. Remove from heat; stir in the remaining ingredients.
2. Press into a 13x9-in. pan coated with cooking spray; cool completely. Cut into squares.

1 bar: 111 cal., 2g fat (1g sat. fat), 5mg chol., 73mg sod., 24g carb. (13g sugars, 0 fiber), 1g pro. **Diabetic exchanges:** 1½ starch, ½ fat.

FROSTY WATERMELON ICE

Here's a fun twist on watermelon. It's refreshing, and you don't have to worry about seeds while you're enjoying it.
—Kaaren Jurack, Manassas, VA

Prep: 20 min. + freezing
Makes: 4 servings

- 1 **tsp. unflavored gelatin**
- 2 **Tbsp. water**
- 2 **Tbsp. lime juice**
- 2 **Tbsp. honey**
- 4 **cups cubed seedless watermelon, divided**

1. In a microwave-safe bowl, sprinkle the gelatin over water; let stand for 1 minute. Microwave on high for 40 seconds. Stir and let stand until the gelatin is completely dissolved, 1-2 minutes.
2. Place the lime juice, honey and gelatin mixture in a blender. Add 1 cup watermelon; cover and process until blended. Add the remaining watermelon, 1 cup at a time, processing until smooth after each addition.
3. Transfer to a shallow dish; freeze until almost firm. In a chilled bowl, beat with an electric mixer until the mixture is bright pink. Divide among

FRUITY CEREAL BARS

COOKOUT CARAMEL S'MORES

These classic treats make a fabulous finish to an informal meal. Toasting the marshmallows extends our after-dinner time together, giving us something fun to do as a family.
—Martha Haseman, Hinckley, IL

- -

Takes: 10 min. • **Makes:** 4 servings

- **4   whole graham crackers, halved**
- **8   large marshmallows, toasted**
- **2   tsp. hot caramel ice cream topping, warmed if necessary**
- **2   tsp. chocolate syrup**

Top 4 graham cracker halves with toasted marshmallows. Drizzle with the caramel topping and chocolate syrup; top with remaining crackers.
1 s'more: 127 cal., 2g fat (0 sat. fat), 0 chol., 119mg sod., 28g carb. (16g sugars, 1g fiber), 1g pro.

BLACKBERRY-TOPPED SPONGE CAKES

The recipe for my blackberry cakes is easy to make your own. You can replace the sponge cake with angel food, pound cake or ladyfingers. And any fruit that has a counterpart liquor can be used.
—Karen Robinson, Woodbury, CT

- -

Takes: 25 min. • **Makes:** 6 servings

- **6   individual round sponge cakes**
- **4   cups fresh blackberries**
- **¼   cup blackberry brandy**
- **1¼ tsp. sugar**
-     **Whipped cream, optional**

1. Place sponge cakes on serving plates. Top each with 3 blackberries. Place the remaining blackberries in a food processor; process until pureed. Strain and discard seeds and pulp.
2. Transfer the puree to a small saucepan. Stir in brandy and sugar. Bring to a boil; cook until liquid is reduced by half, stirring occasionally. Pour over berries. If desired, top with whipped cream.
1 fruit-topped sponge cake: 141 cal., 2g fat (1g sat. fat), 28mg chol., 181mg sod., 26g carb. (15g sugars, 5g fiber), 3g pro. **Diabetic exchanges:** 1 starch, 1 fruit.

CHOCOLATE-DIPPED STRAWBERRY MERINGUE ROSES

Enjoy these kid-friendly treats as is or crush them into a bowl of strawberries and whipped cream. Readers of my blog, utry.it, *went nuts when I posted this recipe!*
—Amy Tong, Anaheim, CA

Prep: 25 min.
Bake: 40 min. + cooling
Makes: 2 dozen

3   **large egg whites**
¼   **cup sugar**
¼   **cup freeze-dried strawberries**
1   **pkg. (3 oz.) strawberry gelatin**
½   **tsp. vanilla extract, optional**
1   **cup 60% cacao bittersweet chocolate baking chips, melted**

1. Place egg whites in a large bowl; let stand at room temperature for 30 minutes. Preheat oven to 225°.
2. Place the sugar and freeze-dried strawberries in a food processor; process berries until powdery. Add gelatin; pulse to blend.
3. Beat egg whites on medium speed until foamy, adding vanilla if desired. Gradually add the gelatin mixture, 1 Tbsp. at a time, beating on high after each addition until the sugar is dissolved. Continue beating until stiff glossy peaks form.
4. Cut a small hole in the tip of a pastry bag; insert a #1M star tip. Transfer meringue to bag. Pipe 2-in. roses 1½ in. apart onto parchment-lined baking sheets.
5. Bake meringues until set and dry, 40-45 minutes. Turn off oven (do not open oven door); leave in oven 1½ hours. Remove from oven; cool completely on baking sheets.
6. Remove meringues from paper. Dip bottoms in melted chocolate; allow excess to drip off. Place on waxed paper; let stand until set, about 45 minutes. Store in an airtight container at room temperature.
1 meringue: 33 cal., 1g fat (1g sat. fat), 0 chol., 9mg sod., 6g carb. (5g sugars, 0 fiber), 1g pro. **Diabetic exchanges:** ½ starch.

RASPBERRY SORBET

With an abundant crop of fresh raspberries from the backyard, I rely on this recipe for a tasty frozen dessert that couldn't be simpler.
—Karen Bailey, Golden, CO

Prep: 5 min. + freezing
Makes: 6 servings

¼   **cup plus 1½ tsp. fresh lemon juice**
3¾   **cups fresh or frozen unsweetened raspberries**
2¼   **cups confectioners' sugar**

Place all ingredients in a blender or food processor; cover and process until smooth. Transfer to a freezer container; freeze until firm.
1 serving: 216 cal., 0 fat (0 sat. fat), 0 chol., 1mg sod., 55g carb. (46g sugars, 5g fiber), 1g pro.

CHOCOLATE-DIPPED STRAWBERRY MERINGUE ROSES

FROZEN
CHOCOLATE
MONKEY TREATS

FROZEN CHOCOLATE MONKEY TREATS

These rich banana bites are nutty and yummy.

—Susan Hein, Burlington, WI

- -

Prep: 20 min. + freezing
Makes: 1½ dozen

- 3 **medium bananas**
- 1 **cup dark chocolate chips**
- 2 **tsp. shortening**
  Optional toppings: Chopped peanuts, toasted sweetened shredded coconut and/or colored jimmies

1. Cut each banana crosswise into 6 pieces (about 1 in. thick). Insert a toothpick into each piece; transfer to a waxed paper-lined baking sheet. Freeze until completely firm, about 1 hour.

2. In a microwave, melt chocolate and shortening; stir until smooth. Dip banana pieces in chocolate mixture; allow excess to drip off. Dip in toppings as desired; return to baking sheet. Freeze at least 30 minutes before serving.

1 treat: 72 cal., 4g fat (2g sat. fat), 0 chol., 0 sod., 10g carb. (7g sugars, 1g fiber), 1g pro.

PEAR BUNDT CAKE

Finely chopped pears and syrup add sweet flavor and prevent the cake from drying out. And since there's no oil added to the batter, this cake is surprisingly low in fat.

—Veronica Ross,
Columbia Heights, MN

- -

Prep: 15 min.
Bake: 50 min. + cooling
Makes: 16 servings

PEAR BUNDT CAKE

- 1 **can (15 oz.) reduced-sugar sliced pears**
- 1 **pkg. white cake mix (regular size)**
- 2 **large egg whites, room temperature**
- 1 **large egg, room temperature**
- 2 **tsp. confectioners' sugar**

1. Drain pears, reserving the syrup; chop pears. Place pears and syrup in a large bowl; add the cake mix, egg whites and egg. Beat on low speed for 30 seconds. Beat on high for 4 minutes.

2. Coat a 10-in. fluted tube pan with cooking spray and dust with flour. Add batter.

3. Bake at 350° until a toothpick inserted in the center comes out clean, 50-55 minutes. Cool for 10 minutes before removing from the pan to a wire rack to cool completely. Dust with the confectioners' sugar.

1 slice: 149 cal., 3g fat (1g sat. fat), 12mg chol., 232mg sod., 28g carb. (16g sugars, 0 fiber), 2g pro.
Diabetic exchanges: 2 starch, ½ fat.

MARVELOUS MELON

Kids love these cantaloupe wedges filled with fruit-flavored gelatin and fresh strawberries. Even guests are impressed with this colorful dish. I experiment with other combinations of melons, gelatin and fruit, too.
—Jillian Surman, Wisconsin Dells, WI

- -

Prep: 15 min. + chilling
Makes: 6 servings

1 large cantaloupe
1 pkg. (3 oz.) strawberry banana gelatin
1 cup boiling water
½ cup unsweetened applesauce
1 cup sliced fresh strawberries

1. Cut melon in half lengthwise from bud to stem end; discard seeds. Cut a thin slice off the bottom of each half so melon sits level; pat dry.
2. In a large bowl, dissolve gelatin in boiling water. Stir in applesauce and strawberries. Pour into the melon halves (discard any remaining gelatin mixture or save for another use).
3. Cover and refrigerate overnight. Just before serving, slice each melon half into 3 wedges.
1 serving: 72 cal., 0 fat (0 sat. fat), 0 chol., 21mg sod., 17g carb. (0 sugars, 2g fiber), 2g pro.
Diabetic exchanges: 1 fruit.

CHEWY COCONUT MACAROONS

These chewy cookies are my husband's favorite. He requests them often. I like to make the macaroons on cold winter days and keep them in an airtight bowl on the kitchen counter. They never last long!
—Peggy Key, Grant, AL

- -

Prep: 10 min. • **Bake:** 20 min./batch
Makes: 32 cookies

2½ cups sweetened shredded coconut
¾ cup all-purpose flour
⅛ tsp. salt
1 can (14 oz.) fat-free sweetened condensed milk
1½ tsp. almond extract

1. In a bowl, toss the coconut, flour and salt. Stir in the milk and extract until blended (mixture will be thick and sticky).
2. Drop by level tablespoonfuls 3 in. apart onto lightly greased baking sheets. Bake at 300° just until golden brown, 18-22 minutes. Cool for 2 minutes before removing from pans to wire racks.
1 cookie: 83 cal., 3g fat (2g sat. fat), 2mg chol., 41mg sod., 13g carb. (11g sugars, 0 fiber), 1g pro.
Diabetic exchanges: 1 starch, ½ fat.

CHEWY COCONUT MACAROONS

FROZEN GREEK
VANILLA YOGURT

FROZEN GREEK VANILLA YOGURT

It's easy to make your own frozen Greek yogurt—you might even want to get the kids in on the fun.
—*Taste of Home* Test Kitchen

Prep: 15 min+ chilling
Process: 15 min+ freezing
Makes: 2½ cups

3 cups reduced-fat plain Greek yogurt
¾ cup sugar
1½ tsp. vanilla extract
1 Tbsp. cold water
1 Tbsp. lemon juice
1 tsp. unflavored gelatin

1. Line a strainer or colander with 4 layers of cheesecloth or 1 coffee filter; place over a bowl. Place the yogurt in prepared strainer; cover yogurt with sides of cheesecloth. Refrigerate 2-4 hours.
2. Remove yogurt from cheesecloth to a bowl; discard the strained liquid. Add the sugar and vanilla to yogurt, stirring until sugar is dissolved.
3. In a small microwave-safe bowl, combine cold water and lemon juice; sprinkle with gelatin and let stand 1 minute. Microwave on high for 30 seconds. Stir and let the mixture stand 1 minute or until the gelatin is completely dissolved; cool slightly. Stir the gelatin mixture into yogurt.

Cover and refrigerate until cold, about 40 minutes.
4. Pour the yogurt mixture into the cylinder of ice cream maker; freeze according to the manufacturer's directions.
5. Transfer frozen yogurt to a freezer container. Freeze 2-4 hours or until firm enough to scoop.
½ cup: 225 cal., 3g fat (2g sat. fat), 8mg chol., 57mg sod., 36g carb. (36g sugars, 0 fiber), 14g pro.

STRAWBERRY SORBET SENSATION

HEALTHY PEANUT BUTTER COOKIES

Only four ingredients and one bowl are needed for these healthy peanut butter cookies. If you want to make this recipe gluten free, make sure the oat bran was made in a certified gluten-free facility.
—*Taste of Home* Test Kitchen

- -

Prep: 15 min. • **Bake:** 15 min./batch
Makes: 2 dozen

- 1 **large egg, beaten**
- 1 **cup creamy peanut butter**
- ¼ **cup oat bran**
- ¼ **cup maple syrup**

1. In a large bowl, mix all ingredients. Roll level tablespoons into balls. Place on ungreased baking sheets; flatten with a fork.
2. Bake at 350° for 15 minutes. Remove to a wire rack to cool.

1 cookie: 78 cal., 6g fat (1g sat. fat), 8mg chol., 49mg sod., 5g carb. (3g sugars, 1g fiber), 3g pro.

STRAWBERRY SORBET SENSATION

On hot days, we chill out with slices of this refreshing dessert. The layered effect is so much fun. Use any flavor of sorbet you like.
—Kendra Doss,
Colorado Springs, CO

- -

Prep: 20 min. + freezing
Makes: 8 servings

- 2 **cups strawberry sorbet, softened if necessary**
- 1 **cup cold fat-free milk**
- 1 **pkg. (1 oz.) sugar-free instant vanilla pudding mix**
- 1 **carton (8 oz.) frozen reduced-fat whipped topping, thawed**
  Sliced fresh strawberries

1. Line an 8x4-in. loaf pan with plastic wrap. Spread sorbet into bottom of pan; place in freezer 15 minutes.
2. In a bowl, whisk the milk and pudding mix 2 minutes. Let stand until soft-set, about 2 minutes. Fold in the whipped topping; spread over the sorbet. Freeze, covered, 4 hours or overnight.
3. Remove sorbet from the freezer 10-15 minutes before serving. Invert dessert onto a serving plate; remove plastic wrap. Cut into slices. Serve with strawberries.

1 slice: 153 cal., 3g fat (3g sat. fat), 1mg chol., 163mg sod., 27g carb. (18g sugars, 2g fiber), 1g pro.
Diabetic exchanges: 2 starch, ½ fat.

HEALTHY PEANUT
BUTTER COOKIES

FIRST-PLACE COCONUT MACAROONS

FIRST-PLACE COCONUT MACAROONS

These coconut macaroons are my husband's favorite cookie and earned me a first-place ribbon at the county fair. I especially like the fact that this recipe makes a small enough batch for the two of us to nibble on without lots left over.

—Penny Ann Habeck, Shawano, WI

- -

Prep: 10 min. • **Bake:** 20 min./batch
Makes: about 1½ dozen

1⅓ cups sweetened
    shredded coconut

⅓ cup sugar
2 Tbsp. all-purpose flour
⅛ tsp. salt
2 large egg whites,
    room temperature
½ tsp. vanilla extract

1. In a small bowl, combine the coconut, sugar, flour and salt. Add egg whites and vanilla; mix well.
2. Drop by rounded teaspoonfuls onto greased baking sheets. Bake at 325° for 18-20 minutes or until golden brown. Cool on a wire rack.
1 cookie: 54 cal., 2g fat (2g sat. fat), 0 chol., 41mg sod., 8g carb. (7g sugars, 0 fiber), 1g pro.

TEST KITCHEN TIP
You can use unsweetened coconut if you prefer. Your cookies won't be quite as sweet, but they will be crispier. You can also mix in additions like nuts or mini chocolate chips.

POMEGRANATE-CRANBERRY SALAD

Juicy pomegranate seeds give cranberry gelatin a refreshing twist. For the crowning touch, add whipped topping and a sprinkling of pecans.

—Lorie Mckinney, Marion, NC

- -

Prep: 15 min. + chilling
Makes: 8 servings

- 1 pkg. (.3 oz.) sugar-free cranberry gelatin
- 1 cup boiling water
- ½ cup cold water
- 1⅔ cups pomegranate seeds
- 1 can (14 oz.) whole-berry cranberry sauce
- 1 can (8 oz.) unsweetened crushed pineapple, drained
- ¾ cup chopped pecans
  Optional: Frozen whipped topping, thawed, and additional chopped pecans

In a large bowl, dissolve gelatin in boiling water. Add cold water; stir. Add the pomegranate seeds, cranberry sauce, pineapple and pecans. Pour into a 1½-qt. serving bowl. Refrigerate for 4-5 hours or until firm. If desired, top with whipped topping and additional chopped pecans.

¾ cup : 190 cal., 8g fat (1g sat. fat), 0 chol., 41mg sod., 30g carb. (21g sugars, 2g fiber), 2g pro. **Diabetic exchanges:** 1½ fat, 1 starch, 1 fruit.

MAKEOVER TOFFEE CRUNCH DESSERT

I cut 90% of the fat and nearly half the calories from one of my most-loved desserts. Try it for yourself. Guests will never suspect that the fluffy layered specialty is on the light side.

—Kim Belcher, Kingston Mines, IL

- -

Prep: 20 min. + chilling
Makes: 15 servings

- 1½ cups cold fat-free milk
- 1 pkg. (1 oz.) sugar-free instant vanilla pudding mix
- 2 cartons (8 oz. each) frozen fat-free whipped topping, thawed
- 1 prepared angel food cake (8 to 10 oz.), cut into 1-in. cubes
- 4 Butterfinger candy bars (2.1 oz. each), crushed

1. In a large bowl, whisk milk and pudding mix 2 minutes. Let stand 2 minutes or until soft-set. Stir in 2 cups whipped topping. Fold in remaining whipped topping.

2. In a 13x9-in. dish coated with cooking spray, layer half the cake cubes, pudding mixture and crushed candy bars. Repeat layers. Cover and refrigerate at least 2 hours before serving.

¾ cup: 177 cal., 3g fat (2g sat. fat), 0 chol., 255mg sod., 33g carb. (12g sugars, 1g fiber), 3g pro. **Diabetic exchanges:** 2 starch, ½ fat.

POMEGRANATE-CRANBERRY SALAD

OLD-FASHIONED
TAPIOCA

OLD-FASHIONED TAPIOCA

My family loves classic tapioca, but I don't always have time to make it. So I came up with this simple recipe. It lets us enjoy one of our favorites without all the hands-on time.
—Ruth Peters, Bel Air, MD

- -

Prep: 10 min. • **Cook:** 4½ hours
Makes: 18 servings

- 8 **cups 2% milk**
- 1 **cup pearl tapioca**
- 1 **cup plus 2 Tbsp. sugar**
- ⅛ **tsp. salt**
- 4 **large eggs**
- 1½ **tsp. vanilla extract**
  Optional: Sliced fresh strawberries and whipped cream

SONORAN SUNSET WATERMELON ICE

1. In a 4- to 5-qt. slow cooker, combine the milk, tapioca, sugar and salt. Cover and cook on low for 4-5 hours.
2. In a large bowl, beat the eggs; stir in a small amount of the hot tapioca mixture. Return all to the slow cooker, stirring to combine. Cover and cook 30 minutes longer or until a thermometer reads 160°. Stir in the vanilla.
3. Serve with strawberries and whipped cream if desired.
½ cup: 149 cal., 3g fat (2g sat. fat), 55mg chol., 86mg sod., 25g carb. (18g sugars, 0 fiber), 5g pro.

SONORAN SUNSET WATERMELON ICE

If you didn't think watermelon and cilantro could go together, this recipe will give you a pleasant surprise! Sprinkle pomegranate seeds and a sprig of cilantro on top for extra flair.
—Jeanne Holt,
  Mendota Heights, MN

- -

Prep: 15 min. + cooling
Process: 10 min. + freezing
Makes: 6 servings

- ½ **cup sugar**
- ¼ **cup water**
- 4 **cups cubed seedless watermelon**
- 3 **Tbsp. lime juice**
- 2 **Tbsp. pomegranate juice**
- 1 **Tbsp. minced fresh cilantro**
  Dash salt

1. In a small saucepan, bring sugar and water to a boil; cook and stir until the sugar is dissolved. Cool completely.
2. Puree watermelon in a blender. Transfer to a large bowl; stir in the sugar syrup and remaining ingredients. Refrigerate until cold.
3. Pour watermelon mixture into cylinder of ice cream maker; freeze according to the manufacturer's directions. Transfer to freezer containers, allowing headspace for expansion. Freeze 4 hours or until firm.
½ cup: 100 cal., 0 fat (0 sat. fat), 0 chol., 246mg sod., 26g carb. (24g sugars, 0 fiber), 1g pro.
Diabetic exchanges: 1½ starch, ½ fruit.

LITTLE ITALY PIGNOLI COOKIES

Both of my grandmas came from Italy. Of all the wonderful desserts they made, these cookies were always my family's favorite. Now I make them for every party and get-together. They're easy and use only five ingredients!
—Fran Green, Linden, NJ

- -

Prep: 25 min. • **Bake:** 15 min./batch
Makes: 5 dozen

- 1 **cup almond paste**
- 1 **large egg white**
- 1 **Tbsp. honey**
- ¾ **cup confectioners' sugar**
- ¾ **cup pine nuts**

1. Preheat oven to 325°. In a small bowl, beat almond paste, egg white and honey until crumbly. Gradually add confectioners' sugar; mix well.
2. Place pine nuts in a small bowl. Shape teaspoons of dough into balls. Roll in pine nuts. Place 1 in. apart on parchment-lined baking sheets. Flatten slightly.
3. Bake 15-18 minutes or until lightly browned. Cool 1 minute before removing from pans to wire racks. Store in an airtight container.
1 cookie: 34 cal., 2g fat (0 sat. fat), 0 chol., 1mg sod., 4g carb. (3g sugars, 0 fiber), 1g pro.

OLD-FASHIONED HONEY BAKED APPLES

My baked apple recipe is old-fashioned but tried and true. It's the best kind of comfort food.
—Rachel Hamilton, Greenville, PA

- -

Prep: 10 min. • **Bake:** 35 min.
Makes: 2 servings

- 2 **medium tart apples**
- ¼ **cup dried cranberries**
- ⅔ **cup water**
- ¼ **cup packed brown sugar**
- 1 **Tbsp. honey**
  Optional: Vanilla ice cream or sweetened whipped cream

1. Preheat oven to 350°. Core the apples, leaving bottoms intact; peel top third of each. Place in a greased 8x4-in. glass loaf pan; fill with the cranberries.
2. In a small saucepan, combine the water, brown sugar and honey; cook and stir over medium heat until sugar is dissolved. Pour over apples.
3. Bake, uncovered, until the apples are tender, 35-40 minutes, basting occasionally with juices. If desired, serve with ice cream.
1 baked apple: 253 cal., 0 fat (0 sat. fat), 0 chol., 13mg sod., 67g carb. (59g sugars, 4g fiber), 0 pro.

OLD-FASHIONED HONEY BAKED APPLES

FRUIT JUICE POPS

FRUIT JUICE POPS

I've used this recipe for years as a refreshing treat. My children enjoyed these pops more than any store-bought ones I ever brought home. They taste fantastic with either pineapple or orange juice. Try freezing and serving in cups made from hollowed-out oranges or lemons.

—Barbara Stewart, Garland, TX

- -

Prep: 25 min. + freezing
Makes: 1 dozen

2	cups water
1½	cups sugar
4	cups unsweetened apple juice
1	cup unsweetened pineapple or orange juice
½	cup lemon juice
12	freezer pop molds or 12 paper cups (3 oz. each) and wooden pop sticks

1. In a large saucepan, combine water and sugar; bring to a boil. Reduce heat; simmer, uncovered, for 3-4 minutes or until sugar is dissolved, stirring occasionally.

Remove sugar syrup from the heat; stir in fruit juices.

2. Fill molds or cups with ¼ cup juice mixture. Top molds with holders. If using cups, top with foil and insert sticks through foil. Freeze until firm.

1 pop: 149 cal., 0 fat (0 sat. fat), 0 chol., 3mg sod., 38g carb. (36g sugars, 0 fiber), 0 pro. **Diabetic exchanges:** 1 starch.

CARAMEL-PECAN APPLE SLICES

STAR-SPANGLED PARFAITS

The best time for this layered dessert is midsummer, when the blueberries are thick and plump in our northern woods. Raspberries can also be added to the mixed berries to brighten the colors.
—Anne Theriault, Wellesley, MA

- -

Takes: 15 min. • **Makes:** 4 servings

- 2   cups fresh strawberries, cut into ½-in. pieces
- 2   cups fresh blueberries
- 4   tsp. reduced-fat raspberry walnut vinaigrette
- ¾   cup fat-free vanilla or strawberry Greek yogurt
- 2   tsp. minced fresh mint
      Unsweetened shredded coconut, optional

1. Place strawberries and blueberries in separate bowls. Drizzle each with 2 tsp. vinaigrette; toss to coat. In a small bowl, mix yogurt and mint.
2. Spoon strawberries into 4 parfait glasses. Layer each with the yogurt mixture and blueberries. If desired, top with coconut.
1 parfait: 172 cal., 7g fat (5g sat. fat), 0 chol., 41mg sod., 24g carb. (17g sugars, 5g fiber), 5g pro. **Diabetic exchanges:** 1 fruit, 1 fat, ½ starch.

CARAMEL-PECAN APPLE SLICES

Here's a warm, decadent side dish for a brunch. Ready to eat in only 15 minutes, the apples are also perfect alongside a pork entree or spooned over vanilla ice cream.
—Carol Gillespie, Chambersburg, PA

- -

Takes: 15 min. • **Makes:** 6 servings

- ⅓   cup packed brown sugar
- 2   Tbsp. butter
- 2   large apples, cut into ½-in. slices
- ¼   cup chopped pecans, toasted

In a large skillet, cook and stir brown sugar and butter over medium heat until sugar is dissolved. Add apples; cook, uncovered, over medium heat for 5-7 minutes or until apples are tender, stirring occasionally. Stir in pecans. Serve warm.
½ cup: 155 cal., 8g fat (3g sat. fat), 10mg chol., 43mg sod., 23g carb. (21g sugars, 2g fiber), 1g pro.

**STAR-SPANGLED
PARFAITS**

BLACKBERRY NECTARINE PIE

BLACKBERRY NECTARINE PIE

Blackberries are a big crop in my area, so I've prepared this pretty double-fruit pie many times. I can always tell when my husband wants me to make it because he brings home berries that he picked behind his office.

—Linda Chinn, Enumclaw, WA

- -

Prep: 25 min. + chilling
Makes: 8 servings

¼   cup cornstarch
1   can (12 oz.) frozen apple juice concentrate, thawed
2   cups fresh blackberries, divided
5   medium nectarines, peeled and coarsely chopped
1   reduced-fat graham cracker crust (8 in.)
    Reduced-fat whipped topping, optional

1. In a small saucepan, mix the cornstarch and the apple juice concentrate until smooth. Bring to a boil. Add ½ cup blackberries; cook and stir 2 minutes or until thickened. Remove from heat.

2. In a large bowl, toss the nectarines with remaining blackberries; transfer to crust. Pour apple juice mixture over the fruit (crust will be full). Refrigerate, covered, 8 hours or overnight. If desired, serve with whipped topping.

1 piece: 240 cal., 4g fat (1g sat. fat), 0 chol., 106mg sod., 50g carb. (32g sugars, 4g fiber), 3g pro.

QUICK MANGO SORBET

Last summer I decided to make a passion fruit and mango sorbet. But fresh fruits require more prep and are hard to find ripened at the same time, so I experimented using frozen fruit and juice. And voila! Both are readily available and inexpensive, too.

—Carol Klein, Franklin Square, NY

- -

Takes: 5 min. • **Makes:** 2½ cups

1   **pkg. (16 oz.) frozen mango chunks, slightly thawed**
½   **cup passion fruit juice**
2   **Tbsp. sugar**

Place all ingredients in a blender; cover and process until smooth. Serve immediately. If desired, for a firmer texture, cover and freeze at least 3 hours.

½ cup: 91 cal., 0 fat (0 sat. fat), 0 chol., 2mg sod., 24g carb. (21g sugars, 2g fiber), 1g pro.

QUICK MANGO SORBET

WINTER FRUIT WITH PROSECCO SABAYON

(PICTURED ON P. 214)
This recipe is special to me because it allows me to treat my dinner guests to a special, unusual dessert. The bright, vivid colors are perfect for the holidays. Omit the Prosecco when serving to children.

—Jerry Gulley, Pleasant Prairie, WI

- -

Takes: 25 min.
Makes: 6 servings (¾ cup sauce)

6   **medium blood oranges, peeled and cut into ¼-in. slices**
1   **vanilla bean, split**
¼   **cup sugar plus 3 Tbsp. sugar, divided**
½   **cup Prosecco or sparkling white wine, divided**
    Dash salt
3   **large egg yolks**

1. Arrange orange slices on a serving platter or individual plates. Scrape vanilla bean seeds into a small bowl. Add ¼ cup sugar, ¼ cup Prosecco and salt; combine and drizzle over oranges. Refrigerate until serving.
2. In a double boiler or metal bowl over simmering water, constantly whisk the egg yolks and remaining sugar and Prosecco until mixture reaches 160° and coats the back of a spoon. Drizzle over oranges. Serve immediately.

1 sliced orange with 2 Tbsp. sauce: 151 cal., 3g fat (1g sat. fat), 92mg chol., 249mg sod., 26g carb. (24g sugars, 2g fiber), 2g pro. **Diabetic exchanges:** 1 starch, 1 fruit, ½ fat.

CHOCOLATE
AMARETTI

CHOCOLATE AMARETTI

These delicate almond paste cookies are like the ones sold in Italian bakeries. My husband and children are always excited when I include these goodies in my holiday baking lineup. But don't wait for a special occasion to enjoy them!
—Kathy Long, Whitefish Bay, WI

Prep: 15 min. • **Bake:** 20 min./batch
Makes: 2 dozen

- 1¼ cups almond paste
- ¾ cup sugar
- 2 large egg whites, room temperature
- ½ cup confectioners' sugar
- ¼ cup baking cocoa

1. Crumble almond paste into a food processor; add sugar and pulse until evenly combined. Add egg whites and process until incorporated. Transfer the mixture to a bowl. Sift together confectioners' sugar and cocoa; gradually add to the almond mixture and mix well.

2. Drop by tablespoonfuls 2 in. apart onto parchment-lined baking sheets. Bake at 350° until tops are cracked, 17-20 minutes. Cool for 1 minute before removing from pans to wire racks. Store in an airtight container.

1 cookie: 92 cal., 3g fat (0 sat. fat), 0 chol., 6mg sod., 15g carb. (13g sugars, 1g fiber), 2g pro. **Diabetic exchanges:** 1 starch, ½ fat.

GRILLED ANGEL FOOD CAKE WITH FRUIT SALSA

GRILLED ANGEL FOOD CAKE WITH FRUIT SALSA

When I need a fast dessert for a cookout, I go with a dressed-up angel food cake. I use a mix of fresh strawberries, blueberries and raspberries in my salsa.
—Glorimar Jimenez, Indianapolis, IN

Takes: 15 min. • **Makes:** 6 servings

- 1½ cups fresh berries of your choice
- 1 medium kiwifruit, peeled and chopped
- 2 Tbsp. sugar
- 1 Tbsp. lime juice
- 1 loaf-shaped angel food cake (10½ oz.), split horizontally
  Whipped topping, optional

In a small bowl, combine the berries, kiwi, sugar and lime juice. Grill cake, cut side down, over medium heat or broil 4 in. from heat 1-3 minutes or until lightly browned. Cut into slices. Serve with fruit salsa and, if desired, whipped topping.

1 slice with ¼ cup salsa: 169 cal., 1g fat (0 sat. fat), 0 chol., 372mg sod., 39g carb. (30g sugars, 2g fiber), 3g pro.

INDEX